Giant Book
of
Garden
Solutions

www.jerrybaker.com

Other Jerry Baker gardening books:
Jerry Baker's Flower Garden Problem Solver
Jerry Baker's Perfect Perennials!
Jerry Baker's Backyard Problem Solver
Jerry Baker's Green Grass Magic
Jerry Baker's Terrific Tomatoes, Sensational Spuds,
*   and Mouth-Watering Melons*
Jerry Baker's Great Green Book of Garden Secrets
Jerry Baker's Old-Time Gardening Wisdom
Jerry Baker's Flower Power!

Jerry Baker health books:
Jerry Baker's Homemade Health
Oddball Ointments, Powerful Potions & Fabulous
*   Folk Remedies*
Jerry Baker's Giant Book of Kitchen Counter Cures
Jerry Baker's Herbal Pharmacy

Jerry Baker home tips books:
Jerry Baker's It Pays to Be Cheap!
Jerry Baker's Eureka! 1001 Old-Time Secrets
*   and New-Fangled Solutions*

To order any of the above, or for more information on
Jerry Baker's *amazing* home, health, and garden tips,
tricks, and tonics, please write to:

Jerry Baker, P.O. Box 1001, Wixom, MI 48393

Or, visit Jerry Baker on the World Wide Web at:

www.jerrybaker.com

Giant Book
of
Garden
Solutions

**1,954 <u>Natural</u> Remedies
to Handle Your
Toughest Garden Problems**

by Jerry Baker,
America's Master Gardener®

Published by American Master Products, Inc.

Published by American Master Products, Inc. / Jerry Baker

Executive Editor: Kim Adam Gasior
Managing Editor: Cheryl Winters Tetreau
Interior Design and Layout: Sandy Freeman
Cover Design: Kitty Pierce Mace
Illustrator: Len Epstein
Indexer: Nan Badgett

Publisher's Cataloging-in-Publication

Baker, Jerry.
 Giant book of garden solutions : 1,954 natural remedies to handle your toughest garden problems / by Jerry Baker.
  p. cm.
  Includes index.
  ISBN 0-922433-51-8

  1. Gardening. I. Title.

SB455.B256 2003   635
     QBI02-200922

Printed in the United States of America
2 4 6 8 10 9 7 5 3   hardcover

Contents

Introduction

It's hard to believe, but I've been helping folks solve garden-variety problems for close to half a century now. And you know what? I still get as big a kick out of it as I did the very first time I showed a neighbor of mine how to send bad bugs to their "just rewards" with my Grandma Putt's Simple Soap Spray. You should have seen the smile on her face when she showed off her pest-free plants—you'd have thought she'd just won the lottery!

And you'll feel like you've won the lottery, too, when you get a load of the fast, fun, and easy solutions I've packed into this book. Whether your trouble is a clear-cut case of munching marauders or a puzzling predicament like why your sweet peas don't smell sweet, I'll show you how to right that wrong faster than you can say "What's going on here?"

We'll start off in my favorite place in the whole wide world: the flower garden. I'll show you all of my super-simple ways to cure whatever ails your annuals, perennials, and bulbs, so you can hit the high road to perfection—or get as close to it as Mother Nature will allow. We'll cover the gamut, from chasing mealybugs from your one-season wonders to transplanting roses that have been around since Grandma Putt wore pigtails.

In Part II, we'll conquer your various vegetable vexations. I'll clue you in on my sure-fire strategies to win the pest-control wars. And the fun doesn't stop there! You'll also find miracle mixes for solving mysterious maladies ranging from hollow taters to brown cabbage, rotting tomatoes, and hot peppers that taste about as steamy as a glass of milk. So, dig in!

Part III is all about fruit—the beautiful, sweet stuff that can deal you a deck full of trouble. In fact, some of the most experienced gardeners I know won't even grow fruit because they think it's too much trouble. But they didn't know the super secrets I'll share with you, including a powerful bug killer that may be sitting in your refrigerator right now, and a common weed that can give you better-tasting berries.

The stars of Part IV are what gardeners call "the workers of the plant kingdom": herbs. In these chapters, you'll learn all about curing herbal woes, ranging from seeds that won't start to plants that are bound and determined to take over your yard—and go on to conquer the world! I'll also let you in on some of my best tips for putting herbs to work, whether its spicing up your favorite recipes, curing what ails you, or adding pizzazz to your handmade treasures.

Finally, we'll look at what it takes to stop garden-variety problems before they start. Part V is chock-full of terrific tricks to keep your plants happy, healthy, and strong. I'll show you how to enlist an army of good-guy critters to fight those bad-guy bugs that assault your garden on a daily basis. I'll also show you how to make no-muss, no-fuss compost. And, I'll even give you my no-dig, almost no-work recipe for the best soil you—or your plants' roots—have ever seen.

So, what are we waiting for? As I always say, "Let's get growing!"

PART I

FLOWER
Fixes

CHAPTER 1

Alluring Annuals

Every gardener's been there at least once: You get your annual flowerbeds planted, you're all geared up for a blaze of color that'll knock your neighbors' socks off, and then, BINGO! Trouble strikes and your color is about as blazing as the ashes in a dead campfire. Well, friends, here's how to re-ignite that flame!

Stricken Seeds 'n Seedlings

Leftover Losers

When you don't use up all the seeds in a packet, it only makes good sense (cents, too!) to save the leftovers for next year. They should perform just as well: Most annual flower and vegetable seeds remain viable for two to three years. If your leftovers aren't even germinating, it could be that they weren't stored properly.

➡ Nothing will revive the nonstarters, but you *can* make sure the problem doesn't happen again. The secret is to keep the seeds cool and dry. Here's a method that's as easy as 1-2-3:

1. Get a container of powdered milk, and some glass jars with tight-fitting lids (one jar per type of seed).

2. In each jar, put 1 part seed to 1 part powdered milk.

3. Seal the jars very tightly, and stash them in the refrigerator (not the freezer). The milk will keep the seeds dry and fresh all winter long. Then, come spring, they'll be set to go!

Just Testing

If you've got some leftover seed, you can't tell whether they're still viable just by looking at 'em.

➡ **Try my sink-or-swim test:** Just pour the seeds into a glass of water. The ones that float on the surface are nonstarters, so throw 'em on the compost pile. The seeds that sink stand a good chance of growing up sleek and sassy. You'll need to plant them soon, though, because they'll have soaked up water and will be sprouting before you can say "Everybody out of the pool!"

Try Again

Old age isn't the only reason a flower seed can fail to germinate. When you've got bare spots where you expected to see healthy, young seedlings, the blame could rest with any number of factors.

➤ **They froze to death.** Some seeds can hold their own in cold, wet ground; others will freeze or rot. Next time, wait until the soil is warm enough to suit your plants. (Check the time and temperature guidelines on the seed packet.)

They floated off. Heavy rains could have washed the seeds away. Or, perhaps you went overboard with the garden hose. When you water a seedbed, use a fine mist. You want to keep the soil evenly moist, but never sopping wet.

They were trapped. Some seeds have thick coatings that are all but impossible for a growing tip to break through without help. To ensure seed-starting success, soak these tough guys in water for 24 hours before you plant: dwarf morning glory (*Convolvulus tricolor*), morning glory (*Ipomoea tricolor*), moonflower (*Ipomoea alba*), hyacinth bean (*Dolichos*

★ Miracle Mix ★

SEED-STARTER TONIC

No matter what kind of seeds you're planting, get 'em off to a rip-roarin' start with this excellent elixir.

1 tsp. of baby shampoo
1 tsp. of Epsom salts
1 qt. of weak tea water*

Mix the shampoo and Epsom salts in the tea. Then bundle up your seeds in cheesecloth or an old panty hose toe (one kind of seed per bundle, unless you're aimin' for a casual mix). Drop the bundles into the liquid, and put the container in the fridge to soak for 24 hours. Your seeds'll come out rarin' to grow!

*Soak a used tea bag in a mix of 1 gallon of warm water and 1 teaspoon of liquid dish soap until the mix is light brown.

lablab), and firecracker vine, a.k.a. Spanish flag *(Ipomoea lobata)*. Annual sweet pea *(Lathyrus odoratus)* likes a full 48 hours in the drink.

They were eaten. Birds and squirrels could have gobbled up your future plants. To put a halt to their dining pleasure, make a shelter (see the "Super Solution" at right).

To make an all-but-instant shelter for your seeds, drive some stakes into the soil around the bed, and drape a sheet of plastic on top.

They were planted too deep. Or maybe not deep enough. Some seeds need light to germinate—press them into the soil just enough to keep them from blowing away. Other seeds must be completely covered. The depth varies, but my rule of thumb is to set a seed into the ground at a depth equal to two times its diameter.

Cut It Out!

It's one of the sorriest sights in all of gardendom: A flowerbed full of seedlings lying on their sides, sliced right off at ground level. The culprit is the King of Seedling Savagery—the cutworm.

➡ Fortunately, cutworms have enemies too, and some of the deadliest are birds, tachinid flies, and parasitic wasps. (Don't worry: These wasps are harmless to humans!) All of these top guns love to hang out in flower gardens. If more than a few of your baby annuals are being felled in the night, my hunch is that the good-guy/bad-guy balance has gotten out of whack. Here's my simple, two-step solution:

Step 1: Read before you spray. Even some pesticides that won't

The parents of cutworms are dark-colored moths that flit around after dark. Way back in Grandma Putt's day, folks called 'em millers, and they had a great trick for luring the culprits to their death. Just fill a wide, flat pan with milk, and set it in the garden. Beside it, place a lighted lantern so that it shines on the milk. The moths will zero in on the glowing target, fall into the milk, and drown!

hurt humans or larger critters can kill off good-guy bugs along with the bad ones. And that'll leave you with more problems than you started with!

Step 2: Attract beneficial insects. Tachinid flies and parasitic wasps are drawn to any pollen- and nectar-packed plants, but they go ga-ga over dill, yarrow, sweet alyssum, and cosmos. So just plant some and watch the posse ride to your rescue! For more tips on culling cutworms—including how to entice pest-eating birds and beneficial insects to your garden—see Chapter 14.

They Just Keeled Over and Died!

It happens to every new gardener (and even not-so-new ones): One night, when you turn out the lights and go to bed, you've got pots of fine-lookin' young seedlings. Come morning, you go to admire your handiwork, and find the plants barely alive. The problem: damping-off. It's a fungus that shoots like lightning through a seedling tray. The prime causes: nonsterilized soil, stagnant air, and dirt from hands, pots, or tools.

➡ If this dastardly disease has felled only a few seedlings in a flat, you can stop it dead in its tracks. You have to act fast, though. Just mix up a half-and-half solution of hydrogen peroxide and water, and saturate the affected soil. To head off future attacks, follow these guidelines:

Say no to soil. Always use a sterile, soilless potting mix that's made especially for starting seeds. You can find it at any garden center.

Clean 'em up. If your containers have been used before, soak them for 15 minutes or so in a solution that's 1 part household bleach to 8 parts hot water. Use this solution to clean any tools that will come into contact with your seeds or starter mix, like tweezers or soil scoops.

Give 'em a shower. When the first bits of green appear above the surface, spray them with my Damping-Off Prevention Tonic (below).

Keep the air moving. Poor air circulation is an open invitation to damping-off (or any other) fungus.

Water from the bottom. Seedlings with wet leaves are prime candidates for damping-off. Set your starter pots into a tray that has no holes, then pour water into the flat. The roots will take up the moisture they need, and the baby foliage will stay nice and dry.

Energize 'em. As your seedlings grow, keep the planting mix moist by adding my Seed-Starter Tonic to the tray (see page 4).

Don't touch! Even if your hands are clean as a whistle, keep

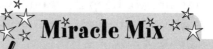

Miracle Mix

DAMPING-OFF PREVENTION TONIC

This wonder drink will say a loud and clear "No way!" to damping-off fungus.

4 tsp. of chamomile tea
1 tsp. of liquid dish soap
1 qt. of boiling water

Mix the tea and soap with the water, and let the mixture steep for at least an hour (the longer, the better). Let it cool to room temperature, then mist-spray your seedlings as soon as their little heads appear above the starter mix.

them off the seedlings—especially the fragile stems. You can injure them without even knowing it, and to a fungus spore, damaged tissue all but shouts "Pick me!" When it's time to transplant your seedlings, lift them from the tray with a small spoon, taking as much of their starter mix with them as you can.

Fan-tastic!

Basements with good air circulation are almost as rare as chickens with fur. Yet, for lots of folks, a basement, with overhead lights, is the only space they have for starting seeds. But we know that poor air circulation encourages the growth of fungus, so *is* the basement a good seed-starting environment?

You *can* use your basement for seed-starting if you turn on a fan or two. Keep them on low, and don't aim them directly at the seed flats—just a soft breeze in the general vicinity will do the trick nicely.

Get Up and Grow!

These easy annuals prefer to start life right in the garden. Just sow the seeds in the spring, and they'll be up and growing in no time at all:

Annual baby's breath (*Gypsophila elegans*)
Annual phlox (*Phlox drummondii*)
Bachelor's buttons (*Centaurea cyanus*)
California poppy (*Eschscholzia californica*)
Celosias (*Celosia*)
Cosmos (*Cosmos bipinnatus*)
Creeping zinnia (*Sanvitalia procumbens*)

Diamond flower *(Ionopsidium acaule)*
Forget-me-not *(Myosotis sylvatica)*
Four-o'clocks *(Mirabilis jalapa)*
Larkspur *(Consolida ambigua)*
Love-in-a-mist
 (Nigella damascena)
Marigolds *(Tagetes)*
Moonflower *(Ipomoea alba)*
Morning glory *(Ipomoea tricolor)*
Moss rose *(Portulaca grandiflora)*
Nasturtium *(Tropaeolum majus)*
Spider flower
 (Cleome hassleriana)
Summer forget-me-not
 (Anchusa capensis)
Sunflowers *(Helianthus)*
Toadflax *(Linaria maroccana)*
Wallflower *(Cheiranthus cheiri)*
Zinnia *(Zinnia elegans)*

PLANT THESE at your PERIL!

While it's true that damping-off can attack any seedling, impatiens and snapdragons are prime targets. Give these babies extra-special care in their seed flats. Better yet, leave the babying to someone else, and buy transplants at the garden center!

Tops for Transplants

This crowd starts out slowly from seed. Unless you live in a warm climate, you'll have a better and longer show if you start with transplants (either home-grown or store-bought):

African daisy *(Arctotis stoechadifolia* var. *grandis)*
Black-eyed Susan vine
 (Thunbergia alata)
Browallia *(Browallia speciosa)*
Canterbury bells *(Campanula medium)*
Common stock *(Matthiola incana)*

English daisy
   (*Bellis perennis*)
Flossflower (*Ageratum houstonianum*)
Geraniums*
   (*Pelargonium x hortorum*)
Gloriosa daisy (*Rudbeckia hirta* var. *pulcherrima*)
Heliotrope (*Heliotropium arborescens*)
Impatiens (*Impatiens*)

Joseph's coat
   (*Amaranthus tricolor*)
Lisianthus (*Eustoma*)
Lobelia (*Lobelia erinus*)
Ornamental cabbage
   (*Brassica oleracea*)
Pansy (*Viola x wittrockiana*)
Petunia (*Petunia x hybrida*)
Salvias (*Salvia*)
Swan River daisy
   (*Brachyscome iberidifolia*)

*Only a handful of varieties come true from seed, but all kinds are easy to start from cuttings.

They Could Try Out for the Rockettes!

If your seedlings look as leggy as dancers in a New York chorus line, there could be two possible problems—and, of course, two simple solutions. The first possible problem is that they're reachin' for the light. This is a common affliction of seedlings that start life under artificial lights. The second possible problem is that they need more calcium in their diet.

➤ **Adjust the lights.** Seedlings can grow up straight and sturdy under fluorescent lights—even in a basement, as long as it's dry. The key is keeping those beams at just the right height: about 3 inches from the tops of the plants. Otherwise, the little tykes will stretch toward the light. Just pick up some inexpensive, adjustable light fixtures, and you'll be good to grow.

Boost calcium levels. Too little calcium tends to make seedlings (or even older plants) grow long and spindly. To boost calcium levels, give 'em my eggshell tea. Almost fill a 1-gallon container with water. (A milk jug with a good, tight lid is perfect.) Then, every time you break an egg, crush the shell, and toss it into the jug—don't even bother rinsing it.

You'll know the tea has brewed to perfection when it smells like, um, rotten eggs. Dilute the brew with an equal amount of water, and pour it on the soil around your plants. They'll start plumpin' up in no time!

GRANDMA PUTT'S
grow-how

My Grandma Putt knew that when it came to buying young annual plants at the garden center, it was best to steer clear of the showy beauties. Why? Because big, beautiful blooming plants are sure candidates for transplant shock. You'd think that they'd just take off and fill up your flowerbed in the blink of an eye. But chances are, they'll just sit there, not doing much of anything. That's because churning out those big, beautiful blooms leaves baby plants plum tuckered out, and they'll have no steam left to put down new roots in your garden. So do what my Grandma Putt always did: Look for transplants that have good, healthy roots, and not so many flowers.

How Corny Can You Get?

Your sweet pea seedlings have just poked their heads out of the soil, and their little seed leaves (a.k.a. cotyledons) have been munched on! What's going on?

➤ They've become the main course for underground diners— seedcorn maggots. These guys are the larvae of an otherwise harmless fly, *Delia platura*. The maggots find most of their victims in the vegetable patch, where they feed on beans, peas, and (of course) corn. Now and then, though, they meander into the flower garden for a sweet pea snack. Some seedlings may have dead or crooked growing tips. Others die before they even reach the surface. Any seedlings that make it to the surface should put on a fine show, though they may grow slowly at first. To safeguard next year's flowery vines, deliver this one-two punch:

1. Add organic matter to your soil in the fall, work it in, and let it age through the winter. That way, you'll foil the female flies, which lay their eggs only in *fresh* organic matter.

2. Wait until the soil temperature has reached 60°F before you plant your seeds. They'll germinate in about nine days, and they'll be growin' great guns before the maggots have a chance to start their feast.

No Room at the Inn

Is your seedling problem simply the fact that you've got no planting space except a weed-choked plot by the back door? And to make matters worse, you've got no time to dig up the weeds and till the soil? Not to worry, my friend: I've got the solution!

Here's how to gain new ground in six easy steps:

Step 1: Mark off your planting site. Use stakes and string if you want a straight-sided bed; otherwise, just arrange a long rope or a garden hose in the shape you want.

Step 2: Mow down tall weeds, but don't fuss with short ones—and don't bother to pull any up.

Step 3: Lay a 1-inch-thick layer of newspapers over the site, overlapping the edges as you go. Then wet them down, so they don't blow away.

Step 4: Spread 1 to 2 inches of peat moss over the paper.

Step 5: Cover the peat with 6 to 8 inches of topsoil and compost, mixed together thoroughly.

Step 6: Plant! If you can let the bed "cook" over the winter, so much the better. But if it's spring and time's a-wastin', just sow your seeds, or set in your plants, and water well. Before you know it, earthworms will break down the newspapers, and you'll have deep, rich soil.

The secret ingredient in this no-dig recipe is the bottom layer of newspaper—it draws earthworms by the droves, and the worms will break organic matter down into good, fertile soil faster than you can say "Go to it, guys!"

Wretched Roots

Too Darn Hot

There's nothing like big containers of annuals to brighten up your outdoor summer scene. But when roots are sitting high and dry in a pot, warm weather can dehydrate 'em in no time flat. If your flowers are flaggin', it's a clue that their living quarters are a tad too hot for comfort.

➡ When you pot up your posies, set each container inside a bigger one. Then fill the space in between with peat moss. The insulation will reduce heat stress on the roots, and keep your flowers in fine fettle all summer long.

Waxworks

A whole lot of things can make a plant lose its get-up-and-grow power. But a plant that seems less than its perky old self—*and* has a white, waxy powder on the soil surface—is entertaining a

crowd of root mealybugs. **These tiny white critters drain sap
from the roots, causing a general decline in the plant's vigor, and
eventually their death. Potted geraniums and fuchsias are especially prone to root mealybug attacks.**

➡ Lift the plant out of its pot, and give the roots a good, thorough
washing in mild, soapy water. Make sure you get *all* the soil off!
Rinse well, then repot the plant in fresh soil and a clean, new
container. Then, bury the infested soil as far away from your
plants as you can. Before you use the pot again, wash it in a
solution of 1 part of household bleach to 8 parts of hot water.
And, just to play it extra-safe, use that container only for plants
that are not root mealybug targets. (These guys also prey on
cacti and other succulents, and on houseplants such as African
violets that are grown in dryish soil.)

Quench Their Thirst

**Here's the dilemma: You want containers of color-
ful annuals to brighten up your deck, but you also
want to go on summer vacation. How do you
keep those potted-up roots from drying out
and dying while you're gone? It's simple.**

➡ At spring planting time, set up an auto-
matic watering system: Before you put
each plant into its pot, run a piece of thick
cotton cord or clothesline through the drainage hole and into
the pot, leaving a long piece lying outside. (Make sure the cord
is cotton; if it's nylon or some other synthetic fiber, it won't
absorb moisture.) Then, before you go away, fill a large container with water, and set the end of the cord into it. The longer
you plan to be gone, the bigger your water container needs to
be. Play it safe, though: Give the system a trial run before you
take off. Then, when departure time rolls around, leave your
plants with at least one-third to one-half more water than they

drank in the trial. That way, the roots will have enough to satisfy their thirst, even if a heat wave strikes, or you get delayed in your travels.

Dear Jerry, I love colorful annuals, but our water bills get higher every month, and my garden is drinking me out of house and home! What can I plant that doesn't need so much moisture? – D.R., Wichita, Kansas

Dear D.R., If it's any comfort, my friend, you're not alone in your water woes! Judging from the letters in my mailbag, folks all over the country are trying to cut back on the H_2O they use in their gardens. Here's a list of annuals that are first-class water conservationists. Remember: Even drought-tolerant plants need a steady water supply until their root systems are established. After that, though, you can watch those water bills plummet!

California poppy (Eschscholzia californica)

Cosmos (Cosmos bipinnatus, C. sulfureus)

French marigold (Tagetes patula)

Globe amaranth (Gomphrena globosa, G. haageana)

Lantana (Lantana camara)

Melampodium (Melampodium paludosum)

Moss rose (Portulaca grandiflora)

Snow-on-the-mountain (Euphorbia marginata)

Vinca, a.k.a. Madagascar periwinkle (Catharanthus roseus)

Zinnias (Zinnia)

They've Joined the Club!

Clubroot can wipe out a whole cabbage-family crop faster than you can say "Please pass the coleslaw." But this rampaging fungus can also run roughshod over flowers that are related to the cabbages, including wallflowers (*Cheiranthus cheiri*), stocks (*Matthiola incana*), candytuft (*Iberis*), and—of course—ornamental cabbage (*Brassica oleracea*).

As with most root disorders, the first symptoms you see will be above ground—and, in this case, usually on a hot, sunny day. Leaves will wilt, and some will turn a tad yellow. Come nightfall, the plant may recover, only to droop again the next day. When you pull up a plant, you'll see a mass of thick, swollen—and downright ugly—roots.

➤ There is no cure for clubroot, so pull up the victims and destroy them. Then, for the next seven years, keep all cabbage-family members out of that soil. To keep your cabbage-family flowers *out* of the club, follow this routine:

Move 'em around. Grow your stocks, wallflowers, and ornamental cabbage in a different spot every year. Besides holding clubroot at bay, you'll foil another family enemy: cabbageworms.

Give 'em sweet soil. Keep the soil pH at 7.2 or above—clubroot loves sour, a.k.a. acidic, soil.

Plant disease-resistant varieties. You'll find 'em listed that way in seed catalogs.

Pot 'em up. If you know that clubroot is hangin' around your area, don't take any chances: Grow your plants in containers. And, to be extra safe, don't buy transplants or seeds that were locally grown. Instead, use plants or seeds that started life elsewhere.

Rhubarb gives off chemicals that repel the clubroot fungus. To safeguard your flowers, bury stalks of rhubarb—leaves and all—in your flowerbeds.

Sickly Stems

Poor Cosmos

When cosmos starts trying to lie down on the job—yet the plants seem healthy otherwise—chances are the problem lies in the real estate. Although these old-time charmers will grow in just about any kind of soil, they prefer to sink their roots into ground that's on the poor side. Soil that's too rich causes weak, floppy stems. That's especially true if the drainage is less than perfect.

➡️ This year, stake your plants to keep them on the up and up—and whatever you do, *don't* feed them! Then, next spring, sow your cosmos seeds in lean, well-drained soil, and get ready for a summer of straight-up color! By the way, nasturtiums *(Tropaeolum majus)* and moss roses *(Portulaca)* also put on their best show in poor soil. (See Chapter 14 for more on plant-pleasing soil.)

But I See Spots!

If your cosmos stems are collapsing, *and* there are dark, sunken spots on the stems and crowns, you've got a serious problem: canker. It develops when fungi in the soil attack the plant's water-conducting tissue. First, the dark spots (a.k.a. cankers) appear, then the foliage wilts and dies. Cosmos are a favorite target, though no plant is completely safe from the disease. It can strike at any time during the growing season, but, like all fungi, it's most likely to occur during wet or humid weather.

➡️ Dig out the afflicted plants and destroy them. If the living quarters look tight, remove some healthy plants, too—there's nothing fungus hates more than good air circulation. Then dig plenty of compost into the soil. (Besides being good for whatever ails a plant, compost gives off ethylene gas, which discourages the growth of fungus.) To fend off future fungus attacks, spray your plants with my Vinegar Fungus Fighter (at left) once a week during the growing season. (For my full fungus-fighting strategy, see Chapter 14.)

Miracle Mix

VINEGAR FUNGUS FIGHTER

This simple-to-make elixir will help keep your plants fungus-free all summer long.

3 tbsp. of apple cider vinegar
1 gal. of water

Mix the vinegar and water, pour the solution into a spray bottle, and let 'er rip—it's as easy as that! Just be sure to spray your plants in the morning, so they have time to dry off before nightfall. Fungal spores *love* dark, damp flowerbeds!

Doggone It!

Rover's done it again—gone rompin' through the flowerbeds, crashin' through the stems. They're all flat on the ground, and he's rollin' on them! Now what do you do?

➡️ Draw the line! Fishing line, that is. Here's how to make a net that will keep the pooch out, and those stems standin' tall:

Step 1: Push stakes in the soil, all around the edges of the planting bed. Then put more stakes in a row down the middle of the bed. They should sit about 7 inches above the ground.

Step 2: Tie nylon fishing line to one of the stakes, about an inch from the top. Then, start weaving the line from stake to stake, across the bed and back

Dear Jerry, I bought some impatiens for my window boxes. According to the little plastic tag in the flat, these plants are supposed to get only 6 to 8 inches tall. Well, they've already topped 10 inches, and they show no signs of stopping! Are they mutant monsters? – R.F., Houston, Texas

Dear R.F., Don't fret, pardner! All is well: In hot, humid climates like yours, impatiens normally grow at least 20 percent taller than usual. If your plants get so high they start blocking your view, move them to pots on the ground. Then, fill up your window boxes with a variety such as 'Super Elfin' that's been specially bred to stay low-down, even in high heat.

again. When you're finished, you'll have a big zigzag pattern. Be sure to keep the openings big enough so you can step into them easily to plant or weed.

Once the pooch gets tangled up in the net a time or two, he won't prance through that bed again! One word of caution: When the plants come up, you won't be able to see the line—so when you're working in the bed, be careful you don't get trapped yourself!

Fascinatin' Fasciation

Fasciation is a disorder that can strike almost any plant, but among annuals, geraniums and petunias are most at risk. And, boy, is this a weird-looking plant problem! Fleshy, flat, almost ribbon-like stems grow out from the main one. Usually, leaves, buds, and flowers carry on business as usual on the distorted stem. Sometimes, though, several fasciated stems bunch together and form a gall-like structure at the soil line. Strange as it looks, fasciation is not a disease and won't spread to other plants. In fact, it rarely affects the overall health of its victim. The cause: injury to the plant's growing tip in its early life. The culprit can be frost, insects, slugs, herbicides, or even (whoops!) a misdirected garden tool.

➡ This is a no-brainer: Clip off the misshapen stems, and toss 'em on the compost pile. Unless, that is, you'd prefer to open a roadside attraction featuring weird and wonderful plants!

Miracle Mix

COMPOST TEA

Compost tea is the healthiest drink a plant could ask for. It delivers a well-balanced supply of all those important nutrients—major and minor—and fends off diseases at the same time.

1 gal. of fresh compost
4 gal. of warm water

Pour the water into a large bucket. Scoop the compost into a cotton, burlap, or panty hose sack, tie the sack closed, and put it in the water. Cover the bucket and let the mix steep for three to seven days. Pour the solution into a watering can or hand-held mist sprayer, and give your plants a good spritzing with it every two to three weeks. *Note:* You can make manure tea (another wonder drink) using this same recipe. Just substitute 1 gallon of well-cured manure for the compost, and use the finished product the same way.

They Won't Perk Up!

When impatiens plants droop, and no amount of water will perk
them up again, look at the stems. If they're turning black near
the base, they're suffering from stem rot. It's caused by a fungus,
and most often strikes plants grown in shade (even when they're
shade-lovers like impatiens). Pansies and dusty miller, though,
can fall victim, even in the sun.

➡ There is no cure for stem rot, so grit your teeth, and dig up the
victims. Then add some good compost to the soil to improve
drainage. If your plants were growing in containers, make sure
the drainage holes are free and clear. Tuck in replacement
plants, and PRESTO!—you're back in business. To guard
against future attacks, water with Compost Tea (at left) every
two weeks throughout the growing season.

Lousy Leaves

Forlorn Fuchsias

A big, hanging basket chock-full of fuchsias is an
elegant sight, alright. That is, until those dark,
glossy leaves turn all yellow and droopy. When
that happens, get a magnifying glass, and take a
gander at the undersides of the leaves. If you see
gauzy, white webbing, it means that your plants are
plagued by spider mites. These guys are so teeny that you can
hardly see them, but they cause elephant-size damage by sucking
juices and nutrients from plant leaves. Fuchsias are their
favorites, but spider mites will drain almost any plant dry.

➡ When spider mites go on the rampage in your flowerbeds and
vegetable garden, your surest move is to buy a passel of preda-

tory mites at the garden center. (For more about these hired guns, see page 314.) For container plants like fuchsias, though, my Mighty Mite Rhubarb Spray (below) works wonders. Try it—they won't like it!

My Geraniums Have Warts!

Wart-like growths on geranium leaves mean one thing: edema. It's caused when the plant takes up more water than its leaves can give off through the process of transpiration. As groups of leaf cells fill with water, they swell up. Over time, they may turn brown and corky-looking. Edema most often develops when humidity is high, and there's too much water hangin' around the roots. Besides striking geraniums, it can also afflict houseplants such as African violets and peperomias.

➡ First, leave those leaves in place! Edema is a cultural disorder, not an infectious disease, so the damage can't spread to other plants. Pulling off the stricken leaves will only reduce moisture loss even more, and make the situation worse. To solve the problem, all you need to do is give the plants less water and more air. Specifically:

❀ Ease off on the hose trigger, improve soil drainage, or both. If

✫ Miracle Mix ✫

MIGHTY MITE RHUBARB SPRAY

This potent potion will make mites mighty sorry they ganged up on your plants!

**1 lb. of rhubarb leaves, chopped
2 tsp. of liquid dish soap
1 qt. of water**

Boil the rhubarb leaves in the water for about half an hour. Then strain out the solids, and pour the liquid into a spray bottle. Mix in the dish soap, and spray away! When you're done, bury the soggy rhubarb leaves near your cabbage-family plants to fend off clubroot. Just one word of caution: Rhubarb leaves are highly poisonous, so never use this spray on edible plants.

your geraniums are growing in pots, make sure they've got big, unclogged drainage holes in the bottoms.

✿ Increase air flow by moving plants farther apart or providing better ventilation. For instance, don't keep pots huddled up against a wall, where breezes can't get at them.

✿ Once big, healthy, new leaves appear, and the plants are growing well, clip off the old, warty leaves, and toss 'em on the compost pile.

Rusty Snaps

Rust can attack any plant, but among annuals, snapdragons are a prime target. In fact, there's a species of fungus that specializes in snaps. When plants have fallen victim to this nasty stuff, you'll see small, dark brown bumps on the lower leaves. Each bump (which is actually a spore-filled pustule) is often surrounded by a yellow halo. These spores need moist surroundings to germinate and spread, so the disease takes its greatest toll in damp weather and humid climates. Rust can strike at any time during the growing season, but usually hits hardest in spring and summer.

☆ Miracle Mix ☆

RUST RELIEF TONIC

Use this terrific tonic to keep your rust-prone plants in the green all summer long.

**6 tbsp. of vegetable oil
2 tbsp. of baking soda
2 tbsp. of kelp extract
    (available at garden centers
    and health food stores)
1 gal. of water**

Mix all of these ingredients together, and pour the solution into a hand-held mist sprayer. Then, give your formerly rusty plants a weekly shower throughout the growing season. Make sure you spray in the morning, though: You want that foliage to dry out before nightfall.

 There's no curing an established rust infection, but if you've arrived on the scene in time, you can head off further trouble. First, depending on the extent of the damage, cut off the rusty leaves, or dig up and destroy the whole plant. Then, do whatever you can to improve air circulation in the bed. (See my general fungus-fighting guidelines in Chapter 14.) Finally, for the rest of the growing season, spray the remaining plants with my Rust Relief Tonic on page 23. Then, next spring, choose rust-resistant varieties and, to be extra-safe, plant them in fresh territory.

Winding Roads

Well, they look like roads, but they're actually tunnels—and they're winding through the leaves of your nasturtiums. The tunnelers, which start their dirty work in midspring, are tiny larvae called serpentine leaf miners. First, the good news: Although these guys cause big-time trouble in the vegetable garden, on nasturtiums (one of the few ornamentals they attack), the damage is mainly cosmetic. Now the bad news: The little no-goodniks do their mining between the upper and lower surfaces of the leaves, where no spray can reach 'em.

Well, the damage may be merely aesthetic, but that doesn't mean you have to take it sitting down! Here's your game plan:

Step 1: Clip off the tunneled leaves and destroy them.

Step 2: Pick up all debris that may be harboring more miners.

Step 3: If the invasion is big and threatening to move into your vegetable garden, spray your plants with neem oil, a safe pesticide that's made from the oil of the neem tree. (You can buy it at any garden center.)

Step 4: If you've only got a few spoiled leaves, just invite some parasitic wasps over for lunch. They'll do a fine job of keeping the population under control. (See page 314 for wasp-enticing guidelines.)

Don't Suck on My Sunflowers!

As garden-variety villains go, aphids are among the most wide-ranging. They do have their favorites, though, and sunflowers top their list. Whatever the target, the damage is the same: The pesky pests suck the sap from plants, leaving shoots, buds, flowers, and leaves distorted and sticky. (You'll usually find the little, pear-shaped critters camped out on the undersides of leaves.)

➡ First, pray for rain. A hard, driving storm will kill the aphids by the boatload! If Mother Nature isn't forthcoming in your hour of need, blast your plants with water from the garden hose. Beyond that, draw on this anti-aphid arsenal:

Repellent plants. Catnip, chives, dill, fennel, mint, and nasturtiums all send aphids scurrying. Beware, though: Catnip and mint will take over your whole yard in the blink of an eye, so don't just turn 'em loose— plant 'em in pots.

Natural enemies. Aphids have legions of them, including aphid midges, big-eyed bugs, damsel bugs, hover fly

✦ Miracle Mix ✦

GREAT-GUNS GARLIC SPRAY

This'll halt an aphid invasion faster than you can say "Hold it right there!"

1 tbsp. of garlic oil*
3 drops of liquid dish soap
1 qt. of water

Mix these ingredients together in a blender, and pour the solution into a hand-held mist sprayer. Then, take aim and fire. Within seconds, those aphids'll be history!

*To make garlic oil, mince 1 whole bulb of garlic and mix it in 1 cup of vegetable oil. Put the garlic oil in a glass jar with a tight lid and place it in the refrigerator to steep for a day or two. To test it for "doneness," open the lid, and take a sniff. If the aroma is so strong that you take a step back, you're ready to roll. If the scent isn't so strong, add half a bulb of garlic, and wait another day. Then, strain out the solids, and pour the oil into a fresh jar. Keep it in the fridge, and use it in any Miracle Mix that calls for garlic oil.

larvae, snakeflies, soldier beetles, and both adult and larval forms of lacewings and ladybugs. Some are hired guns that you can buy in catalogs and garden centers; some will simply show up and start chowin' down if you don't use pesticides. Others need a little enticement in the form of flowers that are rich in pollen and nectar. (For the full lowdown on calling up the pest-control troops, see page 312.)

Death traps. Like a whole lot of insects, aphids are drawn to the color yellow (that's one reason they go hog-wild for sunflowers). To kill the little buggers by the carload, just hang yellow sticky traps on your plants' branches. You can buy traps at any garden center, but it's a cinch to make your own. Just glue yellow paper to cardboard, spray it with cooking oil, and poke a string through the top.

Who's That Imposter?

At first glance, you might think that your petunias have been invaded by thrips or mites. On the undersides of the leaves, white- to bronze-colored spots appear, and then turn to a silvery haze. Plants also lose their get-up-and-grow power, and blossom production falls off. The culprit isn't a critter, though: It's a condition with the tongue-twisting name of peroxyacetyl nitrate (a.k.a. PAN) damage, and it's caused by air pollution. If you live where summertime brings smog alerts and air inversions, sooner or later, you'll see this nasty stuff. It strikes many plants, but among annuals, petunias are especially vulnerable.

Unfortunately, there is no way to control PAN damage. The good news is that some plants can handle the bad-air assault better than others. They vary from one region to another, though, so here are your best tactics:

Any kind of mint will send bad-guy bugs fleeing from your flower patch—and lay out the welcome mat for a full-scale cavalry of good guys. These plants do have their dark side, though: Given their druthers, they'll take over your whole yard faster than you can say "A mint julep, please." To solve your pest problems without begging for a bigger one, grow your mint in containers.

Look around. See which plants are holding up well in your neighbors' yards. If they perform for them, they'll perform for you.

Get in touch. Call your local garden club, and ask what plants their members have had good luck with. (Your Cooperative Extension Service probably isn't your best bet, because they generally cover whole counties, and PAN damage can be a very localized problem.)

Drive less and walk more. Not only will you keep the air cleaner, but your plants will also thank you for it!

It's a Whiteout!

You kneel down to weed your flowerbed, and a white cloud flies up in your face: Look out—it's whiteflies on the rampage! If you look closely at the undersides of the plants' leaves, you'll see the babies (nymphs)—tiny, pearly white specks that look like scales. Both nymphs and adults suck the juices from plants, making them weak and vulnerable to other pests and cultural problems. What's more, as whiteflies feed, they often spread viruses. Almost no plant is safe from these tiny guys.

➡ There are dozens of ways to wipe out whiteflies. If you've got a large cutting garden, just hang out the same yellow sticky traps that work for aphids, and you'll polish off thousands of the pesky flies. (See "Don't Suck on My Sunflowers!" on page 25.) For smaller beds or container gardens, though, there's a faster—and more attractive—way to deal out death and destruction: Get out your hand-held vacuum cleaner, and sweep 'em up on the fly.

Then, to finish the job, spray the plants with my Rhubarb Bug Repellent (see page 104). It'll get any lingering adults, plus all the nymphs, and leave your plants clean as a whistle. Just be sure you saturate the underside of every single leaf!

Their Leaves Are All Covered in Ashes and Soot...

just like Santa's clothes. Your plants didn't pick up this dirt coming down the chimney, though: It's called sooty mold, and it forms in the honeydew left by insects such as aphids, mealybugs, scales, and whiteflies. It most often develops when both temperature and humidity are high. Sometimes, whole leaves will be covered with a papery, black or dark gray layer that you can peel right off. Usually, the stuff occurs in separate patches on a leaf. Sooty mold is ugly, alright, but the damage it does is even uglier. It blocks the leaves' access to light, and sometimes clogs up the pores (*stomata* in scientific lingo) that let water and oxygen pass through the plant tissue.

First, get that stuff off the leaves! If there's not too much of it, just wipe the leaves gently with a cloth dipped in warm water. For larger outbreaks, haul out the garden hose, and blast the plants with water. Then, to get any malingering pests, spray again, this time with Grandma Putt's Simple Soap Spray (see page 94). To *really* say "so long" to sooty mold, though, your best defense is a good offense: namely, a hit squad of good-guy bugs. See Chapter 14 for my no-fail enlistment strategy.

Vampires Got 'Em!

Tarnished plant bugs do their dastardly deeds by piercing and sucking sap from their victims. In the process, the bugs spew out toxic saliva, which results in leaves and flowers that are pinched, scarred, and distorted. (Sounds almost like a B-grade monster movie, doesn't it?) These villains haunt the vegetable patch more than the flower garden, but they do go a-gunnin' for a handful of annuals, including impatiens, marigolds, poppies, and zinnias. You probably won't catch these bugs at their dirty work, because they're both tiny (about ¼ inch long) and shy. The minute they sense a disturbance, they fly away or drop down out of sight.

Unlike most insects, which zero in on anything yellow, tarnished plant bugs are drawn to the color (or noncolor) white. So your solution couldn't be simpler: Spray pieces of white cardboard with adhesive, then hang or stand the traps among your troubled posies. For long-term protection, broaden the palette in your flower garden to include daisies and yarrow. They'll attract minute pirate bugs, who will gladly polish off all the tarnished plant bugs they can find (and other bad guys, besides).

GRANDMA PUTT'S
grow-how

Grandma Putt's flower garden looked just like one of the big, silk-and-velvet crazy quilts she sewed in the winter. Those planting beds were full of so many different kinds of flowers, in so many different colors, that it just about took your breath away. That crazy-quilt mix kept pesky pest problems away, too. That's because most bad-guy bugs have definite food preferences. When they look down on a big patch of their favorite vittles, they'll drop in and chow down. But when they see a whole lot of different plants—some good, some so-so, and some they wouldn't touch, even if they were starving—they generally take their appetite elsewhere.

Failing Flowers

What's With All That Green?

It *is* disappointing: Your annuals are churnin' out healthy leaves and stems galore, but not many flowers. What's going on here?

➡ Their diet's too high in nitrogen—that's what! All plants need nitrogen (N), of course, but to put on their best show, they need a balanced diet that also includes phosphorus (P), potassium (K), and a handful of trace minerals, or micronutrients. (See Chapter 15 for the full lowdown on plant nutrition.) In the meantime, get your babies back on the blooming track by digging wood ashes into the soil; they're a good source of both phosphorus and potassium, as well as micronutrients. If you don't have ashes at hand, choose one phosphorous snack and one potassium snack from the lists below. Be sure to follow the directions on the package: When it comes to fertilizer, more is *not* necessarily better!

Phosphorus: bonemeal, colloidal phosphate, fish meal, guano, rock phosphate.

Potassium: granite dust, greensand, langbeinite, seaweed.

Then, to keep your parade of color marching right through the summer, give your plants a drink of my Flower Power Tonic (at left) every three weeks.

Miracle Mix

FLOWER POWER TONIC

A dose of this tonic will get your flowers up and growing in no time!

1 cup of beer
2 tbsp. of fish emulsion
2 tbsp. of liquid dish soap
2 tbsp. of ammonia
2 tbsp. of whiskey
1 tbsp. of corn syrup
1 tbsp. of instant tea granules
2 gal. of warm water

Mix all of these ingredients together in a watering can. Drench your annuals every three weeks during the growing season to keep them blooming all summer long.

They Weren't Supposed to Stop!

If you think that planting annuals will guarantee you nonstop color from spring 'til fall, think again. In many cases, once an annual plant has produced a good crop of flowers, and they've set seed for the next generation, that's all she wrote. From the plant's perspective, its job is done. That's particularly true of species and old-time varieties (a.k.a. heirloom flowers). So, is there any way to keep the flowers coming?

In a word: Deadhead. This simply means removing flowers before they set seed. The more you clip, the more the plant will churn out. Most annuals will keep right on goin' until frost bowls 'em over. So get out there and clip away! And don't think of it as a chore; think of it as a chance to fill your house with flowers all summer long—and have plenty left over to share with friends and neighbors.

The Petunias Are Peterin' Out

As the season drags on, petunias get leggy, and almost all the flowers appear at the ends of stems. How do you keep the plants trim without calling an intermission in the show?

Go at 'em in thirds. Once a week, cut back one-third of the stems by two-thirds of their length. By the time you've trimmed the last batch, the first set will be goin' great guns, and you'll have show-stopping color all summer long!

How Sweet It's Not!

If you planted what you thought were fragrant flowers and the results have been, well, less than aromatic, I'm not surprised. That's a problem I hear about from lots of folks. There's a very simple reason for it: Over the years, plant breeders have been tinkerin' with sweet old favorites, like flowering tobacco, stock, petunias, and sweet peas. The breeding has produced more new hybrids than you can shake a shovel at. And they have some good things going for them, like improved disease resistance; bigger, showier flowers; more compact plants; and a whole rainbow of new colors. Unfortunately, in many cases, so much of the fragrance has vanished along the way that only a bloodhound could find it!

 There are several things you can do to get those old-time fragrant flowers.

 **Go on a treasure hunt.** The trick is knowing where to look and what to look for. Don't count on finding many of the old-timers at a chain garden center or discount store. You'll have better luck in catalogs and

Dear Jerry, About midsummer, my lobelia starts looking raggedy. So I cut it back and wait for the encore performance. But weeks go by, and nothing happens. What's going on here? – M.T., Fairfield, Connecticut

Dear M.T., What's going on is heat check. It's a flower's version of a summer vacation. Lobelia, alyssum, and French marigolds, in particular, like to chill out when the weather gets steamy. Don't worry: Come early fall, when nights are cooler, your plants will crank up their bloomin' engines, and you'll be knee-deep in flowers again! For now, just keep the plants watered, and keep an eye out for pesky pests. Then, when your plants are back in business, drench their soil with my Flower Power Tonic (see page 30) every three weeks until Jack Frost puts an end to the show.

nurseries that specialize in fragrant or heirloom plants. To find them, call your local garden club, or crank up your favorite Internet search engine, and type in "heirloom plants" or "fragrant plants."

Shop wisely. Beyond looking for old-fashioned, "unimproved" flowers, keep these pointers in mind when you're shopping for plants or seeds:

❀ Look for the word *odorata* or *odoratus* in a plant's scientific name; that means it is (or should be) fragrant.

❀ The most fragrant flowers tend to be white or very pale-colored. If you think back to high-school botany, you may remember the scientific reason for that fact: To reproduce themselves, most flowering plants need to attract birds or insects that will pollinate the blossoms. Those critters are drawn to either bright colors or strong scents. So if you don't have one, ya gotta have the other!

❀ Second in the fragrance line are purple- and mauve-colored flowers. (Don't ask me why *that* is—my botany teacher never mentioned it!)

❀ Thick-textured flowers often have wonderful scents—tuberoses are an example. Yeah, I know: Tuberoses are not annuals in the true sense; they're warm-climate perennials that folks up North grow as annuals—but if you love fragrant flowers, and you've never tried these, you and your nose are in for a real treat!

❀ Many flowers release their aroma only after the sun goes down. Night-scented stock, four-o'clocks, and flowering tobacco are prime examples.

Make a list. Check out my list of favorites in "The Nose Knows" on page 34, and take note of the ones that interest you.

THE NOSE KNOWS

Here are some of my favorite nose-pleasers. Most are annuals, but some are tender perennials that folks in cold climates grow as annuals. (If you see a zone number, it means you lucky ducks in warmer territory can enjoy 'em year-round!)

Angelwing, a.k.a. shining, jasmine *(Jasminum nitidum).* Glossy, dark green leaves and white pinwheel-shaped flowers. Great for hanging baskets. Full sun or partial shade.

Common mignonette *(Reseda odorata).* Somewhat sprawling plants, 1 to 1½ feet tall, with light green leaves and spikes of yellow or copper-colored flowers. Full sun; partial shade where summers are hot.

Common stock *(Matthiola incana).* Plants grow 1 to 3 feet tall, with narrow, gray-green leaves, and flowers in just about any color you can think of. Even the bright shades have a spicy-sweet scent. Grows best in cool climates. Full sun or light shade.

Four-o'clocks *(Mirabilis jalapa).* Mounded, bushy plants that reach 3 to 4 feet high, with trumpet-shaped flowers in red, yellow, pink, and white, often striped or mottled. Reseeds like crazy! Full sun.

Heliotrope *(Heliotropium arborescens).* Plants grow 1½ to 2 feet tall, with flowers in white and all shades of violet and purple. Full sun in cool climates; partial shade where summers are hot.

Night-scented stock *(Matthiola longipetala* subsp. *bicornis).* 1-foot-tall plants with lance-shaped leaves and small, purplish flowers that release a powerful fragrance after dusk. Grows best in cool climates. Full sun or light shade.

Scented geraniums *(Pelargonium).* Plants grow 1 to 3 feet tall, with clusters of small flowers in white or shades of rosy pink. Full sun; light shade in hot climates. Zones 9 to 11.

Sweet peas *(Lathyrus odoratus).* Vines reach to 5 feet or more; bush types grow from 8 inches to 3 feet tall. All have long stems, and spike-like clusters of flowers in every color but yellow. Most perform best in cool weather and full sun.

Tuberoses *(Polianthes).* Plants are 2 to 3 feet tall with long spires of waxy white flowers. Full sun. Zones 8 to 11.

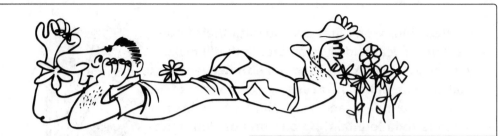

Get a Whiff of This!

If you've planted scented species, but they just aren't all that aromatic, don't despair.

➡ To make the scent of your flowers more potent, try these two tricks:

1. Enclose your garden, at least partially. A wall, solid fence, or vine-covered trellis captures and strengthens the aroma of any flower (not to mention giving you privacy and vertical planting space).

2. Add water in some form—a small pool, a fountain, or even a birdbath will do the trick. Any moisture in the air intensifies a flowery fragrance.

PLANT THESE at your PERIL!

After the sun goes down, flowering tobacco (*Nicotiana*) can fill your whole garden with a sweet, old-time scent, but not if you've planted the wrong kind. When you go to the garden center, you'll likely see table after table full of two popular hybrids: 'Nicki' and 'Domino.' Keep right on walking: These two upstarts were bred to have a wide color range and compact growth habit, but they won't give you a nickel's worth of fragrance. Instead, look for *N. alata* or *N. sylvestris*. When the sun goes down, either one will deliver an aroma that'll make your evening!

Is There a Lemon Phosphate in the House?

Don't confuse scented geraniums with the big-flowered show-stoppers you see in pots and window boxes all over town. The

scented kinds won't impress you with their flowers, but the *leaves* deliver an aroma that'll make your nose think it's died and gone to heaven! Make that aroma*s*, plural. Just set some containers of these on your deck, and you'll think you're in an old-time soda fountain! If your local garden center doesn't have what you're looking for, find a nursery that sells herb plants. Then, mosey on over with this chart in hand.

SCENTED PLANTS	
Apple	*Pelargonium odoratissimum*
Lemon	*P. crispum*
Lime	*P. nervosum*
Nutmeg	*P. x fragrans*
Peppermint	*P. tomentosum*
Rose	*P. capitatum*

Fill 'Er Up

There's nothing like big pots of fragrant annuals to spruce up a deck. There's just one problem: Filling those super-size containers with soil can put a dent in your bank account—and a heavy load on your deck supports.

I've got the solution to both those worries: Before you add potting soil to a large container, set empty soda cans on the bottom. They'll take up the space, and the weight, of a lot of soil. Don't worry that you'll cheat your plants out of growing room—annuals rarely send their roots down to the bottom of a big pot.

CHAPTER 2

Perky Perennials

Lots of folks think that once they've planted a perennial garden, it'll give them year after year of colorful, carefree blooms. But even the hardiest of the hardies can sometimes hand you a wheelbarrow full of challenges! Fear not: Whether your plants are refusing to grow at all, or they're threatening to take over the whole neighborhood, you'll find the answers to your problems right here.

Stricken Seeds 'n Seedlings

Seedy Characters

You say you planted your favorite perennial seeds, followed the packet instructions to the letter, waited what seemed like forever—and then *nothing* happened? I'm not surprised: Many perennials are darn near impossible to grow from seed. Either they need conditions that the casual gardener can't produce, or they take so long to germinate that even Job would run out of patience. (Not to mention the fact that they can fall victim to the same woes that trouble annual seeds. See page 4 for that rundown.)

➡ There's a simple solution to this perennial problem: Choose your seeds from this list of super-easy starters. Sow them indoors in late winter or early spring, or outdoors in late spring or early summer, according to the directions on the seed packet. But before you sow your seeds, give them a bath in my Seed-Starter Tonic (see page 4). It'll get them off to a rip-roarin' start!

Asters *(Aster)*

Black-eyed Susans
(Rudbeckia)

Blanket flower
(Gaillardia x grandiflora)

Columbines
(Aquilegia)

Hollyhock
(Alcea rosea)

Jupiter's beard
(Centranthus ruber)

Lupines *(Lupinus)*

Mountain bluet
(Centaurea montana)

Mulleins *(Verbascum)*

Rose campion
(Lychnis coronaria)

Shasta daisy
(Chrysanthemum x superbum)

Stokes' asters *(Stokesia)*

But I Already *Have* a Mortgage!

For a lot of folks, one of the biggest garden problems is measured not in numbers on a thermometer or a pH scale, but in dollar signs. If you've perused a plant catalog lately, or shopped for perennials in a garden center, you probably got a first-class case of sticker shock. How can you possibly start a new flower garden—or revive the one you've got—without taking out a second mortgage?

➤ Rest easy, friends: You can have a perennial garden that's the talk of the town, and at a cost that'd please old Scrooge himself. Just try some of these budget-pleasing ideas:

Think small. When you're in a hurry to get your garden up and growing, it's tempting to reach for perennials in 1-gallon containers. Don't do it! For what you'll pay for one of those, you can have three or four in 3-inch pots, and once those babies are in the ground, they'll take off. In no time at all, they'll catch up to the big guys.

Get it wholesale. You don't have to own a garden center to buy plants wholesale. A number of catalogs sell to anyone who places a big enough order. Usually, the minimum is 25 to 50 plants of a particular kind—but the price will be less than half what you'd pay at a retail store. If

GRANDMA PUTT'S
grow-how

You know about good-guy bugs, but have you ever heard of good-guy weeds? That was Grandma Putt's name for flowers that reseed like crazy, but are easy to control if they get out of hand. Instead of using weed-killers, she'd sow her good guys anyplace she had weed problems, and then just let 'em go. These were some of the good guys she called on. I still do!

Asters (*Aster*)
Columbines (*Aquilegia*)
Coreopsis (*Coreopsis*)
Forget-me-not (*Myosotis sylvatica*)
Johnny-jump-up (*Viola tricolor*)
Poppies (*Papaver*)
Sweet alyssum (*Lobularia maritima*)
Violets (*Viola*)

you don't need that many plants at any price, team up with friends or neighbors. Wholesale nurseries advertise in many gardening magazines. You can also find them via your favorite Internet search engine.

Hold a swap meet. The concept is simple: Folks come bearing plants, cuttings, bulbs, or seeds from their gardens. Then everyone trades what they've got for what they want. If you're starting from bare ground, and you have absolutely no plant material, offer something else in trade—say, homemade grape jelly, your world-famous chocolate chip cookies, your babysitting services, or even that fancy iron bed frame that's been in the attic since the first Eisenhower administration!

Read all about it. In spring and fall, all over the country, local garden clubs, plant societies, and botanical gardens hold fund-raising plant sales. The prices are generally much lower than they are at garden centers. What's more, the plants sold at most of these affairs started life in your neighborhood, so you know they've got the right stuff to perform on your turf. (For more on choosing native plants, see page 323.)

The Unkindest Cut

A friend gave you cuttings from her prized perennials, and you tucked the shoots into trays filled with sand and potting soil. Now, tiny roots have appeared, and you're counting the days until you can plant the little tykes in your garden. This morning, though, you bent over the trays for a look-see, and you couldn't believe your eyes: The stems were all turning dark at the base! Are your infant plants doomed?

➡ What's going on is called blackleg. It's an infection caused by water- and soil-borne fungi—including some of the same crowd that cause damping-off in seedlings (see page 6). Blackleg strikes before or shortly after roots start to form. There is no cure, but if the nasty stuff hasn't spread through your whole rooting tray, there *is* hope. Just mix up a half-and-half solution of hydrogen peroxide and water, and saturate the rooting mix in the flat. If you're lucky, that'll kill off any lingering fungi, and your babies will be saved. Unfortunately, though, if all the cuttings in a tray are turning color, you'll have to kiss 'em good-bye and start over. When you do, follow the steps below in "A Healthy Send-Off."

A Healthy Send-Off

Your cuttings appeared to get off to a good start, but fizzled fast. Now you're thinking that when it comes to cuttings, you're all thumbs. Is there any way to be sure next year's cuttings will be successful?

You can't just cut 'em, plant 'em, and forget 'em. Here's how to ensure that your cuttings get off to the best possible start:

Use the right stuff. Before you take your cuttings, buy a sack of sterilized rooting medium made especially for starting cuttings and a rooting hormone that contains a fungicide.

Be picky. Take cuttings only from plants that you know are strong and healthy. Otherwise, you're asking for trouble right from the get-go! Cut pieces that are about 4 to 6 inches long from semi-mature stems.

Cut and wrap. Use a clean, sharp knife or clippers; a ragged or torn stem is an open invitation for fungi. After every cut, dip the tool in a solution of 1 part household bleach to 8 parts water. As you cut each group of stem pieces, wrap them loosely in wet paper towels, and tuck them into a plastic bag.

Cut again. When you're back inside, cut each stem about $1/4$ inch below a node (the place where a leaf or pair of leaves meets the stem). Use a sharp knife, dipping it in the bleach solution between cuts.

Pinch. Pinch off the lower leaves so the bottom third to half of the cutting stem is bare. Keep the upper leaves in place, but pinch off any buds or flowers. That way, all the shoot's energy will be directed toward forming roots.

Dip and tuck. Dip the bottom of each cutting in rooting hormone, then tuck the bottom third to half of the stem into the rooting medium. With a spoon (again, dunked in the bleach solution), press the rooting medium firmly around the cutting. Water lightly, then wrap each pot or flat with a plastic bag to keep the humidity high. Take off the cover for an hour or so every day to fend off mildew. Keep the rooting medium moist, but not soggy.

Harden 'em off. When you see new shoots forming (usually within three to five weeks), it means the roots are starting to grow, too. Wait a week or so, then start leaving the plastic covers off for several hours a day. This'll toughen 'em up for life in the great outdoors, come spring.

✬ Miracle Mix ✬

REPOTTING BOOSTER TONIC

Once you've repotted your rooted cuttings, give them a drink of this elixir. It'll give 'em a good start in their new home.

½ tsp. of all-purpose, organic
   plant food
½ tsp. of Vitamin B$_1$ Plant Starter
½ cup of weak tea water*
1 gal. of warm water

Mix all of the ingredients together, and gently pour the mixture through the soil of your repotted cuttings. Let it drain through for 15 minutes or so, then pour off any excess liquid that's in the tray.

*Soak a used tea bag in a mix of 1 gallon of warm water and 1 teaspoon of liquid dish soap until the mix is light brown.

What's Up, Doc?

Your baby perennials are up, that's what. At least they *were* up. Now their new spring sprouts are in the tummies of a bunch of rascally rabbits. What to do?! You could surround your plants with a chicken-wire fence, or set out smelly repellents like the ones you use in the vegetable patch. But this is your *flower* garden! You want it to look and smell like, well, a flower garden.

➤ In this battle, Mother Nature is on your side, my friend! She blessed bunnies with the cutest good looks this side of a teddy bear store, but she forgot to give them good taste. To prove the point: Rabbits *hate* dusty miller *(Centaurea cineraria)*, which to most human eyes is one beautiful plant! What's more, the variety that seems to send 'em scurryin' faster than any other is (in my humble opinion) the prettiest one of all, 'Diamond.' It has velvety white leaves and purple flowers that look terrific in any garden. (There are dozens of plants that go by the name of "dusty miller," so make sure you ask for this one by its scientific moniker: *C. cineraria* 'Diamond'.)

SUPER SOLUTION

Bugs and his buddies can make mischief in your flower garden, alright, but there is one thing I have to say in their favor: They're the only pests I can think of that leave valuable souvenirs behind! Rabbits' hard, brown little pellets are first-class plant chow. What's more, unlike other kinds of manure, this stuff is mild enough to use fresh from the source. Just scatter the pellets on the soil around your plants, water them in, and bingo—nutritious fast food for your garden!

What a Pill!

Probably, when you were a kid, you had fun pokin' a twig in the belly of a pill bug, and watching it curl up in a little round ball. Well, pill bugs, or sow bugs, aren't really bugs at all; they're tiny crustaceans — kissin' cousins of crayfish and lobsters. They usually feed on dead plant material, and, in the process break it down into rich, fertile soil. Once in a while, though, the population explodes, and there's not enough dead stuff to go around. That's when trouble strikes: The hungry hordes sink their chops into tender, young perennial seedlings.

➡ Send 'em back to work! Set out halved cantaloupe rinds; or tuck cabbage leaves, potato peelings, or corncobs under upturned flowerpots. Every few days, check your "traps," and relocate the prisoners to the compost pile. If you don't have a compost pile, just dig a hole in the ground and bury the traps in a place that's far away from your perennial beds.

Who's Digging Up My Garden?

What a way to start the day! You wander out to admire your new perennial bed, and find your young plants lying high

✦ Miracle Mix ✦

HIT THE TRAIL MIX

This spicy concoction will make any critter hightail it away from your garden.

4 tbsp. of dry mustard
3 tbsp. of cayenne pepper
2 tbsp. of chili powder
2 tbsp. of cloves
1 tbsp. of Tabasco® sauce
2 qts. of warm water

Mix all of the ingredients together, and sprinkle the solution around the perimeter of your perennial bed.

and dry, beside their holes. Some no-goodnik dug 'em up in the night and just left 'em there to die! Who would do a dastardly deed like this?

➡ First things first: Tuck those youngsters back into their holes, and give 'em a good dose of my Compost Tea (see page 20). That'll get 'em back on their feet and growin' great in no time. Then, go after the culprit—the most likely suspect is a roving dog or cat. Don't bother to get a positive I.D., though. Just turn up the heat: Fido *or* Fluffy will turn tail and run from the scent of my extra-spicy Hit the Trail Mix (at left). And so will just about any other critter who has a nose to sniff with!

Miracle Mix

FUNGUS FIGHTER SOIL DRENCH

When foul fungi are fussin' around in your soil, polish 'em off with this potent potion.

4 garlic bulbs, crushed
½ cup of baking soda
1 gal. of water

Combine these ingredients in a big pot, and bring the water to a boil. Then turn off the heat, and let it cool to room temperature. Strain the liquid into a watering can, and soak the ground around fungus-prone plants. (There's nothin' fungi hate more than garlic!) Go *very slowly,* so the elixir goes deep into the soil. Then, dump the strained-out garlic bits onto the soil, and work them in gently, so as not to disturb plant roots.

Oh, Shoot!

When young peony shoots wilt and turn brown at the base, you've got a case of (what else?) peony wilt on your hands. It's caused by a botrytis fungus that attacks only peonies. In wet weather, you may also see a fuzzy gray growth at the stem base; on occasion, the damage occurs farther up the stem. Most often, this fungus attacks herbaceous peonies (the kind that die back to the ground in winter), but tree peonies can also be affected.

➡ Look on the positive side: Far worse trouble could've knocked at your garden gate! Not only does peony wilt give other plants the cold shoulder, but if you spring into action pronto, you can save your peonies. Here's the routine:

Step 1: Cut out the infected stems. Make sure you cut all the way back into healthy growth, even if that means going below soil level.

Step 2: Clear out and destroy all plant debris, which is where the fungal spores hide. If the plant showed severe damage, scrape up the top 3 or 4 inches of soil (very carefully, so as not to hurt the roots). Then send that dirt far, far away; otherwise, the fungus could be with you for years to come.

Step 3: Spread 4 inches of good, healthy compost on the planting bed, and carefully work it into the soil. Besides improving drainage and adding nutrients, compost gives off ethylene gas, which hinders the growth of fungus. Then, to wipe out every last, lingering spore, water your plants with my Fungus Fighter Soil Drench (see page 45).

Step 4: From now on, follow the fungus-fighting guidelines" in Chapter 14—they'll help keep your peonies in fine fettle for years to come.

Wretched Roots

Heave-Ho!

Finally, spring has sprung. You're looking at your perennial bed, where you expected to see tiny green shoots. Instead, you're gazing at root clumps lying on the ground, as high and dry as beached whales. What's going on here? Winter heaving, that's what. In places where the weather goes through alternate spells

of freezing and thawing, a plant's roots can be thrown clear out
of the ground. Exposed to the dry, frigid air, they can freeze to
death, or die of dehydration in no time flat.

➡ Tuck the roots back into their holes, give them a long, slow
drink of my Compost Tea (see page 20), and hope for the best.
To make sure the problem doesn't happen again, follow these
guidelines:

❀ When you're shopping for plants, choose varieties that are
proven performers in your hardiness zone (see the USDA
Plant Hardiness Zone Map on page 358).

❀ Water your perennials well all through late summer and
early fall. That'll give the roots the moisture they need to
carry them through the winter. (Once the ground freezes,
rain and melting snow can't get through the soil.)

❀ After the soil surface has frozen, mulch with 6 inches of straw,
pine boughs, or other organic mulch to prevent heaving.

We Need Some Air!

At first glance, your plants seem to be suffering from
pests or disease. Growth is stunted and weak; leaves
are either scorched, burned, or turning yellow. Pale
green blisters or water-soaked spots appear on stems
and leaves. Take a closer look. Are the roots concentrated just under the soil surface, or even creeping above
it? Then your plants are simply getting too much of a
good thing — namely, water. When soil becomes waterlogged, the soil particles clump together, leaving no room
for the oxygen that roots need to survive.

➡ If only one or two plants are suffering, there may be an obvious culprit, like a downspout that floods their root zone every
time it rains. In that case, simply move the waterlogged plants
to friendlier territory. When the damage is more widespread,

you've got a drainage problem on your hands. First, test your soil's drainage according to the guidelines in Chapter 14. Depending on the results, your solution could be as easy as adding a heap of organic matter to the soil, or as complicated (and expensive) as calling in a landscaping contractor.

Gimme a Drink!

When your plants are wilting, growing, and flowering poorly, or their buds are dropping off, it means their roots need water—yesterday!

➡ First, give those guys a good, long drink! Take it slow and easy, though: Drought followed by a sudden rush of water—whether from your hose or the sky—can make stems crack or split. Then, take stock: If only one plant in your garden has a thirst that won't quit, it could be that its roots have been damaged and can't take up enough water. In that case, dig it up and have a look. (Unfortunately, you'll have to kiss that plant good-bye.) If it's affecting your entire planting bed, your soil isn't retaining the moisture your plants need. See "Build a Better Bed" (below) for a simple solution.

Build a Better Bed

You realize that your planting bed is drying out too fast to do your plants much good. Chances are, your soil is simply too light and sandy to retain moisture, so water runs through before the roots can take more than a sip. But what can

you do that doesn't involve digging up your plants while you renovate their bed?

Relax, your plants can stay put while you work on creating a moisture-loving bed. Just follow these four simple steps:

Step 1: Put about a 3/4-inch layer of newspaper on the ground between your plants, and then soak the newspaper thoroughly.

Step 2: Spread about 2 inches of compost on top of the newspaper.

Step 3: Snake a soaker hose through the bed so that it comes within a few inches of each flower clump. This way, when you water, the H_2O will go directly to the plants' roots. (If the hose doesn't want to stay in place, pin it down with wire hoops made from wire clothes hangers.)

Step 4: Top the compost and the hose with 3 to 4 inches of chopped leaves or other organic mulch. Add more mulch as the layer thins out.

HAPPY CAMPERS

If you and your bank account are tired of catering to a crowd of thirsty plants, send the heavy drinkers to a new home. Then replace them with more modest imbibers. For starters, you can't go wrong with any of these:

Black-eyed Susans *(Rudbeckia)*
Blanket flower
    (Gaillardia x grandiflora)
Butterfly weed
    (Asclepias tuberosa)
Coreopsis *(Coreopsis)*
Moss phlox *(Phlox subulata)*
Russian sage
    (Perovskia atriplicifolia)
Sundrops *(Oenothera fruticosa)*
Wormwoods *(Artemisia)*
Yarrows *(Achillea)*
Yuccas *(Yucca)*

The secret to this soil improvement plan is the newspaper: For some reason, it draws earthworms like honey draws bears. As the worms gobble up all the news that's fit to eat, they turn the paper—and all that other organic matter—into soil that's both moisture-retentive *and* well-drained. And that's any root's idea of heaven on earth!

They Just Floated Away!

Finally, after years of mowing your almost vertical front yard, you sent the grass packin' and planted a perennial groundcover. You thought you had it made in the shade! Then, last week, the mother of all rainstorms swept through. It took your hillside for a ride, and the groundcover went with it. Those plants were supposed to hold the soil in place! What went wrong?

 The roots went wrong, that's what! To keep a steep slope in place, you need plants with fine, dense root systems that can grab the soil and hang on for dear life. If your former lawn was garden-variety turf grass, it would have fared no better than your young perennials in a major storm. Controlling erosion is a job that native plants were born for. Your best bet: Restock that mini mountainside with perennials that grow naturally on stream banks, steep hillsides, or windswept places close to your home sweet home. Your local Nature Conservancy office, botanical garden, or native plant society can clue you in to some real winners.

What a Rotten Development

It just doesn't seem fair: Your tall bearded irises have to battle three kinds of rhizome rot. Is there any way to keep your prized beauties safe and sound?

 You can conquer the wretched stuff if you catch it in time, but your game plan depends on which kind of rot you've got. Here's a rundown on the terrible trio:

Bacterial soft rot. Your nose will clue you in to this one: Besides being soft and mushy, stricken rhizomes give off an odor that'll send you runnin' for a gas mask! The bacteria sneak into the plant through wounds made by iris borers or (whoops!) careless cultivation. You may also see withered tips and water-soaked streaks on the leaves.

❀ Dig up the infected rhizomes, then cut out and discard the rotten parts. Dunk the healthy portion in a solution of 1 part household bleach to 3 parts water, and let it dry before replanting.

❀ To keep the bacteria from spreading, dip your tools in 70% denatured alcohol before using them on healthy plants.

❀ Head off future problems by controlling iris borers, which spread the disease (see page 57).

Fungal rhizome rot. The fungus goes by the tongue-twisting name of *Botryotinia convoluta*, and it strikes irises growing in poorly drained soil, especially in cool, wet weather. If your plants up and died in early spring (and you don't have to cover your nose when you go near them), this is the rot they've got.

❀ Dig up the plants, then cut out and destroy the infected parts of the rhizomes.

❀ Before you replant, improve drainage in the bed (see page 307), or move your irises to more hospitable territory.

❀ When you replant, leave about one-third of the rhizome above the soil surface—this fungus *loves* buried rhizomes!

Crown rot. Though technically caused by a fungus, the real cul-

HAPPY CAMPERS

Not all plants need well-drained soil. In fact, a lot of great-looking perennials love living with wet feet. If soggy turf is your problem, plant this crowd: They might just make you decide that your cursed swamp is a blessing in disguise!

Common canna (*Canna x generalis*)
Common rush (*Juncus effusus*)
Horsetail (*Equisetum hyemale*)
Japanese iris (*Iris kaempferi*)
Rose mallow (*Hibiscus moscheutos* subsp. *palustris*)
Siberian iris (*Iris sibirica*)
Variegated cattail (*Typha latifolia* 'Variegata')

prit is simply lack of care. Crown rot usually attacks crowded plants that have gone too long without being divided. It's easy to recognize: When you dig up the rhizomes, you'll see white, thread-like growths and tiny black or brown "fruits" that are chock-full of fungal spores.

❧ Clear out and destroy the rotted plants, along with the soil they were growing in. This stuff spreads like wildfire, so take care not to spread infected soil to other parts of the garden.

❧ Divide your irises every four or five years, or sooner if they're looking cramped. You can do the job any time from flowering until early fall.

The Rotting Crown Affair

It's springtime. Balmy breezes are blowing, birds are twittering, and your tulips and daffodils are bursting into bloom. But your balloon flowers are just sittin' there. Where there should be tiny green shoots, there's just bare ground. On closer inspection, the place where there should be shoots sprouting from the root clump (the crown) is black, rotten, and covered with things that look like white threads. It's a case of crown rot. Balloon flower (*Platycodon grandiflorus*) is a prime target, but crown rot can strike many perennials. Like all other fungal and bacterial diseases, crown rot thrives in poorly drained soil and crowded planting beds.

PLANT THESE at your **PERIL!**

A whole host of perennials can fall victim to crown rot, but in addition to balloon flower, it most often plagues these hapless victims: baby's breath, bellflower, black-eyed Susan, columbine, delphinium, hosta, phlox, and wisteria.

➥ If you reach the scene in time, you can save the day. Just dig up the roots, and cut away the damaged spots. And don't be knife-shy: Slice well back into healthy tissue. Then, before you replant the root clump, dig plenty of compost into the soil; it'll both improve drainage and kill fungal spores. For extra protection, saturate the soil with my Fungus Fighter Soil Drench (see page 45).

Sickly Stems

Fat Phlox

Well, to be more accurate, swollen. If the stems of your phlox plants swell up and even split in early to midsummer, phlox nematodes are to blame. Although there are many kinds of nematodes in gardendom, these guys attack only phlox (both perennial and annual vari-eties). Besides swollen stems, their dirty work results in stunted growth and very skinny leaves at the shoot tips. If the population goes unchecked, plants rot and often die.

➡ The bad news is that you'll have to dig up and destroy the infected plants. The good news is that before you toss them into the trash, you can cut off chunks of the roots and replant them. That's because unlike their close relatives, root-knot nematodes, phlox nematodes don't attack roots, only stems and leaves. They overwinter in dormant buds at the base of the plant, though—so, when you slice into the roots, get rid of *all* the buds. You may have to wait until next year before your phlox blooms again, but bloom again it will!

Bleeding Hearts Broke Your Heart

Your bleeding hearts put on their big spring show, then the plants just turned brown and died. They *seemed* strong and healthy as could be. What did you do wrong?

In short, nothing. Common bleeding heart, *Dicentra spectabilis*, usually dies back after it blooms, especially in hot, dry summers. To prolong the blooming period, keep the soil evenly moist, but not soggy. (If its home ground is wet, *D. spectabilis* will die and *never* come back.) Once the foliage has gone, mark its place, so that you don't accidentally disturb the roots. Meanwhile, give your bleeding hearts some bedmates like astilbes, hostas, or shade-loving annuals that will help to fill the summertime gap.

HAPPY CAMPERS

If you don't want a gap where your bleeding heart used to be, plant fringed bleeding heart *(Dicentra eximia)* or western bleeding heart *(D. formosa)*. The flowers aren't quite as showy as those of *D. spectabilis*, but the foliage—and sometimes the flowers—hangs in there all summer long.

The Not-So-Great Pretender

Your plants are droopin' like there's no tomorrow! You say to yourself "Uh-oh: drought stress," and you give them a long, slow drink. They perk up, and you go on your merry way. Come the next morning, they're all droopy and wilted again! Your plants aren't suffering from drought, my friend: They've got fusarium wilt. It's a fungus disease that blocks the vascular tissue. (In cool, damp weather, you might see fluffy, pale pink or white fungus growing from the blocked spots.) In the case of a partial blockage, some water will

get through, but not enough to keep the plant alive for very
long. This trouble is most likely to invade your garden if you live
in a warm, moist climate.

 Fusarium wilt is nasty stuff, so don't just sit there and ponder
the situation—dig the plant up and get rid of it, pronto!
Remove as much soil as you can from the former root zone,
and send it packin' too. Then, before you plant anything else in
that spot, read my fusarium-fighting guidelines in Chapter 7.

Lousy Leaves

Not You Again!

There's one plant disease that, sooner or later,
shows up in just about every perennial garden: powdery mildew. It's a fungus that first
appears as a grayish white powder on
leaves, buds, or stems. Eventually, plant parts
become distorted and even drop off. The stuff goes
on the rampage anytime days are warm and nights are
cool and humid—most commonly in late summer or early
fall. Powdery mildew plagues a whole host of plants, including
asters, bee balms, black-eyed Susans, and mums. One perennial,
though, has a well-earned reputation as a mildew magnet: That's
garden phlox *(Phlox paniculata)*.

 Powdery mildew might be widespread, but it's not vicious. It
rarely kills a plant, or even causes serious damage—it just *looks*
as ugly as sin. At the first sign of trouble, clip off and destroy
the affected leaves, then spray the rest of the plant with my
Chamomile Mildew Chaser on page 56. If you've happened on
the scene late, and the plant is covered from top to bottom with

white powder, cut the stems back to the ground. Before you know it, new ones will grow back. To fend off future attacks:

✿ Improve air circulation by dividing crowded clumps or thinning out stems.

✿ When you water, aim your hose at the ground, not at the leaves. Better yet, install a soaker hose in the bed.

✿ Spray your plants with my Chamomile Mildew Chaser once a week throughout the growing season.

✿ Grow mildew-resistant varieties. You'll find 'em marked that way on labels and in plant catalogs.

★ Miracle Mix ★

CHAMOMILE MILDEW CHASER

To help keep powdery mildew from pounding your plants, serve them this tea once a week, especially in late summer and early fall.

4 chamomile tea bags
2 tbsp. of Murphy's Oil Soap®
1 qt. of boiling water

Put the tea bags in a pot, pour the boiling water over them, and let it steep for an hour or so, 'til the brew is good and strong. Let it cool, then mix in the Murphy's Oil Soap. Pour the tea into a 6-gallon hose-end sprayer, and fire away! Try to apply this elixir early in the day, so your plants' leaves can dry by nightfall.

Who Spit on My Leaves?

A spittlebug, that's who! These tiny greenish or yellowish nymphs hatch from their eggs in late spring, then spew out a frothy mass of "spit" to protect themselves while they nibble on your plants. Eventually, they grow up into little brown, black, or tan insects called froghoppers.

➡ Their disgusting manners aside, spittlebugs don't do any real damage. Just wipe 'em off, or blast 'em from your plants with a spray of water. As for the froghoppers, they just go about their business and don't bother anybody. (In fact, you'll probably never even see one in your garden.)

Bored to Tears

Very often in the plant kingdom, trouble above ground means trouble below ground. This is a classic case in point: When you see irregular tunnels or mines in iris leaves or flower stalks, it means that iris borers are hard at work, tunnelin' for the rhizomes. When the caterpillars hatch in April or early May, they drill tiny holes in the leaves, a few inches above the soil surface. Then, they crawl in and start chomping. By midsummer, they invade the rhizomes, and eat 'em alive from the inside out. Once they're in the soil, they pupate. Anywhere between August and October, they emerge as night-flying moths with purplish front wings and yellow-brown hind wings.

➡ Your action plan depends on when you first spot the invasion. Here are your best options:

❀ In the happy (but unlikely) event that you catch the larvae just as they hatch in the spring, give 'em a lethal dose of my

Miracle Mix

CATERPILLAR KILLER TONIC

No matter what kind of caterpillars are buggin' your plants, a jolt of this aromatic blend will do 'em in.

½ lb. of wormwood leaves
2 tbsp. of Murphy's Oil Soap®
4 cups of water

Simmer the wormwood leaves in 2 cups of water for 30 minutes. Strain out the leaves, then add the Murphy's Oil Soap and 2 more cups of water. Pour the solution into a 6-gallon hand-held sprayer, and apply to your plants to the point of run-off. Repeat as necessary until the caterpillars are history.

Caterpillar Killer Tonic on page 57. At this early stage, the creeps are slim and greenish in color.

✿ Once they've drilled into a leaf or flower stalk, you can pinch 'em to death. Just take each leaf between your fingers, and squeeze hard, from the base up. When you hear a "pop," you'll know that a borer has bitten the dust.

✿ If the thought of squashing makes you squeamish, cut off the whole fan of leaves, and destroy it. You'll lose this year's big flower show, but you'll save the rhizome from the invasion.

✿ In midsummer—the normal time for dividing irises—dig up the rhizomes and look for tunnels. When you see one, poke a wire into it, and you'll hook the borer. (There's only one per rhizome, though droves of 'em might haunt the leaves—go figure!) Then, dip the rhizome in a solution of 1 part household bleach to 3 parts water, let it dry, and replant. First, though, scrape a few inches of soil out of the planting area, add an equal amount of compost, and mix it in.

✿ To cut down on next year's borer population, invite some bats over to your place to polish off the egg-laying moths. (For the lowdown on these good guys, see page 316.)

PLANT THESE at your PERIL!

Tall, bearded iris is the iris borers' favorite victim, with Louisiana iris a close second. For reasons I can't fathom, the wormy guys rarely bother Siberian iris.

Geometry Quiz

Yellow, geometric-shaped patches in leaves—especially lower ones—point to the early work of foliar nematodes. As these microscopic worms attack tissue between the veins, they

make triangles, semi-circles, and other shapes that start out yellow, then turn brown. Eventually, the whole leaf dies. These tiny
terrors are especially partial to asters, chrysanthemums, and
primroses. They also go gunnin' for dahlias and strawberries, so
be prepared to do battle.

➡ Here's your three-step
action plan:

Step 1: Dig up seri-
ously damaged plants,
and destroy 'em.
Where only a few
parts of a plant have
been attacked, cut
off, and destroy the
affected sections. Make
sure you scoop up any
leaves or stems that
may have dropped to
the ground—nema-
todes multiply like
crazy in plant debris.

Step 2: Get some
good-guy nematodes at
the garden center, or
order them from a cat-
alog, and apply them
according to the direc-
tions on the package.
(For more about these
garden heroes, see page 314.)

Step 3: Mulch around the remaining plants with well-aged
compost; it contains organisms that eat bad-guy nematodes for
lunch. Then spray your plants with my All-Season Clean-Up
Tonic (above).

★ Miracle Mix ★

ALL-SEASON CLEAN-UP TONIC

This excellent elixir will keep your
whole yard and garden squeaky
clean—which is just what pesky pests
and dastardly disease germs hate more
than anything!

1 cup of liquid dish soap
1 cup of antiseptic mouthwash
1 cup of tobacco tea*

Mix all of the ingredients in a 20-gallon
hose-end sprayer, and give your plants
a good shower. Repeat the process
every two weeks throughout the growing season.

*To make tobacco tea, wrap half a
handful of chewing tobacco in a panty
hose toe or a piece of cheesecloth.
Soak it in 1 gallon of hot water until
the water turns dark brown. Pour the
liquid into a glass container with a
tight lid for storage.

It's Crazy Out There!

It's a strange scene, alright: Your plants' leaves are turning yellow along the veins, then pale all over, with brown edges. Too many leaves emerge on a stem, and they're all yellow, spindly, and longer than they should be. Scraggly bunches of stems, like witch's broom, spring out of nowhere. Plants are stunted. If flowers appear at all, they're a sickly yellow-green color, and weirdly deformed. The culprit: aster yellows, a disease caused by a tiny no-goodnik called a mycoplasma-like organism, a.k.a. MLO. This bit of nastiness strikes in early summer, and it spreads its blanket over a variety of flowers, vegetables, and non-woody fruit plants.

Although the MLO does the dirty work, it reaches the crime scene courtesy of aster (or six-spotted) leafhoppers or, sometimes, aphids. It can also be spread by plant-to-plant contact. On the positive front, seeds don't carry the germ, and the MLO can't live long in the soil. If aster yellows has put your plants in sick bay, follow this road back to good health:

✿ Dig up the infected plants. It's okay to put them in the compost pile, but don't let them touch any healthy plants on the way.

✿ To kill any lingering disease-spreaders, saturate neighboring plants with my Lethal Leafhopper Spray (at left). Test a few leaves first, though, just to make sure they're not sensitive to soap. Then, let 'er rip. Cover the plant from top to bot-

Miracle Mix

LETHAL LEAFHOPPER SPRAY

Even hard-to-get bugs like leafhoppers kick the bucket when you hit 'em hard with this stuff.

½ cup of alcohol (any kind will do)
2 tbsp. of liquid dish soap
1 gal. of warm water

Mix all of these ingredients together, and pour the solution into a hand-held mist sprayer. Then, saturate your plants from top to bottom, especially the undersides of leaves, where leafhoppers love to hide.

tom, including the undersides of leaves—you don't want to leave any of these guys standing! Then, repeat the procedure twice more, at three-day intervals.

✿ For long-term protection, recruit an army of good-guy bugs to control your villainous population (see page 314).

Unhappy Trails

Your big, beautiful hosta leaves are full of holes and silvery trails of slime! Only two villains leave this kind of evidence: slugs and their kissin' cousins, snails. These slime-balls slither through shady gardens all over the country, but in cool, damp territory like the Pacific Northwest, they act like they own the place! No plant is safe from their clutches, but in the perennial garden, hostas and delphiniums are high-risk targets.

➡ Every soldier in the slug and snail wars has his own favorite strategy. Here are some of my tried-and-true tactics:

Trap 'em. In the evening, just before the creeps come out to feed, set cabbage leaves or citrus rinds on the ground beside your plants. The next morning, they'll be chock-full of slugs and snails. Just pick up the whole kit and caboodle, and drop it in a tub of hot, soapy water.

Scratch 'em. Both slugs and snails have soft underbellies. When they try to glide over little jagged particles of any kind, they get a lethal cut to the tummy. To safeguard your plants, surround 'em with any of these pricklers: pine needles, wood ashes, crushed egg shells, diatomaceous earth (available at garden centers), or bird grit (available at pet shops).

Serve 'em. For dinner, that is. Encourage some natural enemies to bed down on your turf, and the slug and snail population will plummet. A whole lot of critters dine on the slimers, but toads, turtles, robins, and downy woodpeckers have slug appetites that just won't quit! As for snail specialists, well, given its druthers, the song thrush would *live* on escargot!

Dear Jerry, Last year I moved to Seattle, and bought a house with a wonderful, shady garden full of hostas, ferns, bleeding hearts, and all sorts of great plants. The only problem is that slugs are eating everything in sight! My neighbors tell me I can keep them out by sprinkling something called diatomaceous earth around my plants. What is this stuff, anyway? And if it kills slugs, won't it kill earthworms, too? – J.H., Seattle, Washington

Dear J.H., To the naked eye, diatomaceous earth looks like an abrasive dust, but it's really the fossilized remains of prehistoric algae. Its tiny particles are so sharp that they puncture the skin of any slug that slithers over them. Then, presto: The culprit loses so much water, it dies of dehydration. And don't worry about your friendly neighborhood earthworms; not only can they slither over the particles, but they actually digest the stuff! Diatomaceous earth is also harmless to birds, bees, and mammals. It even contains some trace minerals that your plants need for good health. So hightail it down to your local garden center and buy a big sack— and tell 'em Jerry sent you! (Just be sure you get horticultural-grade diatomaceous earth, and not the kind that's made for use in swimming-pool filters.)

You Could Drink Out of 'Em!

Cup-shaped leaves, often with the veins close together, signal herbicide damage. It works its nastiness on any plant. You see it most often in spring and summer, when folks (and public works crews) are spraying weed-killers on lawns and along roadsides. Other symptoms include stems twisted into spirals, and scorched, brown spots on leaves and stems. Where side shoots should be, you'll find stunted rosettes of short shoots and malformed, strap-like leaves.

➡ First, cut off the damaged areas and destroy them. Don't toss 'em on the compost pile—those chemicals have done enough damage already! Then, to promote healthy new growth, water well, and give your plants a snack of my All-Purpose Perennial Fertilizer (at right). If you know where the herbicides came from, you can probably defend your garden against future attacks. Just call the folks who did the spraying, and ask them (politely) to let you know in advance of their next assault. That way, you can cover up your plants with sheets, paper sacks, or plastic garbage bags until the foul stuff has blown over.

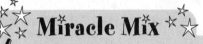

Miracle Mix

ALL-PURPOSE PERENNIAL FERTILIZER

Here's a great recipe for healthy perennials—use it to boost soil before *and* after planting to keep your perennials growing strong.

3 parts bonemeal
3 parts greensand or wood ashes
1 part bloodmeal

Mix the ingredients together. Apply 3 to 5 pounds per 100 sq. ft. before planting and work it into the soil, or scatter 2 tablespoons around each clump and scratch it into the soil surface.

Vamoose, Virus!

The leaves are sort of pretty, with yellow and light green splotches, streaks, and mottled patterns—although you know that's not the way they're *supposed* to look. Then you notice that some of the leaves are cupped, puckered, and distorted, and the plant's overall growth seems stunted. It's a virus at work. Any plant can catch one, but among perennials, asters, columbines, delphiniums, and mums are especially prone to virus attacks.

➡ There are oodles of plant viruses, but all have similar symptoms. Your plan of action is the same, too: Dig up the victim and get rid of it. Then, to keep the rest of your plants out of sick bay, give them my Flower and Foliage Flu Shot (at left). I have to admit that this "drug" is still in the experimental stages, but scientists in California have found that juices squeezed from green pepper plants can protect other plants from viruses. I can't absolutely guarantee it'll work, but it's worth a shot (sorry, I couldn't resist). Meanwhile, for long-term protection, keep a tight rein on the culprits that spread these nasty diseases—aphids, thrips, and other sap-sucking insects (see page 112).

✦ Miracle Mix ✦

FLOWER AND FOLIAGE FLU SHOT

There's no cure for plant viruses, but this "vaccine" *could* help fend off attacks.

2 cups of leaves from a healthy green pepper plant
½ tsp. of liquid dish soap
2 cups of water

Put the leaves and the water in a blender and liquefy. Then dilute the mixture with an equal amount of water, add the dish soap, and pour the solution into a hand-held mist sprayer. Drench your plants from top to bottom.

Failing Flowers

What's With All the Green?

It *is* disappointing: Your perennials are churnin' out healthy stems and leaves galore, but almost no flowers. What's going on here? Their diet's too high in nitrogen, that's what!

➡ All plants need the big N, of course, but to put on their best show, they also need plenty of phosphorus (P) and potassium (K). If your bloomers are bummers, get 'em back on track with these miracle workers. Just choose one from each column, sprinkle them on the soil around your plants, and dig them in gently (so you don't disturb the roots). Then, water well, and slowly, so the chow can start movin' downward toward the roots. Before you know it, buds'll be bustin' out all over! After that, feed your perennials every two weeks with my Flower Feeder Tonic (see page 66).

Phosphorus	Potassium
Bonemeal	Bananas (peels and fruit)
Colloidal phosphate	Granite meal
Rock phosphate	Kelp meal
Seaweed meal	Wood ashes

Nonperforming Peonies

All through the long, cold winter, you wait for your peonies to put on their big spring show. The shoots come up right on schedule in early spring, and almost overnight, leaves pop out. But no buds appear. Come mid-June, when your plants should be chock-full of big, fluffy flowers, there's nary a bloom in sight. What went wrong?

➡ There are three possible causes for nonblooming peonies—and, of course, three possible solutions to the problem.

1. They're planted too deep.

When you set the root clump into the hole, its pink buds ("eyes") must be no more than 1 to 2 inches below the soil surface. Otherwise, the plants just won't bloom—ever. So, early in the fall, dig up each plant. (Go *very* gently, because once peonies set down roots, they don't like to be disturbed.) Then add a half-and-half mixture of soil and compost to the hole until you've got the right depth. Mix the new stuff with the existing soil, set the plant back into its home, and water well. You may not see blooms the following spring— or even the spring after—but within a few years, your efforts should reward you with oceans of flowers.

2. Too much shade.

Although a peony's dream home is in full sun, it'll perform well in partial shade. In gardeners' terms, that means two to five hours of direct sun a day. Anything less (especially in dry soil), and a plant might give you leaves galore, but not a glimpse of a bud. If shade is

★ Miracle Mix ★

FLOWER FEEDER TONIC

Once your plants are churnin' out flowers again, put them back on a well-balanced diet. This healthy mix includes healthy doses of all of the Big Three (nitrogen, phosphorus, and potassium), plus important trace minerals, a.k.a. micronutrients.

1 can of beer
2 tbsp. of fish emulsion
2 tbsp. of liquid dish soap
2 tbsp. of ammonia
2 tbsp. of hydrogen peroxide
2 tbsp. of whiskey
1 tbsp. of clear corn syrup
1 tbsp. of unflavored gelatin
4 tsp. of instant tea granules
2 gal. of warm water

Mix all of the ingredients together. Feed all of your perennials (and bulbs) with this mix every two weeks in the morning. You'll have glorious blooms all season long!

the problem, you need to shed more light on the scene. You may have to prune or remove trees or tall shrubs, or replace a solid fence with lattice panels. If that's not possible, move the plants to a sunnier site. But this maneuver is a gamble; the older the plants are, the less likely they are to survive trans-planting. If you want to ensure the survival of your peonies, your best bet is to take cuttings and root them according to the guidelines on page 41.

3. They're just not ready yet. Peonies are slow starters. They seldom bloom the first year after planting, and sometimes it takes them two or three years to start churnin' out flowers. So, be patient. Given just basic care, your plants should still be struttin' their stuff when your great-grandchildren pick up their first shovels!

It's a Blackout!

When your flowers or buds suddenly turn black, there's one likely suspect: botrytis blight, also known as gray mold. It often gets its first toehold on aging blossoms, then spreads like lightning to leaves and stems. The prime targets are big, billowy flowers like peonies, but I can't think of a single plant that's immune to this das-tardly disease. Botrytis can wipe out a whole garden in a few days. The good news is that the nasty stuff is not hard to control, once you understand how it operates.

➡ Battling botrytis is a two-part process:

Instant action. The minute you spot signs of botrytis, cut off and destroy the infected flowers, leaves, and stems. Whatever you do, don't toss 'em on the compost pile! Then, to control the spread of the fungus, dust the plant with sulfur, or spray the foliage with my Compost Tea (see page 20).

Constant vigilance. The botrytis fungus lives in the soil almost everywhere, but it tends to cause trouble only in certain conditions. It thrives in cool, damp, or humid weather, and it *loves* crowded, shady gardens. The fungus lives through the winter on dead plant debris. Then, come spring, spores form and travel to new plants via wind, water, or dirty garden tools.

To keep the culprit at bay, give your plants enough elbow room to allow good air circulation, and water early in the morning, so flowers and foliage can dry off before nightfall. And when you're working in the garden, be careful where you swing those tools!

The Dirty Turncoats!

You chose your pearly pink columbines because they were *exactly* the color you wanted for a corner of your pink-and-white garden. That was two years ago. Now, baby columbines are springin' up all over the place, and they're every color of the rainbow—except the pink that you started with. What's more, the original plants have disappeared!

First, that disappearing act is business as usual for columbines; they're naturally short-lived plants, and rarely survive for more than two or three years. In the meantime, though, they reseed like crazy, so there are always new plants to replace the old ones. Now, here comes the answer to the color-change mystery—and a mini botany lesson: A species columbine, such as *Aquilegia canadensis,* will produce flowers of the same color from every seed it sets. (The same is true of any other plant species.) On the other hand, hybrids are often the result of very complex breeding programs. For instance, a columbine that's labeled *A.* 'Double Pinkie' in a catalog could have a family tree that includes every color under the sun. When a plant like that throws its seeds to the wind, there's no telling what'll come up! But there are a couple of simple solutions to this colorful dilemma:

✿ Find a species columbine in a color you like, and let it go. It'll give you a new crop of identical seedlings every year. (In fact, it'll give you enough of 'em to share with the whole neighborhood!)

✿ Plant a hybrid that strikes your fancy, and clip off the flowers before they set seed. Then, plant more of that same variety every two years or so. That way, you'll always have the exact shade you want, where you want it.

GRANDMA PUTT'S
grow-how

Sometimes, when trouble strikes, you need to move a plant *pronto*—even if it's a tad too cold to be transplanting anything. When that happens at my place, I do what Grandma Putt did: Before I set the plant in its new hole, I pour in a bucket of hot water. It works like a liquid blanket, so the roots don't shiver their timbers in the cool soil.

But This *Is* the Same Plant!

Here's a variation on the color-change mystery: Last year, you planted a clump of pink-colored daylilies. When you brought 'em home from the garden center, each plant had three or four flower stocks, with plump buds beginning to form. Come July, those buds opened up into deep, peachy pink flowers. This year, your plants bloomed right on schedule—but the flowers were yellow! What went wrong?

➥ In a word: sun. Or, rather, lack of it. I'll bet shillings to shovels that your daylilies are growing in partial shade. As any plant catalog will tell you, daylilies *(Hemerocallis) do* thrive in any amount of light from full sun to partial shade. But here's something they don't tell you: Plant growers have been crossbreeding daylilies for years, and the results have been more gorgeous colors than you can shake a paint box at. Once in a while, though, when the plants are grown in less than all-day sun, the flowers revert to one of their parents' colors—usually basic yellow. Heaven knows why that is, but I sure don't! Because your flowers came true to color the first season, it means that they must have lived in full sun when they formed their scapes (flower stalks). As in the case of the color-changing columbines, you can choose your path:

✿ Leave your daylilies right where they are, and enjoy the yellow flowers. As long as the plants get at least three to five hours of sun each day, they'll be happy and healthy.

✿ Come fall, or next spring, dig 'em up and move 'em to a sunnier spot. Unlike columbines, daylilies are in it for the long haul, so the same plants will give you peachy pink blooms year after year!

Open Up, Bud!

A lot of your flower buds just won't open. The ones that do unfold are covered with odd-colored streaks and speckles. The leaves look strange, too: They've got silvery stripes all over them. The culprits might as well hang out a sign saying "Thrips at Work." These guys are so tiny, you'll probably never see 'em, but they do giant-size damage, sucking the sap from any plant they touch. And they touch a lot of 'em, too! In the perennial garden, though, thrips have a special hankerin' for delphiniums, mums, hollyhocks, peonies, and daylilies.

➡ Fighting an almost-invisible enemy does have its challenges. That's no reason to give up, though—as Grandma Putt always said, you're bigger and smarter than they are! First, cut off all the damaged flowers and leaves, and destroy (don't compost!) all but about 2 cups' worth. Then, stop the invading forces dead in their tracks with my So Long, Sucker Spray (at right). It's a nightmare for thrips, aphids, and other little pests that suck the life out of their victims. Finally, put an end to the thrips' trips by enlisting their enemies— damsel bugs, minute pirate bugs, and hover flies eat the teeny terrors by the bucketload!

They're Fallin' Over!

Just a few days ago, you cut a big basketful of flowers and arranged them in your best vase. Now, they're lookin' as limp as overcooked spaghetti. Is it time to toss 'em?

➧ You may be able to save those blooms from the compost pile, at least for a little while longer. Try this:

Step 1: Fill a clean vase with my Flower Saver Solution on page 72. How

Miracle Mix

SO LONG, SUCKER SPRAY

This fabulous formula is just the ticket for tiny insects like thrips and aphids that are too small to handpick and whirl in a blender all by themselves.

2 cups of thrip-infested flowers or leaves*
2 cups of warm water

Put the plant parts in an old blender, and whirl 'em with the water (tiny bugs and all). Strain the goop through cheesecloth, dilute with 1 gallon of water, and pour the juice into a hand-held mist sprayer. Then spray your plants from top to bottom, on both sides of leaves and stems, and along all runners. Repeat the treatment after rain. If you have any extra juice, freeze it right away before bacteria can get a toehold. Be sure to label it clearly—you don't want to have this stuff for dinner!

*Substitute whatever pests are sucking the life out of your plants. Two notes of caution: Once you've used a blender to make this spray, don't use it again for either human or pet food—ever! And don't make this spray (or any other) from mosquitoes, fleas, or other blood-sucking insects that transmit human and animal diseases, or you'll be asking for some serious trouble.

much you need depends on the size and shape of the vase. You want just enough solution so that all the stem tips are under water, and so the vase is heavy enough not to topple over. Too much liquid will make the stems rot faster.

Step 2: Pull off any leaves that will be underwater in the vase.

Step 3: Hold each flower stem under warm running water. Using a sharp knife or scissors—and with the water still running—cut the stem at a 45-degree angle, about 1 inch from the bottom. Then set the flower into the vase.

Miracle Mix

FLOWER SAVER SOLUTION

This recipe makes 1 quart of solution.

1 cup of lemon-lime soda (not diet)
¼ tsp. of household bleach
3 cups of warm water (110°F)

Mix all of these ingredients together, and pour the solution into a clean vase. It'll make those posies perk right up! Use it from the get-go for all of your cut flowers.

Step 4: When all the flowers are sittin' pretty in the container, put it in the fridge for an hour or two. Just make sure the temperature is above 35°F. Also, keep the bouquet far away from unwrapped fruits and vegetables—they give off ethylene gas, which will make those posies go downhill faster than you can say "Baby, it's cold in here!" If there's no room in the fridge, set them in the coolest spot in the house.

Step 5: Once they've chilled out, move the flowers to a place that's out of direct sunlight, and away from both cold drafts and heat sources.

Step 6: Add fresh doses of Flower Saver Solution as the level goes down, and change it completely every two to three days.

CHAPTER 3

Radiant Roses

The way some folks carry on, you'd think that a rosebush is nothing but a disaster waiting to happen. Well, friends, I'm here to tell you that it just ain't so! Oh, I admit roses can hand you their fair share of challenges. (Do you know a single living thing that can't?) The good news is that with this bag of tricks at your beck and call, roses are as easy to live with as any other flowering shrubs.

Stricken Seeds 'n Seedlings

Get Hip to Ripening

You picked rose hips off your bushes in the hopes of harvesting seeds. But then a gardening friend told you that you didn't wait long enough for the hips to ripen, and so your seeds'll never sprout. How do you know when the hips are ripe?

➡ Rose hips (the firm, fleshy fruit that appears just at the base of the flower) take anywhere from two to four months to ripen, depending on the rose. You know they're ready when they change color—usually to orange or red, though the hips of some wild roses turn shiny black. As the hips turn color, some kinds stay hard, while others turn soft (so don't worry that they're going bad).

Nothin's Comin' Up Roses

At the time, it seemed like a great way to jump-start your rose garden: A friend gave you ripe hips from her favorite rosebushes. You took those little fruits home, sliced 'em open, took out the seeds, and stashed 'em in the fridge in a glass jar. A few days later, when you'd gotten their beds all ready, you planted the seeds. But not a single one came up. What went wrong?

➡ Your storage system, that's what. In order to germinate, rose seeds need two things: constant moisture and a period of cold. Aside from that, though, roses are easy to grow from seed, outdoors or in.

Outdoors. This is the simplest way to get roses up and

growing; in the fall, just set the ripe seed into the ground as
deep as the seed is thick, and Mother Nature will take it from
there. Come spring, add a thin layer of mulch to keep the soil
surface moist, and water lightly if the weather's dry. Of course,
there is one disadvantage to this method: It leaves the seeds
and seedlings wide open to attacks from mice, squirrels, and
bad-guy bugs like cutworms.

Indoors. The seed-starting process is basically the same for
roses as it is for annuals and perennials. There are a few differ-
ences, though—and it takes a while, so you'll need to be patient.
Here's the routine:

Step 1: Gather your
supplies. You'll need
plastic, zippered sand-
wich bags; paper towels;
and water.

Step 2: Fold a paper
towel so that it fits
snugly inside the plastic
bag, and add about 3
tablespoons of water.
Cut open a ripe rose hip,
remove the seeds, and
space them out evenly
on one side of the towel.

Step 3: Seal the bag,
and set it in the refriger-
ator, seed side down. Then, sit back and wait. In anywhere
from 6 to 12 weeks (and sometimes longer), the seeds will
germinate.

Step 4: Wait until you see the first round seed leaves (cotyledons). Then carefully remove each seedling from the bag,
and plant it in its own 2-inch pot filled with light, well-
drained potting mix. Set the pots on a windowsill for the

⋆ Miracle Mix ⋆

TRANSPLANT TONIC

This terrific tonic is perfect for getting roses and all sorts of other transplants off to a super-fast start!

½ **can of beer**
1 tbsp. of ammonia
1 tbsp. of instant tea granules
1 tbsp. of baby shampoo
1 gal. of water

Mix all of the ingredients together.
Then add 1 cup of the solution to
each planting hole at transplant time.

rest of the winter. Use a north-facing window if you can, because the sun from a south or west window can dry out a baby plant. If you don't have a window to spare, put the pots on a table under fluorescent lights for at least 18 hours a day.

Step 5: Keep the soil evenly moist, but not wet, and—to keep your seedlings safe from foul fungi—follow my damping-off prevention guidelines on page 6.

Step 6: When you're sure Jack Frost has vamoosed, move the youngsters to a spot that's light, but protected from wind and direct sun (a covered porch makes a dandy nursery). About a week later, set the plants in their new homes, and give them a drink of my Transplant Tonic (on page 75). They'll be off and runnin' in no time at all!

That's Not the Rose I Expected!

If you planted rose seeds, and they grew into bushes that looked nothing like their parents, I'm not surprised. Most modern roses are hybrids—the result of hundreds of years of crossbreeding. When you plant a seed from one of those babies, there's no telling what'll come up!

➡ Only species roses come true from seed. Fortunately, you've got dozens, if not hundreds, of winners to choose from. What's even better, though, is that if you plant a species rose that's hardy in your climate and happy in your soil, it'll fend off pests and diseases that would knock its modern cousins flat. What's more, species roses don't even need to be pruned, except to keep them within boundaries that you've set. Here are some of my all-time favorite rosy heroes:

Lady Banks rose *(Rosa banksiae)*. A rugged rambler (sprawling climber) with thornless canes that grow 20 to 30 feet. This lady shrugs off salty ocean breezes, says "boo" to diseases that knock other roses flat, and thrives in full sun or partial shade.

There are two versions: one with lightly fragrant yellow flowers *(R. banksiae lutea)*; the other with stronger, violet-scented white blooms and listed in catalogs as either *R. banksiae banksiae* or *R. banksiae alba-plena*. Lady Banks is hardy only in Zones 8 to 10, but in colder territory, she makes a great container plant if you keep her pruned and move her to a sheltered spot for the winter.

GRANDMA PUTT'S
grow-how

Grandma Putt's favorite rose was an old-time climber that Shakespeare wrote about: the eglantine, which most of us know as sweet briar rose *(Rosa eglanteria)*. And no wonder! Eglantine has it all: sweet-smelling, light pink blooms; leaves with the spicy aroma of green apples; and mossy, apple-scented burrs that form along the canes. Plus, this rose churns more hips than you can shake a sonnet at. Grandma Putt picked bushels of 'em every fall and used 'em to make jam and tea (besides tasting yummy, they're chock-full of vitamin C). She didn't stop there, though. She also dried the flowers, leaves, and burrs and used 'em in her special potpourri recipe. Talk about useful plants!

Red-leafed rose *(Rosa glauca)*. A real winner for cold climates. This upright shrub is hardy in Zones 2 through 8, but performs best where winter is serious business. And talk about colorful plants! Young canes are an eye-catching purple (and nearly thornless); foliage is copper to purplish in sunny sites, silvery green in partial shade. Flowers—clear pink with white centers—bloom in late spring, followed by bright red hips.

Shining rose *(Rosa nitida)*. A groundcover with real pizzazz! If you need to anchor a hillside that wants to ramble, this is the rose to reach for. It grows about 2 feet high, spreads like nobody's business, and performs like a trouper, even in poor soil and partial shade. What's more, it'll give you year-round color, with fragrant, pink flowers in spring; glossy green foliage through the summer; scarlet leaves in fall; and bright red hips and reddish brown prickles through the winter. It's hardy in Zones 4 to 6.

Swamp rose *(Rosa palustris scandens).* One of the few roses that not only tolerates poorly drained soil, but actually thrives in it. This winner doesn't demand wet feet, though: It also grows sleek and sassy in ordinary, well-drained garden soil. Hardy in Zones 4 to 8, it has nearly thornless canes that bear fragrant, bright pink flowers and willow-like leaves.

A Cut Below

Here's the plot: You took cuttings from a big, healthy rosebush, tucked 'em into pots filled with rooting medium, and they're just sittin' there, as rootless as desert nomads. How come?

 Roses are a snap to grow from cuttings. In fact, most of 'em will even form roots in a jar of water on a windowsill. You can also root rose cuttings in pots filled with a sterilized rooting medium (see "A Healthy Send-Off" on page 41). Still, whichever method you use, things can go wrong. If your cuttings won't perform, the reason—and the solution—could be right here:

They're the wrong age. A cutting that's too old or too young can be hard to root. For best results, clip a stem that's just bloomed or is just about to bloom.

It's the wrong time. For some reason, cuttings are easier to root early in the season, rather than later.

It's in the wrong place. In order to form roots, rose cuttings need all the light they can get, but direct sun will dry out the stems faster than you can say "Please pass the sunscreen." A north-facing window makes the perfect maternity ward.

They're overdressed. Flowers and too many leaves zap the energy a cutting needs for root development. Before you tuck those little stems into water or soil, snip off all the flowers and all but the topmost set of leaflets.

Wretched Roots

Inside the Box

You bought a few bare-root roses, with each plant neatly packaged in a cardboard box. The label said to plant, box and all, so that's just what you did. That was a month ago, and the bushes aren't growing at all. What's going on here?

➡ My educated guess is that the roots are trapped in the box! Large-scale growers often pack the roots of bare-root roses in moist sphagnum peat moss and then put them in a cardboard box that's about the size of a half-gallon milk carton. This method makes for easy (and cheap) shipping on the grower's end, and a neat, space-saving display at the garden center or discount store. Boxed-up roots can mean big trouble for *you*, though, because more often than not, they never find their way out of the carton, and you wind up with a stunted, poorly growing plant. Is the damage fatal? Maybe, maybe not. If you act fast, you can get that rose off and growing on the right root. Here's what to do:

Step 1: Dig up the plant and *very gently* cut the cardboard carton away from the root ball.

Step 2: Deliver a dose of therapy in the form of my Rose Revival Tonics (at right).

Step 3: Add a half-shovelful of compost to the hole, set the plant back in, and replace the soil.

Step 4: Sprinkle a tablespoon of Epsom salts over the soil's surface—it's chock-full of magnesium that'll make those roots grow long and strong.

Step 5: Mulch the plant with about 2 inches of compost, pine needles, or straw. Then, the next time you go shopping for roses, play it safe: Unless it's late winter or very early spring, just say no to any plants with their roots in boxes or plastic bags.

It Just Got Sick

Sometimes, a newly planted rose just sits there and refuses to get on with life. If you dig the plant up, you'll see that the roots haven't been doing anything, except maybe turning darker than normal, and a

DON'T THINK OUT OF THE BOX!

Why can't you just take the packaging off bare-root roses before you plant? You can, but you don't want to, and here's why: Usually, when you strip away the cardboard or plastic, the peat falls away from the roots. If the rose is still dormant, this is okay. You can just plant it as is, and it'll be up and growin' in no time. But your chances are pretty slim that the shrub is actually dormant. Once it's been in the garden center for a few weeks, it's a good bet that the plant is wide awake and sending out tiny new feeder roots. When the peat drops off, it'll take those baby roots with it. At best, the rose will suffer more transplant shock than it normally would; at worst, it could die. So, once cold weather is leaving your neck of the woods, it's best to buy roses in containers.

few of the finer roots may be rotting. It's obvious that, as Grandma Putt would say, the plant is "feelin' poorly," but there's no obvious cause—no sign of pests or disease, and no drainage problems. Gardeners call this condition rose sickness. Most often, it strikes a rose that's been planted on a site where roses grew before. The exact cause is a mystery, but it's probably a combination of destructive soil fungi, bad-guy nematodes, and nutritional factors. So what do you do?

➤ First, dig up that rose, *pronto*, and cut off any dead stems. Then, take out all the soil in the bed, to a depth of at least 1¹⁄₂ feet, and if you feel up to diggin' deeper, go for it—the deeper, the better! Next, replace that no-good dirt with a half-and-half mix of fresh soil and well-cured manure. Finally, settle the plant back into its bed, and give it a big dose of my Rose Start-Up Tonic (see page 82). That'll get it up and growin' on the right root!

Miracle Mix

ROSE REVIVAL TONICS

This dynamic duo will get your bare-root roses off and growing like champs. First, wash the bushes, roots and all, in a bucket of water with the following added:

1 tbsp. of liquid dish soap
¹⁄₄ tsp. of liquid bleach

Then, for about an hour before planting (or replanting), soak your bare-root rosebushes in a clean bucket filled with the following:

2 tbsp. of clear corn syrup
1 tsp. of liquid dish soap
1 tsp. of ammonia
1 gal. of warm water

Movin' On Up

Here's the scene: You've just bought an old house with a garden that's been neglected since heaven knows when. Among all the overgrown mess, you've found a beautiful, very old climbing rose. The only problem is, it's growing on a broken arbor out behind the toolshed. Can you move the plant to a better site without killing those long-entrenched roots?

 You bet you can! Old climbers are rugged, and they can take some pretty rough treatment. I've moved plenty of 'em, and I've never lost one. In mild climates, the best time for transplanting is midwinter, when roses are dormant. In colder territory, you can do the job in early spring, but I like to wait until late spring, just after the flowers fade. That way, I get to enjoy the big, bloomin' show, and the plant still has several months to get growin' strong again before winter sets in. Here's the game plan:

Step 1: First, get the new planting hole ready. That way, you'll minimize the time the roots are exposed to the air.

Step 2: Cut all the stems back to within a foot of the ground. This will make the plant less prone to dehydration.

Step 3: Dig a circle around the plant, 18 inches out from the stem, and at least 1 foot deep. Then reach under with your shovel, and lift out the plant. A lot of the soil will fall away from the roots, but don't worry about that; just do the best that you can.

Step 4: Rush the old-timer to its new home, and get it in the ground pronto! Then give it a good, deep drink of my Rose Start-Up Tonic (at left). Before you know it, new leaves'll be sprouting all over those old canes!

Step 5: Water the plant every other day for the first few weeks, then once a week for the rest of the growing season.

★ Miracle Mix ★

ROSE START-UP TONIC

Here's the perfect meal to get your roses off to a rosy start.

1 tbsp. of liquid dish soap
1 tbsp. of hydrogen peroxide
1 tsp. of whiskey
1 tsp. of Vitamin B₁ Plant Starter
½ gal. of warm tea

Mix all of these ingredients together in a watering can. Then pour the solution all around the root zone of each newly planted (or replanted) rose.

It's in the Pipeline

You've got a climbing rose growing up the trunk of a tree and into the branches. Problem is, the tree looks great, but the roses don't. Is the tree killing off the roses?

Not exactly. The problem here is that the tree's roots are probably draining off most of the moisture that comes their way, and the rose's roots dry up. Here's a simple way to make sure the rose gets a drink: Just sink a 2-foot length of 2-inch-diameter pipe into the ground near where you've planted the rose. Rain will fall into the pipe and travel straight to the rose's roots. During dry spells, shove your hose nozzle into the pipe, and let it trickle slowly for 15 minutes or so each day.

GRANDMA PUTT'S
grow-how

Every time she planted or transplanted a rose, Grandma Putt tossed a couple of banana peels into the hole before she filled it up with soil. She didn't stop at planting time, though—every time she (or I) ate a banana, she'd bury the peel about an inch deep beside one rosebush or another. She knew that gave her plants plenty of get-up-and-grow power. Now scientists know why: Banana peels are chock-full of nutrients that roses need for good health, including potassium, phosphorus, magnesium, calcium, sulfur, sodium, and silica. Talk about power lunches!

Sickly Stems

The Upper Crust

Your roses have breezed right through the summer without handing you a care in the world. Now it's fall, the leaves have dropped, and—uh, oh! The stems are covered with a grayish white crust! What happened?

Scale happened, that's what. That stuff that looks like a crust is actually the larvae of scale insects. They're sound asleep and harmless right now, but come spring, they'll wake up, full grown, and start suckin' the life out of your roses. The little guys are covered with a tough shell, so they're hard to reach with sprays. Also, you don't want to go sprayin' too much, because, along with the scale, you'll kill off their natural enemies—and they've got plenty of 'em! So here's what you need to do:

Step 1: If the plants could do with a little pruning anyway, cut off the badly infested stems, and destroy them. (Don't put 'em on the compost pile.) That way, you'll get most of the little suckers.

Step 2: Spray the remaining stems with my Oil's Well That Ends Well Mix (at left). That'll smother a lot more of the babies.

Step 3: Come spring, when the survivors wake up and start sippin', let 'em have it with my Hot Bug Brew (see page 133). They'll never know what hit 'em!

Miracle Mix

OIL'S WELL THAT ENDS WELL MIX

This oily potion is just the ticket for wipin' out scale, aphids, and other little pests that can suck the sap out of your roses.

1 tbsp. of Basic Oil Mixture*
2 cups of water

Combine these ingredients in a hand-held mist sprayer, and spray your roses from top to bottom. (Shake the bottle now and then to make sure the oil and water stay mixed!) Repeat the process in seven days. Those scale babies'll never wake up!

*To make Basic Oil Mixture, pour 1 cup of vegetable oil and 1 tablespoon of Murphy's Oil Soap® into a plastic squeeze bottle (an empty ketchup or mustard bottle is perfect). Then, measure out whatever you need for a Miracle Mix recipe, and store the rest for later.

Plop!

When the tip of an otherwise healthy rose cane suddenly wilts, dies, and falls over, there's one likely suspect: a cane borer. To make a positive I.D., look for a swollen band of tissue at the base of the wilted section. Then split that section open with a knife. I'll bet candy canes to rose cones you'll find a white or yellow grub holed up inside. These guys are the larvae of a lot of different insects. Which kind you've got depends on which part of the country you're in. You don't need to name names, though: The good-riddance plan is the same for all of 'em.

Let's Be Buddies

This might seem like an unlikely duo, but roses and garlic are a match made in heaven. How so? Well, it seems that some big-time rose pests don't care for that, um, distinctive, garlicky aroma any more than some folks do. Just plant a bunch of the pungent bulbs in your rose beds, and cane borers'll keep their distance. So will aphids, rose chafers, and Japanese beetles. Talk about makin' a stink!

➡ First, cut off and destroy the infected canes—and the ugly grubs with them. Then, coat each cut surface with a dab of white glue. It'll keep pesky pests and disease germs from movin' into the cane. In fact, I use the glue treatment every time I prune my roses, even if there's no sign of cane borers. As Grandma Putt always said, an ounce of prevention is worth a pound of cure!

Cantankerous Canker

Ah, spring! Balmy breezes are blowin' and new growth is bustin' out all over the garden—except on your rosebushes! Nothing is growin' on them except fuzzy gray stuff. What's more, the stems are turnin' black and purple! What's going on here?

➡ A condition called rose canker and dieback is going on, and it's nasty stuff alright. It's caused by a gang of different fungi that get into the plant through wounds in the stems, usually at the base. Those injuries can be caused by critters or rough weather, but usually, they're the result of a poor pruning job. And if that doesn't make you feel guilty enough, these foul fungi are cheered on by poor growing conditions, such as too-deep planting, a too-thick layer of mulch, or overly wet soil. If the nasty germs run rampant long enough, they'll kill the whole plant. The good news is that if you act fast, you can save the day.

❀ First, prune off all the sick canes, cutting way back into healthy tissue. Next, clear away the mulch or excess soil from the base of the plant.

❀ Next, take a long, hard look at your roses' home ground. If you find that poor drainage was the canker-causing culprit (or one of them), improve drainage in the planting bed. (See Chapter 14 for the low-down on testing and improving soil.) Or move your roses to a healthier home site. (See page 74 for my rose-transplant routine.)

❀ Then, whichever tack you take, give those bushes a healthy dose of my Rose Start-Up Tonic (see page 82). Then, every three weeks during the growing season, give them a drink of my Rose Ambrosia (at left). It'll keep 'em growin' like gangbusters!

✫ Miracle Mix ✫

ROSE AMBROSIA

If your roses could talk, they'd ask for big helpings of this nifty elixir, which gives them just what they need to grow big and strong and fend off trouble.

1 cup of beer
2 tsp. of instant tea granules
1 tsp. of rose/flower food
1 tsp. of fish emulsion
1 tsp. of hydrogen peroxide
1 tsp. of liquid dish soap
2 gal. of warm water

Mix all of these ingredients together, and give each of your rosebushes 1 pint every three weeks. Dribble it onto the soil just after you've watered, so it'll penetrate deep into the root zone.

Lousy Leaves

They Look Like Swiss Cheese!

Your rosebushes seem healthy and happy, but some of the leaves are full of holes. The holes are all different shapes—round, oval, and even scalloped—but they're clean-edged and neat as can be. Who are the delicate munchers? And how do you send 'em on their way?

➡️ Those holes are being made by leaf-cutting bees. And you can relax: The little guys don't harm roses; they just take leaf snippets that they use to build their nests. In fact, scientists think that those holes actually stimulate the plants' immune systems, and help them fend off more serious pests and diseases. What's more, leaf-cutting bees do essential work, pollinating a whole passel of garden plants. So don't even *think* about sending these heroes away!

Public Enemy No. 1

It happens every year: Just when roses are launching their big summertime show, hordes of Japanese beetles appear and start eating everything in sight. Unchecked, they can turn leaves, buds, and flowers to shreds faster than you can say "Hey! I never promised you a rose garden!"

➡️ There's no mistaking these voracious villains: Japanese beetles are about $1/2$ inch long and $1/4$ inch wide; they're a dramatic, metallic copper color with green and white markings. In fact, they're dang good-lookin' bugs. It's a shame they've got such big, ugly appetites! Here are some simple ways to end their dining pleasure:

The shakedown. Fill a wide bowl with water, and add a few drops of liquid dish soap (just to break the surface tension). Then, hold the bowl under a beetle-infested branch, and shake it gently; the pests will tumble into the soapy water and that'll be all she wrote. Just one note: Perform this maneuver in the morning or evening and the beetles will drop straight down; if they're distrubed at midday, they generally fly off.

The cocktail party. If you'd rather not stand around shaking buggy branches, then this is the method for you. Set a pan of soapy water on the ground about 25 feet from a plant you want to protect. In the center of the pan, stand a can or jar with an inch or so of grape juice in it (Japanese beetles go ga-ga for grape juice!). Then cover the top of the can with a piece of window screen. The beetles will make a beeline for the juice, fall into the water, and die happy.

The hit squad. You don't have to fight the beetle wars alone: You have some powerful allies in both the plant and animal kingdoms. Garlic, rue, tansy, catnip, larkspur, and white

Miracle Mix

HOT PEPPER SPRAY

This hot toddy will say a loud, strong "No!" to any Japanese beetle that starts to munch on your roses—and the recipes don't come much simpler than this one.

½ cup of dried cayenne peppers
½ cup of jalapeño peppers
1 gal. of water

Add the peppers to the water, bring it to a boil, and let it simmer for half an hour. (Make sure you keep the pan covered or the peppery steam will make you cry a river of tears!) Let the mixture cool, then strain out the solids, pour the liquid into a hand-held mist-sprayer, and spritz your rose-bushes from top to bottom. You'll have to repeat the process after every rain, but it's a small price to pay for beetle-free roses!

geraniums all release chemicals that send Japanese beetles packin'. A lot of birds eat the pests by the bushel, and two tachinid flies kill 'em off in other ways (you can find the flies in garden-supply catalogs). For the lowdown on enticing winged warriors to your turf, see page 316.

Put a Halt to Hybrids

You've made your lawn a grub-free zone, but Japanese beetles are still buggin' your roses every year. Could they be migrating from neighboring gardens?

Absolutely! Your ongoing beetle problems could mean that other folks in your neighborhood have grub problems. There's not much you can do about what's going on next door, but you *can* cheat the beetles out of dinner at your place: Instead of hybrids, grow species roses. Most of them bloom earlier in the season, before the voracious villains come out to do their munching. But that's not the only reason to go with these winners: Species roses shrug off diseases that lay their hybrid cousins flat, and they never need pruning, except to keep them within boundaries that you've set. (See page 76 for some dandy choices.)

In the Black

Black spot is the most famous or, rather, infamous disease in all of rosedom. It's caused by a fungus that produces round, fringed, black spots on the upper sides of leaves, any time from spring through summer. Eventually, the spotty leaves turn yellow and fall off. A severe attack can strip a bush of its foliage, or even kill the plant. The good news is that if you act fast, it's not hard to stop the nastiness in its tracks, and keep it from coming back.

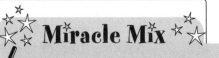

Your emergency response plan depends on how long the fungus has had to do its dirty work. If you reach the scene when spots are first poppin' out, whip up a batch of my Black Spot Remover Tonic (below), and paint every single speckled leaf with it. A more advanced case calls for stronger action. If some leaves are turning yellow and starting to drop, follow this routine:

Step 1: Pick up all of the fallen leaves, clip off those that are about to fall, and put everything in the garbage can (not the compost pile).

Step 2: Rake up the mulch under the plants, and get rid of it, too (it's probably harboring fungal spores). Then replace it with fresh straw, pine needles, or (best of all) compost.

Step 3: Prune your plants so that black spot's worst enemies— fresh air and sunshine—can reach every single leaf.

Step 4: Keep the foul

Miracle Mix

BYE-BYE BLACK SPOT SPRAY

This simple formula works like a charm to head off black spot on roses.

1 tbsp. of baking soda
1 tsp. of liquid dish soap
1 gal. of water

Mix these ingredients together, pour the solution into a hand-held mist sprayer, and spray your roses every three days during the growing season. There'll be no more singin' the black spot blues!

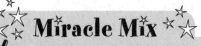

Miracle Mix

BLACK SPOT REMOVER TONIC

At the first sign of black spots on your rose leaves, rush to the rescue with this amazing elixir.

15 tomato leaves
2 small onions
¼ cup of rubbing alcohol

Chop the tomato leaves and the onions into fine pieces, and steep them in the alcohol overnight. Then, use a small, sponge-type paintbrush to apply the mix to both the tops and bottoms of any infected rose leaves.

fungus from coming back by spraying your plants every three days with my Bye-Bye Black Spot Spray (at left). Then also feed your plants with my Rose Ambrosia (see page 86) every three weeks. It'll keep those bushes strong enough to stand up and fight back, no matter what kind of trouble heads their way.

Step 5: Finally, when you water, always remember to aim your hose at the ground, not at the foliage. Better yet, install soaker hoses in your rose beds. Wet leaves, especially leaves that stay wet after dark, are the best friends that black spot, or any other fungus, ever had!

Not Pumpin' Iron

Roses need a steady supply of iron in their diet. When they don't get enough, they develop a condition called chlorosis. The symptoms are easy to spot: The leaf veins remain their normal shade of green, but all the tissue in between turns yellow—otherwise, everything looks fine. Most often, chlorosis is a signal that the soil's pH has gotten out of whack. If a rose's home ground is either too acid or too alkaline, the plant can't absorb the iron that's present in the soil. This problem crops up everywhere, but it's most common out West, in areas where the soil is naturally very alkaline.

➡ First, get a basic, inexpensive soil-testing kit at the garden center, and check the pH in your rose beds. Then, doctor the soil to bring it within the rose-pleasing range of 5.5 to 7.0. The fastest and most common way to do that is to add ground limestone to raise the pH, or sulfur to lower it. That's a sure, quick fix, but I have a better solution: Add the right kind of organic matter. You'll get longer-lasting results, and improve the content and structure of your soil, besides—and that'll take you a long way on the road to trouble-free roses. Here are some of my favorite sweet-and-sour condiments. (For more about testing and improving your soil, see Chapter 14.)

To lower your soil's pH, add:	To raise your soil's pH, add:
Aged sawdust	Bonemeal
Coffee grounds	Ground clamshells
Cottonseed meal	Ground eggshells
Fresh manure*	Ground oyster shells
Oak leaves	Wood ashes
Pine needles	

*If you're making up a new rose bed, this is your best choice, bar none (roses *love* manure). Don't use the fresh stuff on an established bed, though: It'll burn the plants' roots.

Failing Flowers

Their Own Special Brand

It's a sorry sight: a rosebush full of fresh, new buds—and each one of the pretty little things covered from top to bottom with aphids. There are dozens of kinds of aphids, and they go gunnin' for just about every plant under the sun. The one that usually plagues roses, though, is (what else?) the rose aphid, known in scientific circles as *Macrosipbum rosae*.

➤ Aphids are a big pain in the bud, alright, but it's not hard to get 'em under control. First, grab your garden hose, and give those roses a good blast of water. That'll send most of the culprits to a watery grave. Next, spray all the buds and new stems with my Rose Aphid Antidote (below). Finally, to make sure the little suckers don't cause trouble again, lay out the welcome mat for lacewings and ladybugs. (You can read all about these tiny game hunters in Chapter 14.)

Midges on the March

When your rosebuds and new shoots suddenly turn black and die, take a close look. You'll probably find them chock-full of tiny, white maggots, a.k.a. rose midges. The good news is that they don't hurt the plants' overall health. The bad news is that if you don't stop 'em, they'll halt your rose parade in its tracks, from late spring through early fall.

➡️ These little guys travel fast, so don't dawdle! Just grab your pruning shears, cut off all of the infested plant parts, and destroy 'em. Then, spray the bushes with Grandma Putt's Simple Soap Spray on page 94. Before you know it, you'll have a fresh crop of fine new buds!

Miracle Mix

ROSE APHID ANTIDOTE

After you've given your plants a good blast of water from the garden hose, wait about 10 minutes. Then deal the aphids a final death blow with this elixir. The secret ingredient is the citrus oil—it makes rose aphids knuckle right under!

1 lemon or orange peel, coarsely chopped
1 tbsp. of baby shampoo
2 cups of water

Put these ingredients into a blender, and blend on high for 10 to 15 seconds. Use a coffee filter to strain out the pulp, then pour the liquid into a hand-held mist sprayer. Thoroughly spray all the rosebuds and young stems. Repeat after four days, and your aphids will be history.

Chompin' Chafers

Lots of pesky pests prefer to munch on certain kinds of flowers. Well, here's one that chooses its dinner by its *color:* Rose chafers zero in on white blooms. Unless they're really hungry, they give other shades the cold shoulder. These little beetles appear suddenly in late spring to early summer, feast for three to four weeks, then vanish as quickly as they came.

➤ The good news is that rose chafers cause big-time trouble only in years when their population skyrockets. The bad news is that if you don't send 'em packin' in a hurry, they'll eat you out of house and garden! In the fruit and vegetable patch (where rose chafers also do some munchin'), your best defense is to cover your plants with floating row covers at the first sign of trouble. But do you really want to cover up your rosebushes at the very peak of the blooming season? I don't think so! Here are more eye-pleasing options:

Knock down, drag out. Rose chafers eat fast, but they move slowly. To wipe out a whole bush full of 'em, just lay an old sheet on the ground under a bush, then shake the branches. Then gather up the sheet, and dump the buggy contents in a tub of soapy water. (This tactic works best on cool mornings, when the beetles are still sleepy.)

All juiced up. There's nothin' that draws rose chafers faster than the ultra-sweet smell of decaying fruit. Just fill some jars about halfway with water, drop

Miracle Mix

GRANDMA PUTT'S SIMPLE SOAP SPRAY

This old-fangled solution kills off rose midges, mealybugs, thrips, and just about any other soft-bodied insect you can name.

½ **bar of Fels Naptha® or Octagon® soap*, shredded**
2 gal. of water

Add the soap to the water and heat, stirring, until the soap dissolves completely. Let the solution cool, then pour it into a hand-held mist sprayer, and let 'er rip. Test it on one plant first, though—and be sure to rinse it off after the bugs have bitten the dust.

* You'll find Fels Naptha and Octagon in either the bath soap or laundry section of your supermarket.

in some chunks of over-the-hill fruit (any kind will do), and set the jars under your rosebushes. The chafers will mosey on over for a snack, and fall right in.

Head 'em off. Rose chafer babies (grubs), spend the winter in the soil. If your only problem is in the rose garden, just dig down deep and turn the soil over. You'll expose the grubs to the elements—and to hungry birds. If the grubs have moved into your lawn, treat it with milky spore disease or beneficial nematodes (available in catalogs).

Dear Jerry, This spring, some of the buds on my rosebushes never opened, and the outer petals turned pale brown. They were dry and papery, too—almost like pointy, little paper bags. I couldn't find any sign of pesky pests, and the plants seemed healthy and chipper. In fact, a lot of the blossoms opened normally, and the flowers were as big and beautiful as always! I just cut off the paper-bag buds and threw them away. That seemed to solve the problem. But what _was_ the problem? And how do I keep it from happening again? – M.M., Pittsburgh, Pennsylvania

Dear M.M., The problem, my friend, was a condition called rose balling, and it usually appears when a hot, sunny day comes right on the heels of a rainy one. It doesn't harm the plant itself. In fact, as you found, a lot of the rosebuds carry on business as usual. There really isn't any way to prevent rose balling, but you took exactly the right steps to control it. The key here is fast action—if you had let the papery buds stay on the plant, most likely gray mold would have set in, and that would have caused the stems to die back.

CHAPTER 4

Bountiful Bulbs

When it comes to low-maintenance gardening, plants that grow from bulbs are one of Mother Nature's brightest brainstorms. But they can deal you a bucketful of problems, ranging from flowers that refuse to bloom to pesky pests that make off with the goods. Whether you're puzzlin' over balkin' bulbs, tantrum-throwin' tubers, or cantankerous corms, you'll find help right here.

Beat-Up Bulbs

The Show Must Go On!

But this spring, it didn't. Last fall, you planted dozens of bulbs, then sat back, anxiously awaiting their big opening number. The Fourth of July has come and gone, and you're still waiting. Why didn't the curtain rise?

➡️ Spring-blooming bulbs can refuse to take the stage for a whole lot of reasons. Here are some of the most common show-stoppers—and how to make an all-new cast perform like all-stars next year:

Your timing was off. Spring-blooming bulbs are a hardy lot, alright, but they're sticklers for timing. If you put them into the ground when the soil is still warm, they won't form roots at all—though they may send up some top growth in the fall. On the other hand, if you wait too long, the bulbs won't have time to get well-rooted before the ground freezes. The solution: Let your fingers do the testing. After a couple of frosts have hit, shove your hand into the soil. If it's cool, grab your trowel, and have at it!

They rotted. Most bulbs (and all of the more common ones, such as tulips, daffodils, and hyacinths) demand well-drained soil. Before you plant, always add plenty of compost or leaf mold to the bed. (See Chapter 14 for the lowdown on building super soil.) If your home ground is so damp that nothing you can do will change it, grow your bulbs in containers.

They were planted too deep. Or not deep enough. As a rule of green thumb, a bulb should be planted at a depth that's three times its size. That means, for instance, that a 1-inch crocus bulb needs a hole that's 3 inches deep, and a tulip bulb

that's about 2 inches in diameter should be tucked 6 inches into the ground. Like most rules, though, this one needs to be stretched now and then: If your soil is heavy, plant your bulbs just a little shallower than the recommended depth; in sandy soil, go slightly deeper.

They were planted upside down. Unless you find traces of last year's roots, it's not always easy to tell the top of a bulb from the bottom—especially when you're rushing to get dozens of 'em into the ground, and you're runnin' out of daylight! Here's your clue: Generally, the bottom of the bulb is flatter than the top. If you just can't decide which end is up, plant the bulb on its side. A bulb will struggle to its feet from a sideways position, but it'll rarely flip itself over from a headstand.

They starved to death. If your bulbs put on a fine show last spring, but nothing happened this year, it could be that you (or your lawn-mowin' helper) wiped out their food supply, a.k.a. the foliage. It's okay to cut the flowers, but whatever you do, don't touch the leaves until they've turned yellow and started to wither.

WHAT'S IN A NAME?

Technically speaking, a bulb is a swollen, underground stem with a bud in the center. Wrapped around it are scale-like leaf bases that are chock-full of food. Tulips, daffodils, lilies, and onions are true bulbs. However, folks who sell or write about bulbs generally include these other plants that behave the same way, but are not *really* bulbs:

A corm is similar to a bulb, but it carries the bud on top. Every year, the old corm withers away, and a new one takes its place. Gladiolus and crocuses are corms.

A tuber is simply the swollen part of an underground stem. Tuberous begonias, cyclamen, and potatoes are tubers.

A tuberous root is exactly that: a swollen root. In order to produce a plant, the root must have a piece of stem and at least one bud attached. Dahlias are tuberous roots.

Come Out Wherever You Are

Last year, bulbs were blooming, but this year, many of them were no-shows. You think you may have disturbed some hibernating bulbs when you were digging around in the bed. Now what?

➡ Once the top growth disappears, there's no way to tell exactly where your bulbs are lying underground. That makes them prime targets for involuntary plantslaughter. So next year, at the peak of the bloomin' show, take pictures of all of your bulb plantings. That way, you'll know where not to sink your shovel in the ground when you're tending other plants in the bed, or when you're adding more bulbs in the fall.

Some Like It Soggy

You'd love to plant bulbs, but your yard is on the soggy side. Is it a lost cause?

➡ While it is true that the vast majority of bulbs need good drainage, there are some exceptions. This trio all thrive in moist soil:

Camassias *(Camassia)*. Spikes of star-shaped flowers bloom in late spring, in shades of blue and white. Stems range from 14 to 36 inches tall, depending on the variety. These bulbs thrive even in heavy clay soil, but they do need full sun. Zones 5 to 8.

Checkered lilies *(Fritillaria meleagris)*. The flowers look like upside-down tulips on 12- to 15-inch stems, and they really *are* checkered, in either white or green against a base color that ranges from light purple to almost black. They bloom in mid-spring, and like shade and soil that's evenly moist. Zones 4 to 8.

Snowdrops *(Galanthus)*. Bell-shaped white flowers bloom in very early spring on 4- to 10-inch stems. They prefer moist, shady sites, but will tolerate sun. Zones 3 to 8.

Disappearing Daffs

Last fall, you planted dozens of daffodils. This spring, not one speck of green appeared. Your soil scored high marks in its drainage test; you followed the planting instructions to a T; and when you examined the bulbs, there was no sign of pests or disease. What went wrong?

➡️ Those bulbs froze to death, that's what! When it comes to hardiness, daffodils vary enormously. Unfortunately, catalogs and garden centers sometimes overlook those variations when they assign hardiness zone numbers. Next fall, before you place your bulb order, do some homework, and find varieties that have proven themselves in your area. Your best information sources: local garden clubs and botanical gardens, your Cooperative Extension Service, and—of course—your gardening neighbors.

⭐ Miracle Mix ⭐

BULB BREAKFAST

When you plant your bulbs, get the show on the road with this nutritious first meal.

10 lbs. of compost
5 lbs. of bonemeal
2 lbs. of bloodmeal
1 lb. of Epsom salts

Mix all of these ingredients together in a wheelbarrow. Then, before you set your bulbs into the ground, work the mixture into every 100 sq. ft. of soil. If you're planting on a smaller scale, just work a handful of compost and a teaspoon of bonemeal into the soil in each hole before you tuck in the bulb.

They're Tryin' to Escape!

You spent all day planting your bulbs. The next morning, you found them on the ground, right beside their holes, untouched by tooth or claw. Were they trying to make a quick getaway?

Not likely. From the sound of it, the culprit was a chipmunk makin' mischief. How can I be so sure? It's elementary, my dear Watson! That is, once you know a thing or two about chipmunk psychology. When you garden in Chip 'n' Dale country, there are three things you need to remember: These guys are very territorial, they have a terrific sense of smell, and they're curious as all get-out. (Often, they don't *eat* bulbs; they just want to get a good sniff.) In the course of planting, you transferred your scent to the bulbs,

THIS IS *NOT* A RESTAURANT!

The average backyard is full of critters that want to sink their chops into your bulbs—including mice, voles, gophers, squirrels, and, yes, sometimes chipmunks. I've got all kinds of tricks for showing these guys the door, but these tactics work best for protecting newly planted bulbs.

Critter	Control
Gophers	• Before you plant bulbs, line the bottom and sides of holes (or entire planting bed) with $1/2$-inch mesh wire. To keep wire from restricting root growth, set it about 3 inches below the deepest-planted bulbs. • Include bluebells (*Hyacinthoides*, a.k.a. *Scilla*) in your bulb garden—gophers won't go near the pretty little things!
Mice	• Circle the bed with a fence made of fine mesh wire that extends 3 to 4 inches above ground and 6 to 8 inches below. • Don't mulch until after the ground has frozen solid.
Squirrels	• After you've planted bulbs, lay a piece of hardware wire or an old window screen over the bed, and cover with about $1/4$ inch of soil. Once the ground has settled, remove the screen, and put it away until next year. • Plant lots of daffodils—it's the one bulb that squirrels won't touch.
Voles	• Sprinkle Bon Ami® cleansing powder into holes before planting bulbs.

then popped 'em into the ground—thereby invading some chipmunk's territory. So, naturally, the little fella *had* to investigate!

Before you resort to more time-consuming measures, try this simple trick that (kooky as it sounds) has worked like a charm for me: Pop the bulbs back into their holes. Then, lay a bed sheet over the planting bed, and set a few rocks on top to weight it down. Leave it in place for three or four days, then take it off. By then, your scent will have faded, and I'll bet you dollars to daffodils that Chip or Dale won't bother those bulbs again!

Table for Two

Four-footed marauders aren't the only pests that can call a halt to your floral display. A duo of tiny diners can cause banquet-size damage to spring- or summer-bloomers. Most likely, you'll first spot the symptoms above ground: stunted, distorted, or absent foliage and flower stems. To get a positive I.D., though, you'll need to slice a bulb open and examine the evidence.

When bulbs are hurting, these two are the usual suspects:

Bulb mites. These tiny guys chow down on a lot of spring- and summer-flowering bulbs. In the early stages, you'll see large clusters of tiny, white mites; later, corky, brown spots appear on the bulbs. Eventually, these turn to a dry, crumbly pulp.

Narcissus nematodes. Nematodes are even tinier than mites, so you won't see them at all. You will see their damage, though: dark circles or yellow-brown splotches. In addition to their namesake plants (a.k.a. daffodils), these no-goodniks also like to target hyacinths.

Regardless of which culprit you're dealing with, your best response is the same: First, dig up and destroy (don't compost) all seriously affected bulbs, and remove the soil they were growing in. If you've caught the attack in its early stages, you can kill the pests and head off further damage by soaking the bulbs for three to four hours in my Bug-Off Bulb Bath (below). Then, either move your bulb garden to fresh territory, or solarize the infested soil before you plant new *or* treated bulbs. (See Chapter 309 for my simple solarizing method.)

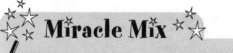

Bulb Busters

Don't ask me how narcissus bulb flies got their name; I just know that they go gunnin' for a whole lot of bulbs, including tulips, lilies, amaryllis, hyacinths, snowdrops, and (of course) daffodils. Your clue that they've attacked is either no spring growth at all, or just a few spindly leaves. If you cut the bulb in half vertically, you'll find a plump, dirty, cream-colored maggot busily eating away at the center of the bulb. (There's usually only one maggot per bulb.) These guys are the larvae of a fly that looks like a small bumblebee, which lays her eggs near the base of bulb leaves in early summer. Can your bulbs be saved?

➡️ Once the maggots have started feasting, your only option is to dig up and destroy the bulbs. You *can* head off

Miracle Mix

BUG-OFF BULB BATH

This spa treatment will help your spring- or summer-blooming bulbs fend off disease germs and pesky insect pests.

2 tsp. of baby shampoo
1 tsp. of antiseptic mouthwash
1/4 tsp. of instant tea granules
2 gal. of hot water (120°F)

Mix these ingredients together in a bucket. Then drop in your bulbs, and let them soak for two to three hours (longer for larger bulbs). Don't peel off the papery skins! The bulbs use them as a defense against pests. Then, either plant the bulbs immediately, or let them air-dry for several days before you store them—otherwise, rot could set in.

✦ Miracle Mix ✦

RHUBARB BUG REPELLENT

Here's a potent spray that'll say "Scram!" to just about any bug.

3 medium-size rhubarb leaves
¼ cup of liquid dish soap
1 gal. of water

Chop up the rhubarb leaves, put the pieces in the water, and bring to a boil. Let the mixture cool, then strain it through cheesecloth to filter out the leaf bits. Mix in the liquid dish soap. Apply with a hand-held mist sprayer. Just remember, rhubarb leaves are highly poisonous, so never use this spray on edible plants.

future attacks, though. In late spring, when the foliage starts to die down, mound up soil around the base of the stem. Because bulb flies prefer to lay their eggs in foliage, not in dirt, they'll probably give your plants a pass. But don't take chances—spray your bulbs' leaves with my Rhubarb Bug Repellent (at left) once a week from late spring through early summer. And pay special attention to the leaf bottoms!

They Took Early Retirement!

For two summers, your lilies were the toast of the town. This year, the foliage turned yellow. When you dug up the bulbs, they were all mushy and smelled like the dickens! Your soil's drainage is close to perfect. How come your bulbs rotted?

➤ This is a case of root rot. It's caused when bad bacteria invade through wounds in the bulbs. Unfortunately, there is no cure; you'll have to dig up and destroy the victims (don't compost them). To head off trouble with the next batch, buy solid, healthy bulbs with no spots or blotches. And when you're planting and tending them, be careful where you shove that shovel! Also, to keep other villains at bay, soak the new contingent in my Bug-Off Bulb Bath (see page 103) for a good five to six hours before you plant them.

They Rotted on the Shelf!

Last fall, you dug up your dahlias and gladiolus, and tucked 'em away for the winter. Then, when spring planting time rolled around, you went to fetch 'em and just about burst into tears. They were all rotten and moldy! You went out and bought new ones, but now you're wondering, should you try storing this crop, or just give up and plant fresh bulbs every year?

Don't give up the ship just yet! Dahlias and glads will keep on goin' for years if you treat 'em right at bedtime. They each like slightly different handling, though. Here's my tuck-in routine for each one.

Gladiolus. Dig up the corms when the foliage turns brown, or any time before the first hard freeze. Then shake off all the soil. The corms you planted in the spring will have all but withered away, but attached to each old corm you'll see one or more chubby, new ones. Then follow these steps:

Step 1: Cut off the tops, and set the corms out to dry for a week or so. (Old window screens propped up on concrete blocks make dandy drying racks.) I like to give my glads one or two days in the sun, then move them to a shady, but airy spot, like a covered porch or dry garage.

Step 2: When the corms are good and dry, gently pull the new ones from

☆ Miracle Mix ☆

BULB CLEANING TONIC

When you take your tender bulbs, corms, and tubers from the ground in the fall, wash them in this timely tonic. It'll keep pests and diseases from moving in over the winter.

2 tbsp. of baby shampoo
1 tsp. of hydrogen peroxide
1 qt. of warm water

Combine all of these ingredients in a bucket, and bathe your bulbs in the mixture. Just be sure to let them dry thoroughly before you put them away for the winter—otherwise, they'll rot.

the old, withered husks, and put these younguns into paper bags (one kind per bag!) with a few tablespoons of medicated talcum powder. Then, tumble the bags around until the corms are well-coated—the powder will keep pests and diseases from invading over the winter.

Step 3: Tuck the corms into paper sacks, mesh onion bags, or old panty hose legs (again, one kind per container), and label each pouch.

Step 4: Hang the bags in a dry place where the temperature stays between 40° and 50°F. A dry, unheated basement or frost-free garage is perfect.

Dahlia flowers come in all shapes, sizes, and colors, but once you've dug up the tubers, they all look alike. Here's a simple way to solve the identity crisis: Get a box of tongue depressors at the drugstore, or save your popsicle sticks. Then, using a wood-burning tool or a waterproof, smear-proof marker, write the name of the dahlia on one side, and the color and height on the other. Drill a small hole in the top of the stick, run a string through the hole, and tie it to the tuber before you store it for the winter. That way, come spring planting time, you won't have to play the guess-the-flower-color game!

Dahlias. The key to success with these guys is to go *very* gently, because the tubers break very easily at the neck. Here's my routine:

Step 1: After the first two or three frosts, carefully dig up the tubers, and cut the stems back to about 3 inches. (Be sure to keep the colors separated!)

Step 2: Brush off any loose soil, then wash the tubers in my Bulb Cleaning Tonic (see page 105). Towel them off, then let them dry out for a week or two (see the glad-drying Step 4 above).

Step 3: Put them in a wooden, plastic, or sturdy cardboard box filled with peat moss, sand, or vermiculite. Cover the top with wire screen to keep roving rodents at bay, then store the box in a dry place at 35° to 40°F.

Sickly Stems

Leanin' Lilies

You ordered your short-stemmed, hybrid lilies because the catalog said they wouldn't need staking, as taller ones do. But they're fallin' over anyway! Did you get defective goods?

➡️ Unless you planted those lilies where gusty winds can get 'em, the problem lies in the soil. A shortage of potassium leads to weak stems that'll topple over even on a calm day. The simple solution: Give those roots a big helping of K (potassium) to munch on. Bananas, granite meal, greensand, kelp meal, and wood ashes are all chock-full of potassium. Whichever one you choose, just make sure you work it into the soil *very* gently, so you don't damage the lily bulbs.

Gall Darn!

Soft, round growths at the base of dahlia stems mean one thing: Crown gall has struck. It's caused by a soil-dwelling bacterium called *Erwinia tumefaciens* that eventually invades the whole stem and kills the plant. Dahlias are favorite targets of this nasty stuff. (It won't bother other bulbs, though.)

➡️ There is no cure for crown gall, so just grit your teeth and destroy the infected plants (don't put them in the compost pile). Get rid of the soil they were growing in,

GRANDMA PUTT'S
grow-how

There's nothing like hyacinths to add a touch of pizzazz to a spring flowerbed. There's only one problem—the big, fragrant heads are so heavy, they tend to nod off. Fortunately, my Grandma Putt had a simple solution to that problem. All you need is a piece of heavy wire about 10 inches long (the straight piece from the base of a wire coat hanger is perfect). Then, just before the flowers open, slip the wire into the top of the spike, down through the stem, and (yep) right into the bulb.

too. Then, to avoid spreading the germs, clean your tools with 70 percent rubbing alcohol, or a solution of 1 part household bleach to 3 parts water, and wash your hands thoroughly. (The bacteria can't hurt you, but you could pass on the disease to healthy plants.) Finally, before you plant replacement bulbs, soak them in my Bug-Off Bulb Bath for two to three hours (see page 103). For more about battling bad bacteria, see Chapter 14.

Dear Jerry, Last fall, I planted dozens of 'Pink Impression' tulips. The catalog description said the stems would grow to be 28 to 30 inches tall, but mine are barely above ground level. (The flowers are gorgeous, though!) What went wrong? – A.M., Savannah, Georgia

Dear A.M., Your climate's wrong, that's what! When tulips don't get a good jolt of cold weather, they produce short, stubby stems. In territory like yours, where winters are generally short and mild, you need to give the bulbs a taste of artificial winter. Just keep them in the vegetable bin of your refrigerator for about 10 weeks, then plant them in late fall. Proper nutrition is important, too, so don't forget to work my Bulb Breakfast into the soil before you set in your bulbs (see page 100). Then, before <u>and</u> after your tulips bloom, feed them a healthy portion of my Out-to-Lunch Mix (see page 113). I guarantee you, your tall, strappin' tulips will be the talk of the town! By the way, hyacinths are prone to the same no-chill, no-thrill condition, but they can make do with a slightly shorter cooling-off period than tulips. Give them six to eight weeks in the fridge before you tuck them into bed.

You No-Good Trespassers!

When dahlia plants suddenly wilt, and their stems rot at the soil line, the culprit is bacterial wilt. There are two kinds, both as ugly as sin—and both can usually be found in the vegetable patch, not the bulb garden. One form, caused by a bacterium called *Pseudomonas solanaecearum*, causes a soft, wet rot at the base of the stems; when you cut into them, syrupy, yellow bacteria ooze out. The other terrible twin, *Erwinia cytolytica*, turns stem bases soft, brown, and foul-smelling outside, and black inside. It also travels into the tubers.

➧ Don't panic! If you reach the scene in time, it's not fatal. At the first sign of trouble, just cut away the affected plant parts with a clean, sharp knife, and destroy them (and don't forget to disinfect your tools before putting them away). Then, clear away any lingering plant debris, rotate your dahlia plantings on a four- to five-year cycle, and don't plant them near any member of the tomato family (the number one target of these bacteria). For more tips on battling bacterial wilt, see page 159.

Lousy Leaves

Dotted Dahlias

They're longish, pale brown spots, with yellow margins, and they're all over the leaves of your dahlias. Those colorful marks are symptoms of dahlia smut, a fungal disease that strikes in midsummer and affects only (surprise!) dahlias. Just for the record, it goes by the tongue-twisting name of *Entyloma calendulae f. dahliae*.

➧ The good news is that, although dahlia smut kills individual leaves, it won't kill the whole plant. Just clip off all of the spotty foliage, and toss it in the trash (not on the compost pile). Then, for the rest of the growing season, spray all of your dahlia plants once a week with my Fungus Fighter Tonic (at right). At summer's end, dig up the tubers, brush off *all* the soil, and soak them in my Bulb Cleaning Tonic (see page 105) before you store them for the winter.

Now, here comes more sobering news: This smutty fungus can live in the soil for up to five years, so when spring planting time comes around, give your dahlias a fresh, new bed of soil to settle down in.

✦ Miracle Mix ✦

FUNGUS FIGHTER TONIC

This terrific tonic works like magic to fend off foul fungi on ornamental *and* edible plants.

1/2 **cup of molasses**
1/2 **cup of powdered milk**
1 **tsp. of baking soda**
1 **gal. of warm water**

Mix the molasses, powdered milk, and baking soda into a paste. Place the mixture into an old panty hose toe, and let it steep in the warm water for several hours. Strain, then pour the remaining liquid into a hand-held mist sprayer, and spritz your dahlias and other fungus-prone plants every week during the growing season.

FIRE! FIRE!

Tulip fire, that is (sometimes called tulip blight). It's the most serious disease that attacks tulips—and attack it *does*! The first sign you see will be red-brown spots on leaves or flowers; later, the spots turn gray and moldy. Foliage may be stunted and pale yellow-green; stems may rot. When you dig up the bulbs, you'll see round, black or dark brown spots all over them.

➡️ Dig up those sick plants and get rid of them, pronto, along with the soil they were growing in. Do it carefully, though; you don't want to scatter those fungal spores around the bed! (I like to throw a plastic bag over a blighted plant *before* I lift it out of the ground.) Then, to protect the remaining plants, spray them every week with my Fungus Fighter Tonic (at left).

Leapin' Leaf Spots!

A quartet of fungal diseases attack daffodils, causing spotted or streaked leaves that die before their time. They're a nasty bunch! Is there any hope for your daffodils?

➡️ First, know your enemy. Here's the lineup:

Fire (*Sclerotinia polyblastis*). At first, red-brown spots and sometimes spores appear on the leaves. As the disease spreads, the leaves die, and flowers rot. Fire most often strikes during hot, humid weather. (Unlike tulip fire, daffodil fire doesn't rot the bulbs.)

Scorch (*Stagonospora curtisii*). Leaves emerge red-brown and scorched—almost as though somebody'd held an iron to them. As the leaves grow, brown spots appear, sometimes surrounded by yellow halos. The fungal spores hide out in the upper scales of the bulb, and the leaves carry them to the surface. The bulb itself, however, shows no symptoms. In addition to daffs, scorch can infect amaryllis (*Hippeastrum*) and snowdrops (*Galanthus*).

Leaf spot (*Didymellina macrospora*). Large spots or blotches develop on leaves after the flowers fade. Stricken leaves die quickly, and if enough of them are affected, the plants can't manufacture enough food for the following year.

White mold *(Ramularia vallisumbrosae)*. This fungus crops up in the Pacific Northwest. It first appears at the leaf tips in the form of tan or white powdery spots, surrounded by unusually dark green tissue. Then it spreads like wildfire, killing both leaves and flower stalks.

The treatment for all four foul fungi is the same. If the disease has gotten a solid foothold, all you can do is dig up the bulbs, along with the soil they were growing in, and destroy the whole shebang (don't even think of heading for the compost pile). However, if you reach the scene early enough, you may be able to save your bulbs. Here's the plan: Cut off all the affected leaves, and get rid of them, pronto. Then, spray the plants every week with my Fungus Fighter Tonic (see page 110), or every two to three days during wet or humid weather. Finally, let the healthy-appearing foliage die down naturally, but once it's yellow and withered, clear it away ASAP.

THE TERRIBLE TINY TRIO

Three pesky little pests that plague the daylights out of annuals and perennials also go gunnin' for bulbs. They're aphids, spider mites, and thrips. Your three-part defense strategy is the same, too:

1. Encourage predators, such as ladybugs, lacewings, and birds.

2. Grow repellent plants, such as mint, garlic, and tansy, among your bulbs.

3. In case of major invasions, let the culprits have it with my So Long, Sucker Spray (see page 71).

Failing Flowers

There Aren't Any!

Finally, spring has sprung. Your bulbs have sent up lush, green foliage that looks as healthy as can be—but there's not a single flower in sight. How come?

➡ This unwelcome condition is something gardeners call "blindness of bulbs." The foliage grows normally, but either no buds form at all, or they're only dry shells, with maybe some shriveled-up flower parts inside. Blindness most often strikes daffodils, especially the double-flowered or multi-flowered types. Occasionally, bulb flies are the culprits, although when they attack, the foliage usually suffers, too (see page 103). Most often, blindness stems from one of the following causes.

They're starved for food and drink. When bulbs don't get enough water and nutrients—or get them on an irregular schedule—they decline in size and fail to produce normal flowers. *Your mission:* Water during dry spells, and feed your bulbs every spring with my Out-to-Lunch Mix (above). And, whatever you do, don't touch the foliage—let it die down naturally after the flowers fade.

⋆ Miracle Mix ⋆

OUT-TO-LUNCH MIX

Every spring, serve up this hearty lunch to your hardy bulbs—it'll give them all the nutrition they need to put on a *really* big show! (This recipe makes enough for 100 sq. ft. of soil.)

10 lbs. of compost
5 lbs. of bonemeal
1 lb. of Epsom salts

Mix all of these ingredients in a large container. Then spread the mixture on the soil where your bulbs are planted, and work it in just under the surface. For an extra treat, add up to 15 pounds of wood ashes to the mix.

Their diet's out of balance. An oversupply of nitrogen makes daffodils—and all other plants—produce lush foliage at the expense of flowers or fruit. *Your mission:* Give those bulbs a booster shot of potassium. Just scratch some wood ashes into the soil around your bulbs. Next spring, you'll have flowers galore!

They're overcrowded. Daffodils are famous as "naturalizers," but that doesn't mean you can just plant them and let Mother Nature take her course. Sometimes, the population gets a little too dense for comfort. *Your mission:* Dig up and divide the bulb clumps, then replant them so they've got some elbow room. In future years, don't wait for blindness to strike. Do your division homework whenever the bloomin' show starts to slack off— which is generally every three or four years. And whenever you tuck those bulbs into their new homes, first put a tablespoon of my Out-to-Lunch Mix (see page 113) in each hole.

Encore! Encore!

If there's one bulb question I hear more than any other, it's "Why won't my tulips bloom year after year the way my daffodils and other bulbs do?" Well, friends, most often the reason is that you've planted the wrong kind of tulip. Plant growers have been cross-breeding tulips for hundreds of years. They've been aiming for bigger, showier blossoms, and, boy, have they hit pay dirt! The trouble is that in the process of producing those rainbow-colored giants, they've sacrificed staying power.

➡ If it's long-term performance you're after, go with species, a.k.a. botanical, tulips. But don't worry that you'll wind up with a bunch of also-rans! In fact, as garden flowers go, these old-timers have a big advantage over the more flamboyant hybrids. Most of them have smaller flowers that blend in perfectly with early-blooming perennials, and shorter foliage that's easier to hide as it's dying down. Furthermore, bloom times vary from February through May, so you can have a parade of color right through the spring. And you won't have trouble finding species tulips—close to two dozen different ones commonly show up in catalogs and garden centers. Here are some of my favorites.

Species	Color	Height (in inches)	Bloom Time
Tulipa acuminata	Pink with a yellow base	4	April
T. biflora	White, with 2 or 3 flowers per stem	6	March
T. clusiana	White with red stripes	12	April
T. eichieri	Scarlet with a yellow and black center	9	May
T. pulchella	Purple with a black or yellow center	4	February through March
T. turkestanica	White with yellow center, and up to 9 flowers per stem	9	February through March

Blast Off!

It's frustrating, alright: Your tulips and daffodils bloomed just fine. Then suddenly, with no warning at all, the buds withered up and fell off! Why on earth would they do that?

➥ They did that because they were hit with bud blast. It generally follows a spell of hot, dry weather in early spring. While it won't affect the overall health of the bulbs, the bad news is that there's not a blasted thing you can do about it except hope for better weather next year!

Nuts to You!

Last fall, you covered your tulip beds with chicken wire to keep the sneaky squirrels out. It worked, too, but only for a while. Now that the plants are up and growing, the vile varmints are stealin' the unopened buds!

➡ Give the little guys a jolt they won't soon forget—a healthy dose of my Hot Bite Spray (below). Spritz your tulips with it every few days, and drizzle some around the plants, too. Feel free to add even more hot stuff to my original recipe—the steamier it is, the faster it'll send squirrels, and even rabbits, scurryin' for cooler territory. Just be sure to wear gloves and long sleeves when you're handling this potent potion.

The Comeback Kids

Even though species tulips are genuine comeback kids, they still need help to perform their best. Once you've chosen your starting lineup, ensure springtime victory with this one-two punch:

➡ **1.** Cut off the flowers as soon as they start to fade. That way, the plant's energy will flow back into the bulb, and not into setting seed.

2. Feed the bulbs before they start *and* after they're done blooming with my Out-to-Lunch Mix (see page 113).

✯ Miracle Mix ✯

HOT BITE SPRAY

When furry munchers are after your flowering plants, whip up a batch of this timely tonic.

3 tbsp. of cayenne pepper
1 tbsp. of Tabasco® sauce
1 tbsp. of ammonia
1 tbsp. of baby shampoo
2 cups of hot water

Mix the cayenne pepper with the hot water in a bottle, and shake well. Let the mixture sit overnight, then pour off the liquid without disturbing the sediment. Mix the liquid with the remaining ingredients in a hand-held mist sprayer. Keep a batch on hand as long as new tulip buds are forming, and spritz the flower stems as often as you can to keep 'em hot, hot, hot! It's strong medicine, so make sure you wear rubber gloves while you're handling this brew.

PART II

VEGETABLE

Victories

CHAPTER 5

Robust Rooters

As food crops go, the ones that form their eatin' parts below ground are about as easygoing as plants can be. But that *doesn't* mean that root crops are trouble-free! In fact, just when you least expect it, they can hand you a cellar full of woes, ranging from woody beets to mushy onions; hollow taters to forked carrots. But don't worry, here's how to solve those lowdown problems and a whole lot more!

Stricken Seeds 'n Seedlings

Where'd They Go?

If you've ever planted carrot seeds, you know the tiny things can be the dickens to work with. It seems that they either fall out of the packet in one big glob, or a breeze comes along and they sail off to who knows where. So how do you get the little rascals into the ground? Here's my favorite method.

➤ When you go out to the garden to plant your seeds, take along a shallow bowl, a bucket of water, and some cotton string. Then pour your seeds into the bowl (one kind of seed at a time). Next, dip a piece of string in the water, and press it into the seeds. Finally, lay the string on the ground, and cover it lightly with soil. The seeds will stay right where they belong. (I use this technique with lettuce seeds, too.)

SUPER SOLUTION

When you're thinning young beets—or any other seedlings—don't pull 'em up. Instead, clip off the tops at ground level with a pair of sharp scissors. That way, you won't disturb the other roots in the bed.

Wide Open Spaces

When you planted your beets, you very carefully spaced them out in neat rows, 2 inches apart. Well, when those little tykes came up, there was a *lot* of empty space between them. Did you get a defective seed packet?

➤ No, my friends: You got a perfectly normal seed packet. Erratic germination is business as usual for beets. When you plant your next crop, follow this four-step road to success:

Step 1: Before you plant your seeds, soak them for 24 hours in my Woody

Miracle Mix

WOODY SEED STARTER TONIC

Seeds with woody coats, like beets and parsnips, get off to a faster start when you treat them to a dose of this terrific tonic.

1 cup of vinegar
2 oz. of liquid dish soap
2 cups of warm water

Mix all of these ingredients together, and soak your seeds in the mixture for 24 hours.

Seed Starter Tonic (at left). It'll soften up the seeds' woody coats and speed up germination.

Step 2: On planting day, forget about rows and spacing. Instead, just scatter the seeds over the whole wide bed. Then cover them with $1/2$ inch of soil. (I like to make repeat sowings every two weeks, until just after the last frost hits.)

Step 3: Lay a piece of burlap over the seedbed. It'll warm the soil, but still let in moisture—giving the seeds the cozy environment they like best.

Step 4: When the little plants are about 2 inches tall, thin them out. Don't be timid—beets need lots of elbow room. Leave 3 to 4 inches between small varieties or for any beets that you plan to pull when they're young, and 6 inches between larger types.

But I Only Want the Tops!

Some folks don't care beans about beet roots—they only want the leafy, green tops. If you fall into that category, read on for your plan of action.

 First, get yourself seeds of a variety that's bred especially for tasty greens, and plenty of 'em. ('Big Top' and 'Early Wonder Tall Top' are two of the best.) Sow 'em the same way you would any other beet, but when the seedlings come up, don't even think about thinning them out. Just clip whatever greens you want to eat, and forget about what's happening underground.

Different Strokes

Don't forget: When you're growing beets for the greens, not the roots, you need to feed them differently.

➡ Every three weeks, give your plants a big helping of my All-Season Green-Up Tonic (below). It'll work wonders for your flowers, trees, shrubs, and lawn, too!

But They Were Such a Bargain!

At least, they seemed like it at the time: You found some great-looking potatoes on sale at the supermarket, so you bought a dozen of 'em, cut 'em into pieces, tucked 'em into the ground— and from then on you had nothing but trouble! First, it took a coon's age for the danged things to sprout. Then, they grew into sick, spindly plants with a yield that wasn't worth beans. What went wrong?

➡ Your seed source, that's what! Commercially grown potatoes are generally treated with a chemical that delays sprouting and limits growth—and therefore, the yield you'll get. What's even worse, in any place that produces a lot of potatoes, there are a *lot* of potato diseases present in the soil. Even when a farmer starts with dis-

✦ Miracle Mix ✦

ALL-SEASON GREEN-UP TONIC

This excellent elixir will supercharge your veggies—and the rest of your green scene—all summer long.

1 can of beer
1 cup of ammonia
½ cup of liquid dish soap
½ cup of liquid lawn food
½ cup of molasses or corn syrup

Mix all of the ingredients together in a large bucket, pour the mixture into a 20-gallon hose-end sprayer, and spray your vegetable plants to the point of run-off every three weeks throughout the growing season. Then mix up another batch to use on your lawn and all of the other plants in your yard!

NOT YOU AGAIN!

Just like any other seedlings, baby root crops are sittin' ducks for cutworms. Rather than put protective collars around all my little rootlings, though, I keep the culprits at bay by mulching the beds with wood ashes or finely chopped oak leaves. (For more ways to battle these malevolent munchers, see page 5.)

ease-free seed potatoes, there's a good chance that many of the tubers will become infected as they're growing. Eating the spuds won't hurt you, but if you plant them, the nasty germs will spread into the soil and spell trouble for your crop—and maybe your neighbors' crops, too.

Fortunately, the solution to this tale of woe couldn't be simpler: Always buy certified, disease-free seed potatoes from a reliable dealer!

What a Rotten Development!

When you live in an area where the growing season is short and spring is cold and damp, getting a good crop of spuds can be a real challenge—the little seed taters tend to rot before they have a chance to sprout. What can you do?

➤ The solution: a technique called "green sprouting." This is a neat trick the pros use, and it works like a charm! Here's all there is to it:

Step 1: About 30 days before your planting date, set your seed taters in a warm, dark spot (70° to 75°F).

Step 2: As soon as you see sprouts, move the potatoes to a well-lit place where the temperature stays between 50° and 55°F, and keep them there for about three weeks. During that time, the sprouts should gradually grow to about 1/2 inch long. If they start growing too fast, move your future crop to a spot that's either cooler (42° to 45° F) or gets more light.

Step 3: At the end of three weeks, pop your spuds in the ground.

POTATO PICKS

Growing Conditions	Good Performer
Hard, clay soil	'Cherokee': Late-season, medium-sized spud with smooth, thin, light tan skin and white flesh. Good for boiling; stores well.
Hot, dry climate	'Jemseg': Very early, with tan skin and white flesh.
Cold, dry climate	'Denali': Midseason variety from Alaska; good baked or mashed.
Damp coastal climate	'Nooksack': Late-season russet type; good for baking; stores well.
Very cold	'Alaska Frostless': Midseason, flat, oval tubers with tan skin and white flesh. Plants are hardy to 27°F!
Very hot or very cold	'Norgold Russet': Matures early, before high heat in the South or frost in the North. The downside: It doesn't store well.
Hot weather and heavy soil	'Red Pontiac': Mid- to late-season variety with dark red skin and white flesh; good for mashing or boiling.

Super Simple Spuds

You say you're hankerin' to grow a crop of great-tasting taters, but you don't have the space in your garden? Or you've got soil from you-know-where? Or maybe you just don't want the work of digging up the tubers at harvest time?

➡️ Not to worry, folks—here's the perfect answer to all three dilemmas: Grow your spuds in containers! Anything that's at least 18 inches deep and has (or can be given) holes for

HAPPY CAMPERS

Any tater can find happiness in a container. But if you're taking the trouble to grow your own, why settle for the same kinds you can buy in any supermarket? Here's a trio of my favorites:

'All Blue': Blue outside, purple inside, with a wonderful, nut-like flavor and an added treat— beautiful blue flowers. (If you want a hard-workin', great-lookin' pot plant for your deck, this spud's for you!)

'Cherries Jubilee': A small, round Swedish heirloom with smooth, cherry-red skin and pink flesh.

'German Butterball': Smooth, golden skin, butter-yellow flesh, and a taste made in heaven.

drainage will do the trick. I've used fancy terra-cotta urns, plastic nursery pots, bushel baskets, wooden barrels—even trash cans. For ease and convenience, though, my hands-down favorite is a stacked-bin composter. Here's how it works:

1. Find an open, sunny spot that's big enough to hold the composter.

2. Unstack the bins, set the first section on top of your mini-plot, fill it with compost (either homemade or store-bought), and set in your seed potatoes. Then cover them with more compost.

3. As the plants grow, add the second and third sections of the composter (also filling them with compost).

4. Any time you want tender, new spuds during the growing season, just reach through the compost, and pluck out a few. Before you know it, more tubers will spring up in their place.

5. When cold weather comes, take the sections apart, and bingo! Your harvest'll fall at your feet— with no muss, no fuss, and no digging!

Uh-Oh!

There's trouble in onionville: Some of your seedlings are coming up with long, dark, thickened splotches at the base. As the leaves grow, they get even thicker and bend downward. What's going on?

The culprit is onion smut. It's a fungus that attacks only onions. (On plants that are starting to bulb, you'll see black lesions near the base of the scales.) Fortunately, all is not lost. First, get rid of any infected plants. Then, to safeguard the rest of your seedlings, spray them with my Vinegar Fungus Fighter (see page 18) every week for the rest of the growing season. And be sure to follow my fungus-fighting guidelines in Chapter 14.

Wretched Roots

But I Planted Round Ones!

Some kinds of beets are naturally long and tapered. But if you planted a round variety and the roots are turnin' out, well, rather long and tapered, it means they don't have enough potassium in their diet.

The quick-fix solution: Spray those plants with fish emulsion, *pronto*, and sprinkle wood ashes on the soil in the bed. Then, every three weeks during the growing season, feed your plants with a liquid organic fertilizer that's low in nitrogen and high in phosphorus and potassium.

Think Pink

Every single member of the onion family can fall victim to a disease called pink root, which stunts the roots and turns them red or pink. (Your first clue that this nasty stuff has struck will be wilted top growth). There is no cure, so what can you do?

First, you'll have to pull up all of the infected plants, and destroy them. Then, keep onion crops away from that spot for at least six years—that's how long the fungus can live in the soil. Now for two pieces of good news: First, pink root strikes commercial growers far more often than it does home gardeners. Second, this vile stuff is a lot easier to fend off than it is to deal with *after* it strikes. Here's how:

Give 'em great drainage. I grow all my onions (and their relatives) in raised beds with plenty of organic matter worked into the soil.

Cultivate with care. Any wounds in onion skins are open doors for pink root fungus.

HOLD THE N!

No matter what kind of root vegetables you're growing, go easy on the manure, and avoid fertilizers that are high in nitrogen. Too much of the "big N" encourages lush top growth at the expense of the eatin' parts underground.

Control onion maggots. Their tunnels let the fungus creep into the plants (see page 130).

Shop carefully. Look for varieties with some tolerance to pink root (you'll find 'em marked that way in catalogs). Tolerance doesn't guarantee safety, but it does mean that if the disease strikes, you'll stand a better chance of getting a decent harvest.

Rotate your onion crops every year. For more on this garden-variety safety measure, see Chapter 6.

Scrub Scab

Both beets and potatoes are prime targets for a fungus disease called scab. In beets, you'll see corky spots on the roots. Stricken taters will have rough, brown splotches that may be sunken, raised, or level with the skin surface. Fortunately, eating a scab-infected veggie won't hurt you—it doesn't even affect the flavor. Still, you don't have to put up with the ugly stuff.

➡ To say "Scram, scab!" just grow your beets and potatoes in highly acidic soil. A pH of 5.3 or lower hinders the growth of fungus. To make your soil more acidic—and improve its grow-power at the same time, dig in one or more of these:

- ✿ Coffee grounds
- ✿ Cottonseed meal
- ✿ Fresh manure

- ✿ Oak leaves
- ✿ Pine needles

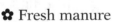

Tiny Taters

There's no better eatin' than small, new spuds fresh from the garden. But if your potatoes are smaller than they should be, it's a sign of calcium deficiency. It occurs most often in highly acidic soil—which, of course, you want to maintain for your taters!

➡ Quick! Sprinkle wood ashes around the plants. They'll start to break down pronto, sending calcium right to the tubers. Then, for the rest of the growing season, give your plants a drink of Compost Tea every couple of weeks (see page 20). Finally, after you harvest your crop in the fall, till a good, slow-release calcium source into your soil. Any of these will do the trick:

- ✿ Aged manure
- ✿ Bonemeal
- ✿ Calcitic limestone
- ✿ Clam or oyster shells

- ✿ Dolomitic limestone
- ✿ Gypsum
- ✿ Rock phosphate

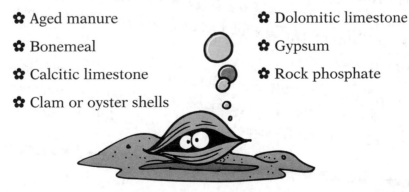

Dear Jerry, I grew carrots for the first time this year. They tasted great, but a whole bunch of them were misshapen. Some of them were short and stunted; others branched off in two directions—they looked just like little pairs of trousers! What went wrong? – M.M., Bennington, Vermont

Dear M.M., From the sound of it, your carrots simply encountered a few obstacles and behaved true to form! If the growing tip comes in contact with so much as a leaf or a tiny twig, the root's liable to fork or even stop growing. Next year, here's what I want you to do: First, till your soil to a depth of at least 12 inches, and rout out every single stick, stone, and piece of straw that you find along the way. Then, loosen up the soil by digging in plenty of finely sifted compost. Finally, to play it extra-safe, choose your carrots from one of these shorter-growing categories:

Amsterdam types grow to be 3 to 5 inches long and about as thick as your index finger. 'Little Finger' and 'Minicor' are both as tasty as can be.

Chantenay varieties are chunky, and range in length from 4 to 8 inches. 'Kinko' is one of the sweetest carrots you'll find anywhere. 'Oxheart' is flavorful, too, and performs like a champ, even in heavy soil.

Paris Market carrots are little globes about $1\frac{1}{2}$ inches in diameter. 'Thumbelina' is the best I've found. It's perfect for containers and matures extra-early—sometimes right along with the peas!

A Heart of Black

Potatoes, beets, and turnips can all suffer from a problem called black heart. Rather, I should say problems, plural, because it's really two different conditions. Potatoes with black heart are splotched inside in shades of purple, dark gray, or black. It's a disease that strikes when too little oxygen reaches the center of the tubers. The cause: waterlogged soil, or temperatures that are too high.

In beets and turnips, black heart strikes when the soil contains too little boron. The roots turn dark brown or black inside, and the leaves become distorted and die back. You're most likely to see this problem if you live in parts of the Northeast, Midwest, or Northwest, where boron is often AWOL.

There is no cure for potatoes suffering from black heart. To fend off the nasty stuff, give your spuds extra-good drainage, and don't leave them in, or even sitting on top of, soil that's warmer than 90°F. As for ailing beets and turnips, spray their foliage with seaweed extract every two weeks until the symptoms disappear. Then, before you plant next year's crop, get a soil test, and add whatever nutrients are needed (see Chapter 14).

Miracle Mix

WILD MUSTARD TEA

Potato beetles, cabbage moths, and cabbage loopers will all give your garden a wide berth if you spray your plants with this tangy tea.

4 whole cloves
1 handful of wild mustard leaves
1 clove of garlic
1 cup of boiling water

Steep the cloves, mustard leaves, and garlic in the boiling water for 10 minutes. Let the elixir cool, then pour it into a hand-held mist sprayer, and let 'er rip!

Another Heart Problem

Potatoes that have cavities at their centers are suffering from a disorder called hollow heart. Actually, you could call it an eating disorder: They're being overfed!

➡ Spuds rank among the lightest eaters in all of veggieville. Just work some compost into the soil at spring planting time, and your crop'll be good to go. If you want to give 'em a snack, wait until the plants bloom, then spray their leaves with liquid seaweed extract two or three times during the growing season. (For more on plant nutrition, see Chapter 15.)

Sickly Stems

Mosey On, Maggots!

Onion maggots go gunnin' for just two victims: onions and radishes. Early in the season, the danged pests burrow into the stems; later, they start feeding on the bulbs below ground. In the process, they open the door to pink root and other diseases.

➡ Here's your two-pronged action plan:

First response. Pull up the invaded plants, and toss 'em on the compost pile. (Don't worry about spreading trouble; the slime-balls can't survive the winter in the pile.) To get rid of any malingering maggots, spray your patch with my Hot

GRANDMA ❦ PUTT'S
grow-how

If you're a big tea drinker, reach for Grandma Putt's favorite anti-maggot weapon: used tea leaves. She saved 'em up all winter long, then worked 'em into the soil before she planted her onions and radishes. It worked like a charm! (Tea bags'll do the trick too; the paper coverings dissolve lickety-split.)

When it comes to carrot rust flies, my motto is "When all else fails, procrastinate." If you're tired of doin' battle with the thugs, just hold off planting your carrots until midsummer. By then, the adults will have laid all their eggs elsewhere and flown the coop, and your crop'll be home free. When you do plant, consider planting coriander, pennyroyal, rosemary, sage, or wormwood nearby. They all stand up and shout, "Flee, Fly!"

Bug Brew (see page 133). Then, pick up some beneficial nematodes at the garden center, and apply them according to the directions on the package. They'll polish off any underground muggers. Finally, sprinkle wood ashes or diatomaceous earth on the ground among your plants. It'll discourage the adults (brown, hairy, humpbacked flies) from laying another generation of eggs.

Long-term protection. Next year, plant your onions and radishes in a different place. After that, rotate the crops every other year. (For more on crop rotation, see Chapter 6) For added protection, encourage birds, toads, spiders, and ground beetles to take up residence—they all feast on maggots (see Chapter 14).

Time Enough

An old-time technique for protecting onions from maggots is to plant a big bed of radishes (their favorite food) nearby. It works, too: The squirts throng to the radishes and leave the onions alone. But what if you want radishes for eatin', not for sacrificial guard duty?

 When it comes to protecting radishes, time is on your side, friends. Because these tangy tubers grow so fast, you can outwit the maggots with a little fancy footwork. Here's how:

Plant early. If you can get a mature crop by

June 1, you'll be all but certain of beating the maggots to the munch.

Plant a midseason crop, and let 'em go to seed. After the seeds mature, till the plants into the ground. Before you know it, seedlings will come up willy-nilly, and produce radishes well into the fall. By then, the maggots will have turned into moths and left town!

All Wired Up

When beets, potatoes, or sweet potatoes suddenly wilt—and even die—the likely suspects are wireworms. And that means trouble down below.

These vile villains go gunnin' for the roots of most garden fruits and vegetables, and in each case, your best strategy is the same: Trap 'em with taters. Just spear chunks of potato with sticks and bury them 2 to 4 inches deep, leaving enough stick above ground so you can find 'em later. Keep the traps in place for a week, then dig 'em up and destroy the whole shebang.

Rustle Up Some Rust Flies

Carrot rust flies are just about the worst enemies a carrot ever had. (But these villains don't stop with carrots—they also run roughshod through parsnip, celery, and parsley beds.) The first sign of trouble will be above ground: Your plants will be stunted, and you may see rot around the stems. That's because underground, the flies' babies (yellowish white maggots) have been chewin' the daylights out of the roots.

Unfortunately, once your crop has been attacked, all you can do is pull up the roots, and destroy them. Fortunately, there's plenty you can do to head off problems next year. Here's a trio of tactics to choose from:

❁ At the end of the growing season, clear out all plant debris. Then till the soil to bring up hibernating maggots. Birds will zero in and help themselves to lunch. They won't get 'em all, but they will help reduce the population.

❁ Go after the culprits. They're small black flies, about $1/5$ inch long, with yellow hairs and yellow heads and legs. They're attracted to anything that's yellow-orange, so they're a snap to trap with sticky boards (see page 26). Don't just stand there and wait for the flies to flock to the boards, though; if you see any flittin' around your plants, let 'em have it with my Great-Guns Garlic Spray (see page 25).

❁ Keep 'em outta there! Wood ashes sprinkled on the ground will keep carrot rust flies from laying eggs on your plants. Better yet, interplant lots of onions among your carrots, and you'll keep the tricksters away altogether!

Miracle Mix

HOT BUG BREW

This potent beverage will deal a death blow to maggots, grown-up flies, and any other bug that's buggin' your plants.

3 hot green peppers (canned or fresh)
3 medium cloves of garlic
1 small onion
1 tbsp. of liquid dish soap
3 cups of water

Purée the peppers, garlic, and onion in a blender. Then pour the mixture into a jar, and add the dish soap and water. Let stand for 24 hours. Strain out the pulp with cheesecloth or panty hose, and use a hand-held mist sprayer to apply the remaining liquid to bug-infested plants, making sure to thoroughly coat the tops and undersides of all the leaves.

Lousy Leaves

They're Nothin' But Skeletons!

Moderate leaf nibbling won't hurt much, but when Colorado potato beetles get down to serious business, their aboveground shenanigans can all but destroy your underground crop. Here's what to do (these tactics work just as well on the culprits' other targets—tomatoes and eggplant):

➡ **Get 'em on their way to breakfast.** In the fall, or very early spring, dig a trench about 8 inches deep around your potato patch, with the sides vertical or steeply sloping (at least 45°). Then line the trench with plastic. When the beetles wake up in the spring, they're too weak to fly, so they have to walk to your plants. They'll get as far as the trench, fall in, and—thanks to the slippery plastic—they won't get out (not alive, that is!). Before you know it, they'll be in the stomachs of some hungry birds.

Turn 'em off. Plant catnip, coriander, tansy, or basil among your spuds. Scientists have found that the first three herbs act as repellents. Basil works because Colorado potato beetles find their food by smell, and the herb's strong scent masks that of the tater plants.

Give 'em the shakes. If it's too late for preventive measures, spread some old sheets or shower curtains

HAPPY CAMPERS

When it comes to potato pests, 'Sequoia' says "Bug off!" to some of the peskiest. These big, white, tan-skinned tubers fend off Colorado potato beetles, flea beetles, and leafhoppers. 'Sequoia' *is* susceptible to aphids, but, hey, nobody's perfect. If aphids are cuttin' up rough in your spud patch, look for 'British Queen', 'Irish Daisy', 'De Soto', 'Early Pinkeye', or 'Houma'.

on the ground under your plants. Then brush the leaves with a broom to send adults, larvae, and eggs tumbling down. Gather up the whole shebang, and dump the varmints into soapy water. Then, to keep the troops from movin' back in, spray your plants with my Wild Mustard Tea (see page 129)—no tater beetle worth his chops will go near your garden!

Miracle Mix

PEPPERMINT SOAP SPRAY

This brew is a nightmare-come-true for hard-bodied insects like weevils. The secret ingredient: peppermint. It cuts right through a bug's waxy shell, so the soap can get in and work its fatal magic.

**2 tbsp. of liquid dish soap
2 tsp. of peppermint oil
1 gal. of warm water**

Mix the dish soap and water together, then stir in the peppermint oil. Pour the solution into a hand-held mist sprayer, take aim, and fire! Those weevils'll never know what hit 'em!

By the Light of the Silvery Leaf

When the leaves of your onions turn silver and start to wither, blame it on onion thrips. The critters are so tiny (about $1/25$ of an inch long) that you'll never see them without a microscope. But you can still do 'em in!

➤ Unlike most insects, which are drawn to the color yellow, thrips go for blue in a big way. Just glue a piece of blue paper to cardboard, and spray it with adhesive, or coat it with petroleum jelly. The thrips will throng to their death!

The Case of the Missing Carrots

Carrot weevils chew their way through a carrot bed until there's nothing left but stems and the ribs of leaves. Meanwhile, below ground, their babies—cream-colored grubs with brown heads—

tunnel through the roots. (Like carrot rust flies, these weevils also attack carrots' relatives, including parsnips, parsley, and celery.) What can be done to foil these felons?

  First, zero in on the grown-ups. These brownish insects are about ¹/₅ inch long and, like all weevils, have a long snout and a hard shell. My So Long, Sucker Spray (see page 71) will kill 'em in droves, but if you'd just as soon not run a bunch of bugs through the blender, reach for my Peppermint Soap Spray (see page 135). To send the grubs packin', drench the soil with beneficial nematodes (see page 314).

Then, to head off damage next year, do a super-thorough fall clean-up—adult weevils sleep through the winter in grass and plant litter, and you don't want to leave any potential parents on the scene! Come spring, do everything you can to enlist predatory help. Toads, turtles, and scores of songbirds eat full-grown weevils and their grubby offspring.

Fight Blight!

The word *blight* strikes terror in the hearts of spud growers everywhere. This dreaded fungal disease comes in two forms: early and late. (It was late blight that caused all the trouble in Ireland about a century and a half ago.) In both cases, the early warning signs are similar: You'll see dark lesions on leaves, leafstalks, or stems. Eventually, decay spreads to the tubers.

There's good news here, folks! You can fight this nasty stuff and win. You don't even need to make a positive I.D., because the treatment for both blights is the same. At the first sign of trouble, start spraying your plants every seven days with my Blight Buster Tonic (at right). It's adapted from a recipe developed by the horticulture folks at Cornell University, and it also works on blight's other targets—celery and tomatoes. Avoid growing potatoes, tomatoes, or celery in that spot for at least three years.

And Stay Out!

Okay, so you can stop blight from destroying your crop, but can you keep it from striking in the first place?

➡️ There's no way to guarantee safe passage, but these measures come close:

✿ Practice my guidelines for good garden health in Chapters 14 and 15.

✿ Grow resistant varieties. Check the descriptions in plant catalogs, or try some of my favorites: 'Alaska Red', 'Atlantic', 'Bison', 'Brigus', 'Cherokee', 'Chieftain', 'Kennebec', 'Onaway', 'Pink Pearl', and 'Sebago'.

✿ Keep an eye on the weather. **Early blight** tends to spread during periods of warm temperatures accompanied by heavy dew or rainfall. It can crop up anyplace in the country. **Late blight** is most common in the north central, northeast, and Atlantic states, and it strikes only after the plants bloom. Favored conditions: Rainy, foggy weather, with temperatures of 70° to 80°F during the day and 40° to 60°F at night. If these conditions persist for more than a few days, reach for the Blight Buster Tonic (at left). Spray your plants every seven days, without fail, until the weather improves.

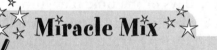

Miracle Mix

BLIGHT BUSTER TONIC

At the first sign of blight on your potatoes, tomatoes, or celery, haul out this powerful weapon.

**1 tbsp. of light horticultural oil
    (available at garden centers)
1 tbsp. of baking soda
1 gal. of water**

Mix all of these ingredients together, pour the solution into a hand-held mist sprayer, and spray your plants to the point of run-off.

Failing Flowers

A Rabbit Wouldn't Even Eat 'Em!

If your fresh-pulled carrots taste tough and woody, rather than sweet and crunchy, don't despair. The solution is simple!

➡ The blame could lie in one of two directions:

The soil was too dry. Carrots grow up sweeter and less fibrous in soil that stays moist, yet drains well. Make your soil work for you by digging in my magic bullet—plenty of finely sifted compost.

They stayed in the ground too long. In the summer, to catch carrots at their peak of flavor and tenderness, you need to pull them within two or three days of the time they turn bright orange (normally 60 to 80 days after planting, depending on the variety). Once the weather turns cool, though, they can stay in the ground for weeks without declining in taste or appearance.

Happy Campers

If you're one of those folks who *really* likes to plan ahead, I've got the carrot for you: It's a fairly new variety called 'Merida.' You can plant it in late September or early October, it'll grow right through the winter, and you can harvest it May through June. Talk about winter keepers!

An Off-Color Joke

When you raise 'em right, beets are the sweetest, juiciest, prettiest vegetables a body could ask for. On the other hand, when you don't give your crop the conditions it needs (or when

Mother Nature throws you a curveball or two), you can wind up with a bunch of tough, stringy, cracked, or off-colored roots. And to a beet lover, that's no joke.

➡️ Here's my 1-2-3 for beets that you can't beat:

1. Raise 'em up fast in spring or fall, while the weather's cool. Hot, dry weather makes beets tough, stringy, and often discolored.

2. Give 'em steady, even moisture (they need about an inch a week). On-again, off-again watering can crack the roots and make rings form inside.

3. Feed 'em every three weeks with a liquid organic fertilizer that's low in nitrogen and high in phosphorus and potassium. (For more about plant nutrition, see Chapter 15.)

Miracle Mix

ALL-PURPOSE ORGANIC FERTILIZER

This well-balanced diet is the best stuff your beets (or any other veggie plant) ever had.

5 parts seaweed meal
3 parts granite dust
1 part dehydrated manure
1 part bonemeal

Combine all of these ingredients in a bucket, then side-dress your plants with the mixture, and water well. Serve it up two or three times during the growing season.

What a Pain in the Neck!

You stroll into your root cellar to grab some onions and find the necks rotting and covered in a dense, gray fungus. *Yuck!* Your bulbs are suffering from a common disease known as onion neck rot; it's caused by a fungus called *Botrytis allii*. Symptoms generally don't appear until the crop is in storage, but the foul stuff gets its toehold in the garden.

➡️ If you *do* happen to catch the damage in the garden, dig up and destroy the victims pronto, and water your soil thoroughly with my Fungus Fighter Soil Drench (see page 45). Then, every week until harvest time, spray your onion plants with my Vinegar Fungus Fighter (see page 18). To make sure the problem doesn't come back next year, follow this protection plan:

✿ Whether you choose to start from seeds, sets, or transplants, buy them from a reliable source.

GRANDMA PUTT'S
grow-how

Grandma Putt knew that when it came to onions, she'd have the best success growing the red and yellow kinds. Why? Because even though no onion is completely resistant to onion neck rot, the red and yellow kinds are less susceptible than the white ones.

✿ Before you plant, work plenty of compost into your soil. Besides improving the drainage, it provides protection against fungi and other disease organisms. (For more on building strong soil, see Chapter 14.)

✿ Avoid high-nitrogen fertilizers, and cut off the food supply entirely about a month before harvest time, or as soon as the necks start feeling soft.

✿ Give your plants steady, even moisture until the tops start turning yellow. Then stop watering completely, so that the skins can dry out.

✿ When the leaves are all yellow, and about a quarter of them have toppled, bend the rest of the tops over with a rake. This trick will direct the plants' energy from the tops to the bulb.

✿ Clean up thoroughly at the end of the season, and don't leave any onions in the ground. (This fungus spends the winter on onion debris or in the soil around onion plants.)

✿ Rotate your crop at least every two years.

Treat 'Em Right

Botrytis allii isn't the only thing that can make onions go belly-up in storage. Improper storage techniques also play a part.

➡ In addition to following the tips in "What a Pain in the Neck!" on page 139, these will keep you in good eatin' all winter long:

❀ At harvest time, loosen the soil around each bulb and pull or dig it up carefully; damaged onions rot quickly.

❀ Spread the bulbs—tops intact—on a flat surface above the ground, and leave them until the skins are crisp and the tops have withered completely. That'll be anywhere from 2 to 10 days outside, or roughly two weeks indoors in a well-ventilated spot.

❀ Cut off the tops, but leave an inch or so of stem.

❀ Tuck the bulbs into mesh bags or old panty hose legs, and hang them in a place that's cool (35° to 40°F), dry, and well-ventilated.

❀ Check your stash frequently; if any bulbs are sprouting, use 'em as soon as possible.

They're Green!

Green spuds mean just one thing: Those tubers grew at least partly above ground. Exposure to light causes the formation of a toxic chemical called solanine.

DON'T FORGET ABOUT ME!

It's not only spuds that turn green when they see the light. You need to keep your carrots covered up, too. Otherwise, they'll go green at the shoulders.

➡ My food-expert friends say that cooking destroys most of the toxins, so if your potatoes show only a few greenish spots, go ahead and eat 'em. On the other hand, if they're as green as a bagel in Boston on St. Paddy's Day, don't take chances—toss 'em on the compost pile, and start fresh next year. And next time around, make sure you keep the tubers completely covered as they're growing. It doesn't matter what you cover them with—soil, leaves, straw, compost, or a combination of all four. Just don't let those roots see the light!

Growers, Keepers

Back in Grandma Putt's day, most folks kept their root-crop harvest in (where else?) the root cellar. For my money, you still can't beat these old-fashioned spaces for long-term storage. But what if you don't have a root cellar?

➡ Most root veggies will keep just fine in an unheated toolshed, garage, or covered porch. You can even use a window well. Just line it with hardware cloth to keep mice and other critters from raiding your stash. Then put down a layer of straw, tuck in your containers of veggies, and add more straw. You're good to go!

SUPER SOLUTION

Some root veggies—namely, leeks, carrots, and parsnips—keep better and stay sweeter when you leave 'em in the ground through the winter. After the first frost, just cover the plants with a fluffy, foot-deep blanket of hay or straw, and extend the mulch about a foot beyond the bed in every direction. Then, whenever the mood strikes, pull back the covers, and dig up some roots. Just make sure you get em' all out before the weather warms up in spring; otherwise, they'll spoil.

One more tip: Drive some stakes into the ground to mark the bed. That way, you'll be able to find your stash, even if a deep snowfall covers it up. (I've learned this the hard way, folks!)

CHAPTER 6

Fabulous Fruiters

I s some mysterious terror taking its toll on your tomatoes? Are your cucumbers crawling with creepy customers? Is some beast beating you to the bean harvest? Or is your problem hot peppers with about as much firepower as a jar of baby food? In this chapter, I'll show you solutions to these and a bushel full of other garden-variety troubles.

Stricken Seeds 'n Seedlings

They Didn't Make the Move

You started a fine crop of seedlings indoors, then when the weather was warm enough, you planted 'em in the garden—where they all up and died! They didn't look sick, and no pests got 'em. So what went wrong? Was it something you did?

➡ From the sound of it, the problem isn't what you did; it's what you *didn't* do. Before baby plants can stand up to life in the great outdoors, they need to go through a process called hardening off. It's as easy as pie, but it can mean the difference between life and death for your fruiting crop. Here's my method:

Step 1: A week before transplanting time, stop feeding the seedlings and cut back on watering.

Step 2: Take your seedlings outside to a partially shady spot for part of each day. A covered porch works great; so does the area under a big shade tree.

Step 3: Start with a couple of hours in the afternoon, and gradually work up to a full day. But the minute a heavy rain starts or a strong wind comes along, rush the little guys back indoors.

Step 4: Just before you're ready to set your seedlings in the garden, water them with a

JOIN THE FAN CLUB

While your seedlings are growing up indoors, brush 'em lightly with your hand a couple of times a day, or aim a slow-turning fan in their direction for a few minutes so they get a nice, gentle breeze. The motion helps the plants produce a hormone called cytokinin, which makes for thicker, sturdier stems.

solution of 2 ounces of salt or baking soda per gallon of water. This elixir will temporarily stop growth and increase the plants' strength so they can face anything Mother Nature throws their way (well, *almost* anything).

Step 5: As soon as you've tucked your baby plants into the soil, give them a drink of my Seedling Transplant Recovery Tonic (at right). It'll ease the stress of moving day and make 'em feel right at home.

★ Miracle Mix ★

SEEDLING TRANSPLANT RECOVERY TONIC

Give your transplants a break on moving day by serving them a sip of this soothing drink. It'll help them recover more quickly from the shock of transplanting.

1 tbsp. of fish emulsion
1 tbsp. of ammonia
1 tbsp. of Murphy's Oil Soap®
1 tsp. of instant tea granules
1 qt. of warm water

Mix all of these ingredients together, and pour the solution into a hand-held mist sprayer. Then mist your little plants several times a day until they're off and growing on the right root.

On the Other Hand...

Although most fruiting vegetables are a snap to transplant, some—namely beans, corn, cucumbers, okra, peas, and squash—hate like the dickens to have their roots tampered with. If your unfortunate seedlings were among that crowd, no amount of hardening off would have eased the transition from their nursery pots to the wide-open spaces of your vegetable garden.

➤ The secret to success with these reluctant travelers: Wait until both the soil and air temperature have warmed up enough, then sow the seeds exactly where you want them to grow up. (Plants differ greatly in their need for warmth, so check your seed packets for specific guidelines.)

It's Not Fair!

Is Mother Nature cheating you out of your favorite vegetables? Not to worry, my friends: Even if your growing season is too short for direct sowing, you can still grow your favorite homebodies. How?

➡ Just start your seeds indoors in what Grandma Putt used to call "travelin' pots"— little containers that can go right into the ground come planting time. For my money, the very best travelin' pots are the ones you make yourself from old newspapers. Garden catalogs sell a nifty wooden gadget that you can use for the purpose, but you don't really need one. This method works just as well, and it doesn't cost a dime! All you need is some newspaper and an aluminum can (a soft drink can is just the right size). Then follow these steps:

Step 1: Cut a strip of newspaper about 1 foot long and 6 inches wide.

Step 2: Wrap the paper around the can lengthwise, with about 4 inches covering the can and 2 inches hanging over the bottom.

Step 3: Fold that extra piece onto the bottom of the can, and press it tightly with your fingers.

Step 4: Pull out the can and presto—you've got a pot!

COLLAR 'EM

Your baby plants need protection from Seedling Enemy Number 1: the cutworm. So, corral each of your new transplants with a collar that reaches about 2 inches into the ground and 3 inches above. Cardboard tubes from paper towels are perfect; so are old aluminum cans minus the ends. I'll bet your house is full of castoffs just waiting to be recycled for garden guard duty. (Think of it as a chance to exercise your creative juices!)

Then, once your seedlings have outgrown their collars (and it won't be long!), sprinkle a scratchy substance on the soil around each plant. The cutworms won't slink across anything that prickles their skin. These are some of my favorite rib-ticklers:

- Chicken manure
- Eggshells
- Hair (human or animal)
- Kitty litter (unscented)
- Shredded oak leaves
- Wood ashes

Step 5: Make as many as you need, fill 'em with seed-starting mix, and tuck 'em into flats with holes in the bottom for drainage. (Just be sure to pack 'em in tightly, so that the paper doesn't unravel.)

Once they're in the ground, those pots'll break down in the blink of an eye, and your seedlings'll be gallopin' skyward before you can say "Jack and the Bean Stalk!"

Too Darn Cold

You say your very favorite vegetables need higher temperatures, for a longer period of time, than your climate can deliver? Don't fret: While it is true that some veggies are naturally hot-blooded, er, hot-sapped, some varieties take to cool territory better than others.

➤ Here's a sampling of veggies that'll go with the flow. Either they can handle lower temperatures better than most varieties, or they mature fast, so you can plant 'em and get a harvest in before the mercury plummets:

Beans (dry): 'Soldier' (bred to perform in cool climates).

SUPER SOLUTION

A terrific way to protect seedlings from the cold is with a gadget called a tee-pee. It's made of hollow, upright plastic cylinders fastened together to form a circle. You fill it with water and set it over a plant. It works great, but if you've got a lot of heat-lovers like peppers, squash, and tomatoes, you could spend a fortune keeping them warm! That's why I came up with my wall-o'-bottles. All you do is tape quart-sized plastic bottles together in a circle and fill them with water. They work just as well as the store-bought kind, and they're free!

Beans (snap): 'Black Valentine' (green, 50 days to maturity); 'Pencil Pod' (yellow, 53 days).

Corn: 'Early Sunglow' (yellow, 65 days); 'Trinity' (bicolor, 68 days); 'Sugar Snow' (white, 70 days).

Eggplant: 'Baby Bell', a.k.a. 'Bambino' (dark purple, 45 days).

Peppers: 'Yankee Bell' (sweet, green-to-red, 65 to 85 days); 'Early Jalapeño' (hot, green-to-red, 70 to 90 days).

Tomatoes: 'Oregon Spring' (red, vining type bred to thrive in places with cool, short summers).

One Tomato, Two Tomato...

Or maybe none. A lot of things can make your tomato crop go belly-up, but most of them aren't caused by pests or diseases—they're a result of misdirected care.

Here's a rundown of my simple secrets for growing the best danged tomatoes in town:

1. Plant local color. Don't settle for whatever tomatoes the local garden center has in stock. Instead, find tomatoes that are proven performers in your area. Not only will they mature in the time you have in your growing season, but they'll grow up stronger and better able to fend off pests and diseases. And they'll taste better, too! (For more tips on growing good-tasting tomatoes, see "More, Please!" on page 167.)

2. Site em' right. To do their best work, tomatoes need full sun and fluffy, fertile soil that's chock-full of organic matter with a pH of 5.8 to 7.0. If you can, get their beds ready in the fall by digging in plenty of manure and chopped leaves. If you must wait until spring, add lots of compost to the soil at planting time.

3. Don't rush the season. Tomatoes crave warmth. Period! So don't even think of putting your plants in the ground until the soil temperature is at least 55°F, and the night-time air temperature is holding steady at 55°F or above. And even then, keep plenty of covers on hand just in case a cold snap hits.

4. Serve dessert first. Add a spoonful of sugar to each planting hole. Your tomatoes will be so sweet and so lip-smackin' good, you'll want to eat 'em for dessert!

5. Give 'em a hearty breakfast. After you set your transplants into their holes, give them a big helping of my Timely Tomato Tonic (below). It'll help ward off many of the more common tomato diseases.

6. Add a security blanket. Mulch your plants with a 2-inch layer of high-quality compost. Not only will it help keep weeds out and moisture in, but as it breaks down, it'll add valuable micronutrients to the soil.

7. Satisfy their appetites. Tomatoes are big eaters and drinkers. To ensure a bumper crop, spray the plants with fish emulsion or my All-Season Green-Up Tonic (see page 121) four times during the growing season: first, two weeks after transplanting; second, after the first flowers appear; third, when the fruits reach the size of golf balls; and fourth, when you spot the first ripe tomato.

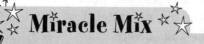
Miracle Mix

TIMELY TOMATO TONIC

This powerful powder will help your tomato plants fend off dastardly diseases.

3 cups of compost
1/2 cup of Epsom salts
1 tbsp. of baking soda
1/2 cup of nonfat dry milk

Combine the compost, Epsom salts, and baking soda in a bucket, then add a handful of the mix to the planting hole. After planting, sprinkle a little of the dry milk on top of the soil. Repeat every few weeks during the growing season.

Peas are some of the coolest customers in veggieland. In fact, you can put 'em in the ground when the soil temperature is just 40°F and they'll still germinate—but it'll take 'em a good seven weeks. And in that time, the seedcorn maggots could demolish your whole crop! So take my advice and be patient. Wait until your soil thermometer reads a whopping 60°F, and then plant your seeds. They'll germinate in about nine days, and take off like a bat out of you-know-where—and you'll be pluckin' sweet, green pods as early as you would if you had tried to rush the season!

They're Comin' Up Eaten!

When corn, pea, or bean seedlings come out of the ground with chewed leaves or dead or crooked growing tips, there's one likely suspect: the seedcorn maggot. These wormy guys are the baby version of a fly, *Delia platura*, which looks a lot like a common housefly. The culprits feed on germinating seeds, making holes in the infant stems and cotyledons (the first, false leaves that show above the surface). Sometimes, the seedlings are killed before the shoots even poke their heads above ground. That's the bad news; the good news is that the seedlings that *do* make it through the soil surface usually survive, though they may grow a bit slowly at first.

Seeds that take their time germinating are this maggot's prime victims, so always wait until the soil has dried out and warmed up before you sow. That way, those seeds will be off and runnin' before the worms can chow down. In the case of corn (and beans, too), the soil temperature should be at least 55°F. (If you're planting one of the super-sweet hybrid corns, the soil needs to be at least 65°F.)

Another way to foil these noxious nibblers is to add organic matter to your soil in the fall, rather than in spring. That's because the female flies like to lay their eggs in organic matter that's nice and fresh—but once the stuff has aged through the winter, the maggot mommies will give it the cold shoulder.

The Crow's in the Corn

And everything else, too. The brazen wingers are pullin' up your seeds and seedlings right before your eyes. Short of spending all day in the garden, waving your arms and shouting "Get outta here!," what's a body to do?

➤ There are lots of things you *could* do, but here's my favorite crow chaser: Collect a bunch of plastic grocery bags—the more colorful, the better. Fill 'em with air, tie 'em shut, and fasten 'em to the top of stakes about 5 to 6 feet tall. Then, push the stakes into the ground all around your garden. I set mine in a random pattern, 10 to 15 feet apart. When the bags bob in the breeze, they look like people bending over, and the crows don't like that one little bit!

Leapin' Lizards!

Actually, they're leapin' flea beetles, and they're chewin' the daylights out of your seedlings. The leaves were just fine yesterday. But today, they look like some miniature Annie Oakley's been using 'em for target practice. (There's no mistaking these culprits: Every time you go near them, they bounce up like tiny, black rubber balls.) So what do you do?

➤ Act fast, that's what! A big crowd of flea beetles can kill a young plant early in the season. What's more, they spread viruses that could cause more trouble down the road. Fortunately, these teeny guys have two big weaknesses: beer and the color yellow. Just set yellow sticky traps (see page 26) or shallow pans filled with beer in your garden. The beetles'll bounce themselves to death!

The Nose Knows

Flea beetles find their targets by scent, and most of the beetles are host-specific (which means they focus on a particular kind of plant). Here's a quartet of ways you can use that knowledge to your advantage—and their demise.

Confuse 'em. Instead of planting rows of individual crops, combine several kinds of plants in small beds (a technique known as interplanting). All the aromas will mingle, and the beetles won't have a clue what's going on. So they'll go elsewhere for dinner.

Dust 'em off. Flea beetles hate powdery stuff like wood ashes and diatomaceous earth. So gather up whatever you've got on hand, and sprinkle away!

Disgust 'em. Surround your garden beds with plants that send 'em packin', such as marigolds, wormwood, mint, and catnip.

Lure 'em in. Plant a big patch of radishes or Chinese cabbage. The beetles'll make a four-point landing there and ignore everything else. (For more on lure crops, see Chapter 15.)

Let's Be Buddies

Here are a couple of news items for all you folks who pooh-pooh the whole idea of good-buddy plants:

• The scientists at Cornell University's School of Agriculture have proven that when you interplant tomatoes with collards, the flea beetle population plummets.

• Researchers in England planted sunflowers and corn together. The result: Armyworms stayed away in droves, the corn yield increased, and up to 50 percent fewer bad-guy beetles bugged the sunflowers.

So there!

Wretched Roots

From Top to Bottom

If your cornstalks are lookin' sickly, wilting, and maybe even falling over, there's a good chance the roots are being munched on. Dig up a plant, and take a good look. If you see little white maggots, your diners are corn rootworms, which are the larvae of both spotted and Western cucumber beetles. If the slimy guys you find are long, shiny, orange worms, you're entertaining a crowd of wireworms, the baby version of a tawny brown insect called the click beetle. (Except for producing obnoxious offspring, the adult beetles are entirely harmless.) How do you get rid of these unwanted guests?

➡ Once you've identified the culprit, spring into action in one of these two ways:

 When wireworms are ridin' rough-shod through your garden, my can-o'-worms traps are a neat, clean way to round 'em up and clear 'em out. Here's all you need to do: First, gather up some big cans (like large juice or coffee cans), and punch a lot of medium-size nail holes in the sides. Fill the cans about half full with cut-up potatoes or carrots, then bury the traps among your target plants so that the tops are just above ground. Cover the openings with small boards, then toss a little mulch on top. Once or twice a week, pull up the cans, empty the contents into a bucket of soapy water, then toss the wormy liquid onto the compost pile (the slimy squirts can't hurt anything once the soap's done 'em in). Then, rebait your traps, and you're back in business.

Corn rootworms: You can foil these babies simply by rotating your corn with crops they don't hanker for—which is just about everything else in the garden. To reduce future populations, lay out the unwelcome mat for their parents, which cause trouble all over the veggie patch. (See my simple anti-beetle tactics on page 159.)

Wireworms: Besides having a monster-size appetite for corn, wireworms love potatoes. They'll also chew their way into the roots of a whole garden full of other fruits and vegetables, including beets, carrots, lettuce, muskmelons, onions, peas, snap beans, strawberries, and sweet potatoes. To round up baby wireworms, bury a bunch of my can-o'-worms traps (see "Super Solution," page 153). Polish off the grown-up crowd by drizzling corn syrup, honey, or molasses on fence posts or thick wooden stakes. Then, when the beetles fly in to sip the syrup, pick 'em off and drop 'em into soapy water. Whatever you do, though, don't lace the sweet bait with poison: It'll kill the click beetles alright, but it'll also kill honeybees, butterflies, and other good-guy bugs that show up for a snack.

An Ounce of Prevention

Wireworms cause the most trouble in gardens that have been converted from turf grass within the past couple of years. So, if you're thinking about replacing part of your lawn with a vegetable garden, it pays to take precautions.

➤ Dig up your future plot in late summer or early fall. Then, turn the soil over once a week for four to six weeks. That way, you'll bring the wireworms to the surface, where birds can get at 'em. Better yet, if you're lucky enough to know someone who has chickens, invite a few of the cluckers over for lunch. They'll clear out the foul felons in no time flat. Trust me on this, folks. I've tried it more than once—thanks to a neighbor who has some very sociable pet hens—and it works like magic!

SUPER SOLUTION

If you grow asparagus, or even buy it at the supermarket, then you've got an A-1 nematode chaser at hand. Every time you finish cooking some of the scrumptious spears, let the water cool down, then pour it onto the soil around your trouble-prone plants. Nematodes can't stand asparagus juice!

Dig Those Nematodes!

Your garden plants are sickly, turning yellow, and wilting—and they don't spring back when you water them. A whole lot of problems can cause those symptoms. But when you dig up the plants and find the roots all covered with galls that you can't break off, it means just one thing: You've got root-knot nematodes at work. These all-but-invisible worms come in two kinds: Northern and Southern, both of which ransack the roots of many garden plants. Fortunately, they both respond to the same good-riddance methods.

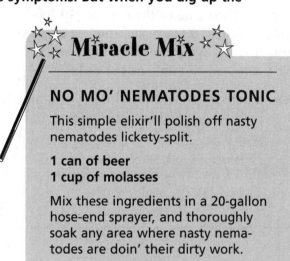

Miracle Mix

NO MO' NEMATODES TONIC

This simple elixir'll polish off nasty nematodes lickety-split.

1 can of beer
1 cup of molasses

Mix these ingredients in a 20-gallon hose-end sprayer, and thoroughly soak any area where nasty nematodes are doin' their dirty work.

Here's a trio of ways to say "No, no, nematodes!"

1. Feed their sweet tooth. Spread 5 pounds of sugar over every 50 sq. ft. of planting area. The nematodes will choke on the stuff.

2. Bring on the enemy. Load your soil with things like eggshells, shrimp hulls, and seafood meal. They all contain chitin, which is what nematode eggs are covered with. Chitin eaters from near and far will show up to feast on the free lunch you've given them—and then start right in on the nematode eggs.

3. Give 'em a drink. Soak infested areas with my No Mo' Nematodes Tonic (above). It'll deliver the final knockout punch!

Don't Join This Club

If your Brussels sprouts, broccoli, cauliflower (or cabbage) plants are stunted, wilted, and turning yellow, dig 'em up, and look at the roots. There's a good chance they've caught the cabbage family disease: clubroot. There's no mistaking the symptoms: The roots will be thick, swollen, and ugly as the dickens.

 There is no cure for clubroot, so pull up the sick plants, and destroy them. And be quick about it—this stuff spreads like wildfire! Then, don't plant any member of the cabbage (*Brassica*) family in that spot for at least seven years: That's how long the fungus can live in the soil.

It's an Epidemic!

Even if clubroot is runnin' rampant in your neighborhood, don't give up—you can still treat yourself to home-grown cole crops.

 Just follow these guidelines:

✿ Grow resistant varieties.

✿ Don't buy transplants or seeds that were grown locally. Instead, order seeds that were grown elsewhere.

✿ Rotate your cabbage-family crops every year (besides guarding against clubroot, you'll also foil another family nemesis: cabbageworms).

✿ Keep the soil pH at 7.2 or above—the clubroot fungus thrives only in acidic soil. (For more on pH, see Chapter 14.)

✿ If you plant in late summer for a fall harvest (and you should, since all the brassicas love cool weather), solarize your soil first. See my simple method on page 309.

Sickly Stems

Support Your Local Vines

Plants that sprawl across the ground are disasters waiting to happen. Pests and diseases of all kinds can stroll right out of the soil and onto (or into) their stems, leaves, and fruit. So what do you do?

Support those stems, that's what! But if you want to really give your crops a helping hand, use stakes or trellises that are made of metal—especially copper. The reason has to do with an old-time kind of gardening called electroculture. To see it in action, just look at your lawn after a thunderstorm. Notice how much greener it is? That's because the electricity flying around in the air teamed up with oxygen and nitrogen to form nitric oxide—a first-class wonder drug for plants. To put electroculture to work in your garden, here's all you have to do:

✿ Use only metal poles for staking or trellising.

✿ Grow cucumbers, indeterminate tomatoes, and other vining crops on metal fences.

✿ If you normally grow peas or other lightweight vines on string trellises, use wire instead.

✿ Tie up your plants with old panty hose, or strips cut from old nylon dress slips. (Nylon attracts electricity.)

SUPER SOLUTION

To give a big, beautiful kick to an ornamental edible garden, grow your plants on copper arches. Just get some flexible copper tubing, cut it into the lengths you need, and bend them into shape. Or, if you loved playing with Tinkertoys® as a kid, get creative and build a copper trellis. First, find a simple trellis plan in a garden magazine or building-project book. Then, instead of wood and nails, use copper pipe, standard connectors, and plumber's cement. (Just make sure you buy your gear at a plumbing-supply store; it'll cost a fraction of what you'd pay at a hardware or building-products store.)

Give 'Em a Lift

What if you're growing crops like winter squash or pumpkins that are just too heavy to tie to a trellis? Here's the solution to that little dilemma.

➡ First, get some hardware cloth or construction-grade wire mesh (you can find both at hardware or building-supply stores). Cut the mesh into 3- by 5-foot pieces, bend each piece into an arch, and set it in place on your planting bed. Then, plant your seeds along the sides, and train the young plants up the sides. If you think your crops' mature weight will be too much for the structure to bear, support the center with bricks or blocks of wood. Better yet, use pieces of metal drainpipe—they'll attract even more electricity!

Staighten Up!

Do your cornstalks keep tryin' to lie down on the job? Well, don't panic—they're not sick. The problem is simply that even with a healthy root system, most cornstalks are so tall that they just naturally tend to fall over; it's a condition called lodging.

➡ This one couldn't be simpler to fix: Just pull soil up around the base of the plants to give them more support. And, if you get tired of doin' that, next year, plant a mini-variety like 'Baby Asian', 'Candystick', or 'Golden Midget'. These stalks rarely get more than 4 or 5 feet tall, and (here's another bonus) each one'll give you four or five tiny ears of corn. With the big guys, you almost never get more than two!

Lousy Leaves

Not Just for Cukes

With a name like "cucumber beetle," you'd expect these guys to be specialists, but these vile villains go after more plants than you can shake a seed packet at. And the worst of their damage isn't the holes the beetles chew in leaves and fruits; it's the nasty diseases they spread, including bacterial wilt and mosaic virus. Once they get a toehold, usually all you can do is pull up your plants and send 'em to that great garden in the sky. Fortunately, there's plenty you can do to battle the beetles *before* they take over.

➥ First, know your enemy. The adults have shiny yellow wing covers with either three black stripes or 11 black spots. They sleep through the winter in dead vines or garden litter, and hit the chow line about the time cucumber seedlings emerge in the spring. Larvae (which eat the roots of young plants) are thin, whitish grubs with a black or brown head. Here's a terrific trio of beetle-bustin' tricks:

1. Mix ½ cup of wood ashes per 2 gallons of water, and pour it over your plants. The beetles'll scram! (Just one note of caution: Wood ashes are highly alkaline, so if your soil is naturally on the sweet side, go easy with this routine.)

2. Set big, wilted squash leaves on the ground among your plants. The cuke beetles will crawl under the leaves to escape

ALLURING LURES

Garden centers and catalogs sell traps that lure cuke beetles to their death with pheromones, a.k.a. sex hormones. They work really well, but as with all powerful lure traps, you're likely to draw a bigger crowd than you had to begin with. It's your call, though.

the hot sun. Then you can stroll through the garden, casually stepping on the leaves, and squashing all the varmints in the process.

3. In the case of a full-scale invasion, don't pull any punches: Mix up a batch of my So Long, Sucker Spray (see page 71), and let 'er rip!

Show 'Em the Door!

Once you've said good riddance to cucumber beetles, make sure they don't come back.

 Use these tried-and-true methods for keeping the beetles at bay:

Grow your crops in old tires. Something in the rubber repels cuke beetles (and squash bugs, too).

Move in masses of marigolds. They'll make the lowlifes scurry in a hurry. What's more, they'll say "Shove off!" to a lot of other varmints, including Mexican bean beetles, squash bugs, tomato hornworms, whiteflies, and even nasty nematodes.

Draft some soldier beetles. There's nothin' they like better than a mess hall full of cucumber beetles! To call up the troops, let some goldenrod or milkweed spring up among your veggies, or set pots of catnip among the plants. (Don't plant it in the ground, though, because it'll take over the whole neighborhood.)

Battle of the Bugs

Cuke beetles aren't the only vile villains gunnin' for your cucurbits (a.k.a. the squash and cucumber family). If the leaves and stems of your squash, cucumbers, or melons turn black, wilt, and die, you can blame it on squash bugs. Besides sucking the life out

of the foliage, they can also take a toll on the fruit. So what's your best battle plan?

➥ Once the culprits have descended, they're prime targets for handpicking and drowning in a pail of water with a little kerosene in it. They're also a snap to trap. In the evening, lay boards on the ground among your cucurbit crops. After a night of carousing, the bugs will crawl under the boards to sleep. Come morning, go out to the garden, and step on the boards. Then, what have you got? Squashed squash bugs, that's what!

Miracle Mix

KNOCK-'EM-DEAD INSECT SPRAY

This potent mixture will deal a death blow to squash bugs or any other foul felons that are after your veggies.

6 cloves of garlic, finely chopped
1 small onion, finely chopped
1 tbsp. of cayenne pepper
1 tbsp. of liquid dish soap
1 qt. of warm water

Mix all of these ingredients together, and let the mixture sit overnight. Strain out the solids, pour the liquid into a hand-held mist sprayer, and knock those buggy pests dead!

The Unwelcome Mat

So you've sent this year's squash bugs to the insect graveyard, but how are you going to keep next year's generation at bay?

➥ The easiest thing to do is add a few new plant friends to your garden. Interplant your cucurbits with nasturtiums, onions, marigolds, or tansy. Squash bugs won't go near 'em! You can also mask the scent the bugs are zeroing in on—which is on the leaves of the curcubit plants. My favorite method is to spray the leaves with a half-and-half solution of water and artificial vanilla flavoring. (Of course, real vanilla extract will work, too, but why waste the good stuff on the enemy?)

Seeing Spots

When you see powdery orange spots on the undersides of your plants' leaves, there can be only one diagnosis: rust. This nasty stuff is caused by a fungus—or, rather, a whole lot of closely related fungi called *Uromyces phaseoli*, each of which zeroes in on a specific kind of plant. So, for instance, corn rust can't infect beans, and rose rust can't infect corn. These fungi strike during damp, mild weather (temperatures in the 70°F range), when a plant's leaves have been wet for several hours.

If you reach the scene in the early stages, you can probably save your crop. Just pull off the infected leaves, and destroy them. Then, if your plants are growing close together, thin them out so the foliage can dry off more quickly. But if the weatherman's callin' for a sustained spell of wet weather, you may need to bite the bullet, pull up the whole shebang, and wait until next year. Then, replant in a different area, and rotate your crop every year, period. Most often, rust attacks plants that have been grown in the same soil or in adjoining plots for several years running. So give your plants plenty of elbow room, and—for the best chance of success—grow rust-resistant varieties.

I Was *Only* Trying to Help!

Here's a problem that can be very tough to diagnose. The symptoms range all over the ballpark, and they're easy to confuse with trouble caused by pests, diseases, nutrient deficiencies, and weather stress. There's a highfalutin name for this condition: *phytotoxicity*. In plain English, it refers to the damage done to plants by pesticides. Although pesticides can hurt—and even kill—all plants, the most at risk are seedlings and young transplants. Even plant-based pesticides like pyrethrin and rotenone can cause big-time trouble. So can good old-fashioned soap solutions. Too many sprayings can make leaf edges turn brown and curl up, and can damage growing tips, delaying maturity. And any soap spray is likely to reduce crop yield (or, in the case of ornamentals, flower output).

➡ Don't use chemicals unless you've got no other choice! Throughout this book, you'll find boatloads of tips, tricks, and Miracle Mixes that'll keep your plants safe from the jaws of pesky pests a good 99 percent of the time—without giving you more problems than you had to begin with. When you're faced with an all-out invasion, and soap spray seems the only answer, follow these guidelines:

Aim carefully. Keep the soap solution away from the plants' growing tips.

Wash it off. A few hours after you spray, give your plants a good hosing to remove any soap residue.

Walk on the mild side. When you're chomping at the bit to send bad bugs packin', it's tempting to throw in more soap than a Miracle Mix may call for. But don't do it: A stronger solution is no more effective at killing pests, and it can cause big-time damage to your plants.

Let's Be Buddies

You might think of a radish as just another tidbit on the relish tray, but it's really a pest-control powerhouse! These tangy tubers protect tomato plants from spider mites and keep cucumber beetles away from squash, melons, and cukes. Planted as a "lure crop," radishes draw flea beetles and aphids away from peppers, and draw maggots away from everything under the sun. When you want your radishes to stand guard duty, sow them among the plants that need protection, then let them flower and go to seed. Plant a separate patch for harvesting and eating.

Failing Flowers 'n Veggies

Breezin' Along

If your corn isn't forming silks (its equivalent of blossoms), your problem is poor pollination, and I'll bet you dollars to donuts that your crop was planted in rows. Corn is pollinated by the wind, and natural breezes just don't do an efficient job when they have to travel in a straight line.

 Next time, sow your seeds in square blocks. I like to make a grid pattern of raised beds that are each about 30 inches square. Then I plant my seeds 1 inch deep and about 8 inches apart down the center of the bed. It works every time!

Birds Do It, Bees Do It...

Lots of beneficial bugs do it. Pollinate your crops, that is. If your veggies are servin' up a measly harvest— or even none at all—the problem could be that their male and female flower parts aren't getting together. (Unlike corn, which is pollinated by the wind, most fruiting vegetables rely on birds and insects to do the job.)

Here are some sure-fire ways to get the boys and girls together:

Don't use pesticides. They take care of the bad guys alright (at least temporarily), but they'll also kill your powerful pollinatin' pals.

Take the lid off. Covering young plants is a great (and sometimes the only) way to protect them from cold weather and early pest invasions. But as soon as the flowers bloom, you need to whisk those covers off. Otherwise, the pollinators can't get in to do their stuff.

Water their feet, not their heads. Overhead watering can wash the pollen right out of the flowers, besides encouraging fungal diseases. So deliver moisture directly to the roots with a soaker hose or drip irrigation system.

Mix it up. By planting a mixed bag of vegetables, along with flowers, herbs, and even trees and shrubs, you'll attract pollinating critters of all kinds—and as far as your bloomin' maternity ward is concerned, the more, the merrier!

Sweet-talk 'em. If the winged matchmakers aren't showing up as fast as you'd like, entice 'em with my Sweet Success Spray (at left). It works like a dating service for vegetable plants!

✸ Miracle Mix ✸

SWEET SUCCESS SPRAY

This sugar-packed spray will lure bees to your veggie plants and ensure pollination. What's more, it'll kill nasty nematodes in the soil, so with this mixture, you get two benefits for the price of one!

**½ cup of sugar
2 cups of water**

Pour the sugar into the water and boil, stirring, until the sugar is completely dissolved. Let the mixture cool, dilute it with 1 gallon of water, and pour the solution into a hand-held mist sprayer. Then spritz your bloomin' plants. Before you know it, willing winged workers will fly to your rescue!

Turn Up the Heat!

So, you've been tryin' to grow hot peppers, but they're not turnin' out as steamy as you'd like? Well, maybe you just need to reach for a different kind of pepper.

➡ What makes a pepper hot is certain heat-producing chemicals, the prime one being capsaicin. How much capsaicin a pepper has—and therefore, how much firepower it delivers—is measured in Scoville Heat Units. (They're named for the scientist, Wilbur Scoville, who came up with the system back in 1912.) Here's Dr. Scoville's scorecard. You might want to keep these numbers in mind when you're whippin' up Miracle Mix recipes that call for hot pepper!

Pepper Type	Scoville Heat Units
Anaheim chile	250–1,400
Jalapeño	4,000–6,000
Serrano chile	7,000–25,000
Cayenne	30,000–35,000
Chile piquin	35,000–40,000
Tabasco	30,000–50,000
Habañero	200,000–350,000

Sweeter and Hotter

Whether you prefer your peppers candy sweet or steamy hot, it's no fun when they don't live up to your taste buds' expectations.

➡️ Here's a pair of tricks for packin' more flavor into your peppers:

Sweet. Harvest most of the peppers while they're still green, leaving just a few on each plant. All the energy will go into those few fruits, and they'll grow even sweeter than usual as they turn from green to red, orange, yellow, purple, or chocolate brown (depending on the variety).

Hot. Just before you're getting ready to harvest your hot peppers, flood their beds. A deluge just at that time stresses the plants' roots and sends out a signal to "turn up the heat."

Dear Jerry, When I visited a friend in Santa Fe last year, he gave me some seeds from his favorite hot peppers. The plants grew well enough in my garden, but the peppers took forever to mature! What's worse, when I did pick them, they weren't nearly as hot as the ones I tasted at my friend's house. His just about sent steam rolling from my ears! I grew the plants exactly the way my friend told me to. What went wrong? – F.D., Portland, Oregon

Dear F.D., Nothing really went wrong; those peppers were just behaving according to plan—_their_ plan, that is! It is true that some kinds of peppers are naturally hotter than others (see "Sweeter and Hotter," at left). But then geography enters the picture in two ways: First, a jalapeño that's grown in hot, dry territory like New Mexico will always be hotter than the identical variety grown in the Northwest, where the soil's a tad richer and the weather is cooler and damper. Second, the cooler the weather, the longer it takes a pepper to mature. A pepper that takes 70 days to mature in northern New Mexico might take up to 100 days in Portland. Just thank your lucky stars you've got that nice, long growing season!

More, Please!

Want more flavor from your tomatoes, squash, and cukes? Well, it is true that some varieties are naturally more flavorful than others. The secret to finding those winners lies in reading catalog descriptions carefully, asking your gardening friends, and sampling the offerings at local farmers' markets.

➥ But, whatever variety you're growing, here's a simple way to give it more flavor: About three days before you plan to har-

Want a super-simple way to get a bigger veggie harvest? Just plant bigger seeds—no kidding! In any given batch, the larger seeds germinate faster and produce stronger seedlings than the smaller ones do, and that grow power translates into a bigger yield. The reason is simple: Larger seeds contain more food to boost the baby plants along.

vest, go cold turkey on the water. How on earth can that make a difference? Well, these veggies are about 85 percent water to begin with. If there's too much water in the soil, it seems to go right into the fruits and dilute the flavor.

Bigger Is Bitter

Not better—at least, not when it comes to summer squash and cucumbers. A zucchini or a cuke the size of a baby seal might knock your neighbors' socks off, but it's all but guaranteed to taste stringy, seedy, and bitter.

➡ The secret to great eatin' with these crops is to get 'em while they're young, tender, and sweet. For summer squash, that generally means about 50 days from planting. For cukes, size is your cue: Pluck picklers off the vines when they're between 3 and 4 inches long; slicers are at the peak of flavor when they're 6 to 8 inches long. (Winter squash, on the other hand, just seem to get better with age; you can leave them on the vine until just before the first frost arrives.)

Have They Lost Their Heads?

No, they haven't formed any—your broccoli plants, that is. The culprit: Mother Nature. Broccoli likes cool temperatures, especially at night. If the weather's too hot for its liking, it won't perform, period. And it turns out its biggest,

best harvest when daytime temperatures hover in the upper 60°F range. So does that mean if you live in warmer territory, you're doomed to a life of supermarket broccoli?

➡ Not at all. Just time your planting so the crop grows up when your weather is (or should be) cool. Cover the beds with organic mulch to help keep the soil cool, and if a heat wave hits, put up a screen to shield the plants from the sun. With a weather wimp like broccoli, I can't guarantee that you'll get a bumper crop, but (barring other disasters) you will have enough to give you braggin' rights at the dinner table—not to mention mighty fine eatin'!

HAPPY CAMPERS

When it comes to success broccoli style, timing is everything. For spring planting, I reach for seeds of 'Green Comet' or 'Arcadia'. They both grow fast and can take some heat as harvest time approaches. In midsummer, when I put in my fall crop, I want a variety that can handle high temperatures when the plants are young. 'Green Jewel' fills the bill here.

Get Your Teeth Off of My Ears!

When you stroll out to your corn patch and find that something's been chewing on the silk and the ends of the ears, you can be sure that caterpillars have come a callin'. If the leaves are also sporting ragged holes, it's most likely your vile villains are armyworms; otherwise, blame the damage on corn earworms or European corn borers.

➡ There's no need to get a positive I.D. You can deal with all of these culprits the same way: Pick 'em off the plants and drown 'em in soapy water (or hire a posse of neighborhood kids to do the job). Then spray your plants with my Caterpillar Killer Tonic (see page 57). It'll knock off any lingering worms and keep their cousins from moving in.

That's Not All

Armyworms, corn earworms, and European corn borers don't let their voracious appetites stop with corn. They chew up a lot of other vegetable plants, too.

➡ Regardless of which crop they're gunnin' for, hand-picking is your best option to control these creepy guys. To keep the culprits from comin' back, spray your plants with my Orange Aid (at right). Believe me, caterpillars can't stand the stuff! For long-term control, call up the troops (this terrible trio has a *lot* of powerful enemies). For the full roster—and tips on signing them up—see Chapter 14. Here's a look at the damage they cause.

Miracle Mix

ORANGE AID

You'll love the aroma of this citrusy spray—but caterpillars *hate* it!

1 cup of chopped orange peels*
¼ cup of boiling water

Put the orange peels in a blender or food processor, and pour the boiling water over them. Liquefy, then let the mixture sit overnight at room temperature. Strain the slurry through cheesecloth, and pour the liquid into a hand-held mist sprayer. Fill the balance of the bottle with water, and spray your plants from top to bottom.

* Or substitute lemon, lime, or grapefruit peels.

Villain	Likely Victims	Damage
Armyworms	Beans, beets, cabbage, cucumbers, lettuce, peanuts, peas, peppers, spinach, and tomatoes	Ragged holes in leaves and fruit
Corn earworms, a.k.a. fruitworms or tomato hornworms	Beans, okra, peas, peppers, potatoes, squash, and tomatoes	On tomatoes: holes at the stem end. On pinhead-size peppers: holes. On other crops: leaves and buds with chunks missing.
European corn borers	Beans and all members of the tomato family	Same type as corn earworms cause

Hey! That's *My* Asparagus!

Voles *love* asparagus. If you grow what Grandma Putt used to call "the queen of all vegetables," you've probably learned this the hard way. I know I have! Is there any way to keep these rascals away?

➤ Yup. I've come up with a vole-proof protection device. Here's how to make one:

Step 1: Build a wooden frame that's 8 to 10 inches high, and the size of your asparagus bed. I use plain 1-inch yellow pine, but any kind of wood will do. (Just don't use pressure-treated wood; it'll leach toxic chemicals into the soil, and from there into your asparagus!)

Step 2: Get a piece of welded-wire mesh (hardware cloth) to fit the frame, and staple it to the bottom. You can find hardware cloth at (where else?) a hardware store. Make sure the openings in the mesh are 1/4 inch or smaller.

Step 3: Set the frame on your plot, fill it up with soil and compost, and plant your asparagus. The roots'll grow down through the mesh and into the soil, but the voles can't shoulder their way up to eat the shoots. And you're home free!

HOLD IT!

Don't cut off any living asparagus fronds—at least not until very late in the fall. The foliage provides food for the roots, so they can produce more tender, juicy spears the following spring.

Trouble Above

There's another critter that's bound and determined to feast on your asparagus spears, and the ferny leaves, too: asparagus beetles. Unlike voles, which are up to no good all over the garden, these guys are true specialists: They eat only asparagus. The adults are shiny, colorful guys, about 1/4 inch long with (depending on the species) blue, black, brown, or russet bodies and black or cream-colored spots. They lay their eggs on the young spears, and when the larvae hatch in early spring, the whole family has a feast.

➥ In most cases, all you need to do is take aim with the garden hose, and blast 'em off the plants. Then, scoop 'em up and send 'em to their just reward. If that doesn't do the trick, whip up a batch of my So Long, Sucker Spray (see page 71), and let 'em have it. Come fall, clear out and destroy any old, dead fronds and any plant litter you find (that's where the beetles spend the winter). Finally, to halt future feasts, encourage the pests' natural enemies. Birds, ladybug larvae, and spined soldier bugs all eat asparagus beetles and their larvae (see Chapter 14).

Let's Be Buddies

Parsley is the best friend an asparagus bed ever had. It repels asparagus beetles, and generally makes the plants stronger and healthier. Furthermore, if you let some of the parsley flower, it'll draw beetle-eaters and other good-guy bugs from near and far.

Deer, Oh Deer

Of all the letters in my mailbag, most of the cries for help concern these beautiful brown-eyed bruisers. But don't you worry, friends, because I've got the answer for deterring deer.

➥ This is the one sure-fire way I've found for keeping deer out of my vegetable garden: erect two fences. Each should be at least 5 feet high. Place the second fence 4 feet away, running parallel to the first. Deer can jump high, and they can jump far, but they can't do both at the same time.

Repel with Smell

If building a deer-proof barrier (see "Deer, Oh Deer," at left) is out of the question, don't despair. You can still do a decent job of keeping deer on the run.

➡️ Hang any of these repellents on your present garden fence, or scatter them among your plants:

❀ Bars of strong-smelling soap, like Dial® or Irish Spring®

❀ Cheesecloth or panty hose pouches filled with human or dog hair

❀ Cotton cloths sprinkled with baby powder or athlete's-foot powder

❀ Dirty laundry, smelly socks, old shoes, or messy diapers (anything that reeks of fearsome humans)

PLANT THESE at your PERIL! Whatever you do, never plant corn and tomatoes anywhere near one another. Corn earworms and tomato hornworms are almost the same critters, and they'll leap from one plant to the other faster than you can say "Jumpin' jackrabbits!"

Flour Power

Some four-footed bad guy is eating your veggies, but try as you might, you can't catch him in the act. To mount your best defense, you need a positive I.D. Will you have to stand at the window day and night?

➡️ Not at all! Just sprinkle a little flour on the ground in the victim's bed. When the thug returns to the scene of the crime, he'll leave his footprints in the powdery white stuff. If you don't recognize them by sight, get out your Audubon field guide, and match those prints. Then you're ready for action!

JERRY'S TOMATO TROUBLESHOOTING GUIDE

At first glance, your tomatoes might look like they've been attacked by pesky pests or dastardly diseases. But hold on: Don't reach for your spray gun just yet. You might find your problem—and the solution—right here.

Symptom	Problem	Cause	Solution
The bottom end of the fruit suddenly collapses and rots.	Blossom-end rot	**1.** Too little calcium in the soil **2.** Soil that's alternately wet and dry	**1.** Add crushed eggshells, bonemeal, or gypsum to the soil. **2.** Water consistently, and apply organic mulch to keep soil moisture constant. **3.** Use a commercial spray such as Rot Stop.
Fruits never mature properly and have yellow-gray patches.	Blotchy ripening	Cool temperatures	Grow a variety that's bred to perform in cool climates (see page 148).
Circular cracks develop on top of the ripening fruit.	Cracking	**1.** Variations in soil moisture **2.** Excess nitrogen	**1.** Water consistently, and apply organic mulch to keep soil moisture constant. **2.** Switch to a lower-nitrogen fertilizer.
Blistered skin; light patches that eventually rot.	Sunscald	Extended exposure to direct sun	Don't prune too much! Keep enough leaves on to shade the fruit. In very intense sun, shade fruits with screens or floating row covers.
Thin, dark lines running from the stem to the bottom of the fruit.	Zippering	Cold temperatures at the time of pollination	Keep young plants warm early in the season with floating row covers or my wall-o'- bottles (see page 147).

CHAPTER 7

Glorious Greens

For my money, there's no tastier treat than a big salad of fresh-from-the-garden greens. Unfortunately, plenty of disasters can befall those luscious leaves *before* they ever reach your salad bowl. Well, worry not. Here are my tried-and-true techniques for keeping your greens free of dastardly diseases, out of the jaws of wily worms and other pesky pests, and even safe from Mother Nature's practical jokes!

Stricken Seeds 'n Seedlings

Where'd They Go?

Spinach, lettuce, Swiss chard, kale, and lots of other leafy greens can be put into the ground even before the last frost. There's just one problem: The seeds will take their sweet old time germinating, so it's easy to lose track of where you put 'em.

➡️ The solution: Sprinkle radish seeds around your plantings to mark the beds. The radishes will spring up before the other seedlings do, so you won't dig up your future greens by mistake.

GRANDMA PUTT'S
grow-how

Grandma Putt always planted onions among her lettuce and other greens. In fact, she kept lettuce seedlings all ready for transplanting. Then, every time she pulled up a young onion, she'd pop a little lettuce plant into the hole. She said her method paid off in two ways: It saved space in the garden, and the onions kept rabbits and other pesky pests away from her greens.

Ah, Dry Up!

Although the seeds of most greens are happy as clams in cold soil, they can't handle home ground that's both cold *and* wet. So if your early sowings aren't coming up, chances are the seeds are rotting before they germinate.

➡️ Fortunately, help is as close as your local garden center—or even your garage. When you put in your next crop, make a shallow ditch, and fill it with sterilized potting mix or compost (whichever is easier to come by). Then sow your seeds, and cover them with more potting mix to the depth recommended on the seed

packet. (You want to barely cover lettuce seeds, though, because they need light to germinate.) Before you know it, you'll see little green shoots poking their heads above the soil!

Chill Out!

Because lettuce and spinach come and go in a flash, it's a good idea to make successive sowings every 10 days throughout the growing season. That way, you'll always have tender, young leaves on hand. There's just one problem with that routine: Lettuce and spinach seeds don't germinate worth a darn once the weather turns hot.

Here's a simple solution: Before you sow your seeds, set them in the refrigerator overnight. Then, once you've tucked them into their garden beds, set ice cubes on top of them, and put up a screen to shade the patch from the sun. Those greens will be out of the ground and in your salad bowl faster than you can say "Balsamic vinaigrette, please!"

The Relief Pitchers

If your summers are too hot to grow spinach even with Grandma Putt's cold-storage treatment (see "Chill Out!" above), don't give up: You can still have home-grown spinach salad all season long. How?

Just grow one of these stand-ins. They're not really spinach, but they taste so much like it that even Popeye wouldn't know the difference.

New Zealand spinach (*Tetragonia tetragonoides*). Sow the seeds as soon as it's safe to set out tomatoes and peppers. Later,

DIFFERENT STROKES

Spinach will be off and runnin' even faster if you soak the seeds in my Seed-Starter Tonic (see page 4). With lettuce, it's a different story: Because those seeds are so tiny, you're better off keeping them dry until planting time. Once they get wet, they're all but impossible to work with! (See page 119 for my favorite small-seed sowing trick.)

clip the leaves anytime you want them, and use them just as you do "real" spinach.

Malabar, a.k.a Indian or Ceylon, spinach (*Basella alba*). As you can guess from its common names, this plant will take all the heat it can get. It's a twining vine, so give it a trellis or fence to climb on (a metal one, of course!). It's also a great-looking plant, so if you've got an eyesore to cover as well as weather woes, this is the spinach to reach for. Just plant your trellis in front of the object of your displeasure, and before you know it, that ugly view will be history!

Any Volunteers?

The ground has barely thawed, and you've got volunteer seedlings springing up like crazy—weeks before you expect to see anything you've planted on purpose. The only trouble is, those baby plants are coming up in all the wrong places. Now what?

➡️ Your immediate solution is a no-brainer: Just dig up those little guys and tuck 'em in where you want 'em to grow. Then next spring, choose your site and sow seeds in the fall, *before* the ground freezes. Use raised beds, with plenty of organic matter, to give the seedlings good drainage, and cover the seedbeds with a couple inches of shredded leaves (for the lowdown on planting, see Chapter 14).

That's Not What I Wanted!

It seemed like a good idea at the time: You wanted to grow some of the fancy mesclun greens they sell at the supermarket, so you bought a packet of mixed seeds and sowed them in your garden. When they came up, though, most of those greens weren't what you wanted at all!

➡ This isn't a problem, folks— it's a chance to let your creative juices flow! First, decide exactly what kind of greens you want to grow. If you know which of the tasty leaves you like best, but you don't know their names, ask the store's produce manager, or take the leaves to a good garden center and ask for a positive I.D. For more ideas—and to find out what greens will grow best in your region— peruse a few books and catalogs that specialize in salad greens. You'll be surprised at how many there are! Then, follow this simple routine:

1. Narrow your choices to five or six different greens that have the same planting requirements and thrive in the same growing conditions. (By the way, there's nothing exotic about mesclun; it's just garden-variety greens that are picked when they get about 4 inches tall.)

2. Order a packet or two of each kind of seeds. When they arrive, empty all of them into a big glass jar, and mix 'em up.

3. Prepare your seedbed, indoors or out (see Chapter 14). Then reach into the jar, take a generous

---

PLANTER BEWARE!

Baby greens can fall victim to the same dastardly duo that targets every other seedling: damping-off disease and cutworms. If you start seeds indoors, follow my damping-off prevention guidelines on page 6. To keep cutworms at bay, corral your transplants with protective collars, and, for good measure, surround each one with a scratchy repellent like crushed eggshells or chicken manure.

pinch of seeds, and drop them onto the soil. If you're direct-sowing your seeds, space your pinches 6 to 8 inches apart; if you're starting your seeds indoors, use that same spacing for your transplants. Then, sow more pinches every week to 10 days throughout the growing season.

4. The result: instant mixed salad whenever you want it. When the greens are as big as you like 'em, just cut off a clump, toss 'em in a bowl, and add your favorite dressing.

GRANDMA PUTT'S
grow-how

Grandma Putt had a simple trick for giving her cabbages a good start in life: Just before she tucked the transplants into their holes, she dipped the roots in a good, thick mixture of well-cured cow manure and water. Some of the goo stuck to the roots and gave them instant nutrition. (Grandma thought of it as a stick-to-your-ribs breakfast, vegetable style!)

Who's Got the Cabbage?

Cabbage seeds not performing? I'm not surprised. Cabbage almost never does well when the seeds are sown directly in the garden. In fact, the days-to-maturity numbers on seed packets always refer to the time from transplanting—not sowing—to harvest.

➡ Start the seeds for your spring crop indoors, four to six weeks before you expect the last frost. Follow my simple seed-starting guidelines in Chapter 15, and be sure to use my Seed-Starter Tonic (see page 4). Then, at transplant time, set the seedlings into their holes so that the bottom two leaves are covered. New roots will sprout from the buried leaf nodules, and give the plants more get-up-and-grow power.

Wretched Roots

Rhizo...What?

Rhizoctonia root rot. It's a fungus (*Rhizoctonia solani* in scientific lingo) that attacks several greens, namely, lettuce, cabbage, Chinese cabbage, kale, and collards. An afflicted plant turns pale and wilts, often without warning. The lower leaves and stems rot. When you dig up the plant, you may see that the roots are dark and rotted—even though the soil is loose, well-drained, and fertile. This stuff sounds deadly! Is it?

➡ Not if you reach the scene in time. Of course, if all the leaves are wilted and the roots are a blackened mess, your only option is to kiss that plant good-bye. On the other hand, if only some of the leaves are drooping, spring into action this way:

❀ Remove the droopy leaves.

❀ Make sure the plants have the moisture they need, but no more—this fungus thrives in warm, moist soil.

❀ Mulch the soil to keep it cool.

❀ Create some shade for your plants, especially during the hottest part of the day.

❀ Saturate the soil with my Fungus Fighter Soil Drench (see page 45).

❀ In midsummer, before you plant your fall crops, solarize your soil (see page 309).

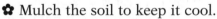

But They're Not Carrots!

Chard isn't even in the carrot family (it's a kissin' cousin to beets), but it's a prime target for carrot weevils. The larvae—cream-colored grubs with brown heads—tunnel into the roots and crowns. The adults strip the leaves bare, from the bottom up.

➡ Send weevils packin' with this one-two punch:

Clear 'em out. Handpick the larvae, drown 'em in water with a little alcohol added, or drench the soil with beneficial nematodes (see Chapter 14 for more on these garden-variety heroes). Then, give the adults what-for with my Peppermint Soap Spray (see page 135).

Stop 'em in their tracks. A thorough fall clean-up will make a big dent in next year's weevil population—the egg-laying adults spend the winter in dead plant material and other garden debris. Then, next spring, invite some weevil enemies into the garden. Birds, toads, and turtles all eat the vile villains (see Chapter 14).

Miracle Mix

JERRY'S LIME RICKEY

Back in my Uncle Art's day, lime soda pop rickeys were all the rage. Well, this rickey isn't made with soda pop, but it *will* make cabbage maggots rage!

1 cup of lime
1 qt. of water

Stir the lime into the water, and let it sit overnight. Then, pour the solution around the root ball of each maggot-plagued plant. Before you can say "Put a nickel in the jukebox," those maggots'll be history!

Mosey on Out of Here, Maggots

Talk about monsters! The cabbage maggot is one of the most notorious no-goodniks in all of veggiedom—and for good reason. It chews its way into the roots and stems of cabbages and their relatives, destroying tissue and leaving the plants wide open to dastardly diseases. The aboveground symptoms are similar to those of many other plant predicaments: wilting, stunted growth, and dark-spotted leaves. Look just under the soil, though, and you'll find the culprit—a white, legless worm about ¼ inch long.

➥ Fortunately, although these guys are vile, voracious villains, they're a snap to outsmart. Here's my modus operandi, maggot style:

Let's Be Buddies

Cabbage flies hate sage even more than they love mustard. So plant lots of the pretty, pungent herb. Your cole crops and your nose will thank you!

✿ Spread about ¼ cup of wood ashes on the soil around each plant, and gently work it in. It'll kill the marauders on contact.

✿ If you prefer liquids to powders, give the maggots a Jerry's Lime Rickey (at left). It'll perform the same deadly magic.

And Don't Come Back!

Protective coverings will keep cabbage maggots' mommies (flies called *Delia radicum*) from laying their eggs on your cabbage family plants. Just make sure you bury the edges of the covers in the soil, so the flies can't sneak under them. Collars, like the ones that fend off cutworms, will guard young transplants from maggots that do show up (see page 146 for my favorite collar makin's).

➥ Here's a duo of other deterrents:

Cut the mustard. The adults are drawn to wild mustard like bears are drawn to honey. So keep the stuff well away from your garden.

Bring on the mustard. If you've got a big piece of property, plant a lure crop of mustard in an area that's farthest from your garden. The flies will flock to it and leave your cole crops alone.

Sickly Stems

Crack!

When the stems of Swiss chard crack, it means just one thing: a shortage of boron. (Cabbage has a craving for boron, too; when it doesn't get enough, the leaves turn brown.)

➡️ The quick fix: Spray your plants' foliage with seaweed extract, or sprinkle borax on the soil, and water it in. Repeat every two weeks until the symptoms disappear. Then, before you plant next year's crop, get a good, thorough soil test, and add whatever nutrients the results call for (for more on testing and doctoring up soil, see Chapter 14).

Color Me Yellow

When your lettuce plants are stunted, wilting, and lopsided, suspect fusarium yellows, a.k.a. fusarium wilt. The plants don't turn yellow, though. Instead, the hearts turn white, and the veins turn brown. This is a fungal disease that likes warm, dry weather. It rarely strikes when soil temperatures are below 60°F or above 90°F. That's the good news. The bad news is that this nasty stuff can live in the soil for as long as 20 years, and no Miracle Mix—and no chemical fungicide—can kill it. Does that mean your garden is doomed?

➡️ Not at all, my friends. It *is* true that your only treatment option is to pull up and destroy the infected plants. But there's plenty you can do to keep trouble from coming back. Here's the routine:

Grow resistant varieties. There are many, and you'll find them marked as such in seed catalogs and comprehensive garden books.

PLANT THESE at your PERIL! When you grow lettuce, cabbage, celery, spinach, asparagus, muskmelon, peas, potatoes, radishes, tomatoes, and watermelon, be prepared to deal with fusarium yellows. In most cases, your only option is to destroy the victims. There is at least a ray of hope, though: Infected fruiting plants may still offer up some goodies, and it's perfectly safe to eat them. You won't get a bumper crop, mind you, but at least your garden labors won't have been in vain!

Solarize your soil before you plant fall crops. (See page 309.) This won't kill all the fungi, but it'll help control them.

Practice my guidelines for good garden health. Get the lowdown in Chapters 14 and 15.

Control striped cucumber beetles. These doggone demons spread the disease. (See page 159 for my cuke beetle battle plan.)

They've Bottomed Out

When the stems and bottom leaves of your lettuce and cabbages turn into a brown, slimy, yucky mess, there's only one possible culprit: bottom rot. It's caused by a kissin' cousin of the fungus that causes rhizoctonia root rot. This one thrives in wet weather, high temperatures, and high humidity. It's especially active where there's a lot of salt in the soil. But you can save the day—why, you can even have a harvest.

➤ The bottom line is you gotta act fast! If you spot the early symptoms—brown spots on the lower leaves—just pull up the plants, pluck off the sick leaves, and eat the good parts. In more advanced cases, destroy (don't compost) the victims. If the remaining, healthy plants are crowded, thin them out to provide better air circulation. Then give the soil a big dose of my Fungus Fighter Soil Drench (see page 45). To head off future trouble, follow these guidelines:

✿ Grow resistant varieties. You'll find plenty of tasty ones in garden catalogs.

❀ Plant in raised beds, and keep the soil chock-full of compost. Besides providing good drainage, it helps wipe out disease-causing fungi of all kinds.

❀ If salty soil is a real problem in your area, grow your greens in containers. (For other container planting tips, see page 278.)

❀ Spray your plants with my Compost Tea (see page 20) every two to three weeks during the growing season. Besides keeping diseases at bay, it'll provide the kind of well-balanced nutrition that greens need.

HAPPY CAMPERS

Bottom rot most often strikes plants with leaves that rest on the ground. If you want to avoid all the hassle of fighting this fungus, forget about head lettuce, and grow leaf types instead. There are literally hundreds to choose from, in more shapes and color combinations than you can shake a salad fork at!

They're Fallin' Over!

Your collards were doing just fine until you harvested the lower leaves. Now the plants are toppling over. Should you reach for a Miracle Mix?

➡ No, just grab some stakes. Collards have shallow roots, and once you pluck off the lower leaves, the plants get top-heavy. Gently sink a stake into the ground beside each plant (watch those roots!), and tie it loosely to the stem. If you want to keep the stems upright and give your plants more grow-power at the same time, use metal stakes, and strips cut from panty hose or an old nylon petticoat. They'll attract electricity from the air and give those greens a good jolt of nitrogen (see the electroculture lesson on page 157). To prevent leaning towers of collards next year, perform this staking operation in the spring, when you thin your seedlings to their final spacing.

Lousy Leaves

Slugs: A Continuing Saga

To a slug, a bed overflowing with tender greens is heaven on earth. And, of course, to a grower of greens, a garden full of slugs is a battlefield. Well, folks, here's how to win that battle—and make your home ground safe for future salad crops (and all your other plants besides).

➡️ I've got more anti-slug tactics than anyone I know. But when I'm facing an all-out invasion in a contained space—or a space I want to contain—this is the battle plan I use:

Step 1: Clear it out; you don't want to put up a barrier that'll keep slugs inside with your plants! Shortly after dark, when the slugs come a callin' for dinner, go out to the garden armed with a flashlight and a spray bottle filled with a half-and-half solution of vinegar and water. Then pick 'em off, one by one. Depending on the size of the slug population, you may need to repeat this search-and-destroy mission two or three times.

(Slug bounty-hunting is a dandy job for a posse of youngsters. Just give 'em loaded squirt guns, and turn 'em loose. The vinegar solution won't hurt the kids or your plants, but it'll stop the slugs dead in their tracks.)

Salt has a well-earned reputation as the mother of all anti-slug weapons. It works, too! A sprinkle or two from a shaker will make a slug melt just like the wicked witch in "The Wizard of Oz." The trouble is, a concentrated dose can make some plants shrivel up, too—so if you use it, aim carefully!

Step 2: Surround the plot with a mini-fence of copper strips, 4 to 6 inches high. Slugs get a jolt from the metal when they try to slither over it. Don't buy your copper from a garden center or catalog, though;

you'll find sturdier—and much cheaper—stripping at an auto salvage shop or plumbing supply store. If you really want to pinch pennies, buy a sheet of lightweight copper and cut it into strips with metal cutters.

Step 3: Just to be on the safe side, set out a few traps baited with beer or grape juice to lure the slimy buggers. A few slugs may have escaped the nighttime raids, and you want to get them *before* you sow your seeds.

Step 4: Plant your seeds, and enjoy your slug-free bounty!

The Dynamic Dastardly Duo

Talk about notorious villains—cabbageworms and cabbage loopers have made the "Most Unwanted List" in gardens all over the country! The worms target only members of the cabbage family, while the loopers extend their crimes to beans, peas, potatoes, and tomatoes. Both are pale green caterpillars that chew the daylights out of leaves and other plant parts—and both knuckle under to the same good-riddance routine.

➡ At the first sign of trouble, dust your plants with my Cabbageworm Wipe-Out Tonic (at right). It'll rout both worms and loopers. To say "Stay out!" to the egg-laying moths, call out the predators (see page 316) and plant plenty of herbs among target plants. Cabbage moths are turned off by rosemary, sage, thyme, and hyssop.

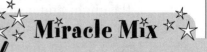

Miracle Mix

CABBAGEWORM WIPE-OUT TONIC

Whip up a batch of this terrific tonic for all cabbage family plants in your garden

1 cup of flour
2 tbsp. of cayenne pepper

Mix the ingredients together, and sprinkle the results on young cabbage family plants. The flour swells up inside the cabbageworms and bursts their insides, while the hot pepper keeps other critters away.

It's Been Headed Off!

Your head lettuce isn't forming heads, the leaves are mottled yellow and green, and the plants are stunted. The diagnosis: mosaic virus. (You'll see the same poor growth and mottled foliage in sick leaf lettuces, too.)

➡ In advanced cases, you'll need to grit your teeth and destroy the victims. If you reach the scene early, though, just pull off the mottled leaves and get rid of them (don't compost them). Then, regardless of which tack you've taken, spray every nearby plant with a mix of 1 part milk and 3 parts water. Repeat every few days. And from then on, follow my guidelines for good health in Chapters 14 and 15, and control aphids, leaf miners, and other disease-spreading pests.

Failing Fruits 'n Vegetables

What They're Cracked Up to Be

When cabbage heads crack, it's a sign that they've gotten too much water all at once.

➡ Here are a couple of ways to "head off" trouble:

Do the twist. If a heavy rain comes after an extended dry spell while the heads are still forming, put both hands on each cabbage, and give it a sharp quarter turn. Some of the roots will break, and they won't be able to take in enough moisture to cause damage.

Raise 'em up. Grow your cabbages in raised beds filled with lots of organic matter, and plant a "living mulch" of low-growing plants like nasturtiums or radishes. That way, you'll keep the soil's moisture level up—and stave off pests.

Help 'Em Keep Their Cool

Lettuce and most other greens are cool customers. When the weather gets too hot for their liking, they bolt—in other words, send up flower stalks, form buds, and go to seed. But that's not the worst of it: The leaves develop a bitter flavor that you *definitely* don't want in your salad bowl!

In biological terms, bolting is business as usual, so there's nothing you can do to stop it entirely. But there is plenty you can do to keep it under control. Here's a trio of ways to keep fresh greens coming longer:

✿ Look for varieties that can take some heat. They're in big demand, so you'll find a good assortment in catalogs and garden centers.

✿ Avoid planting your greens in rows; instead, give them wide beds, with a thick layer of organic mulch. This way, you'll keep the plants cooler and slow down moisture loss.

✿ Plant your crops in light shade, away from drying winds. I like to grow my cool-weather greens at the bottom of trellised crops, like cucumbers, tomatoes, and peas. You can also put up screens to shield the plants from sun and wind.

HAPPY CAMPERS

Believe it or not, there are some mighty tasty greens that stand right up to summer heat *and* winter cold. My two favorites: kale and collards. Both will not only sail right through the steamiest summer, but they'll keep on going through the winter in most climates. You can even dig down through the snow and pluck crisp, tasty leaves! Both of these troupers are much less troubled by the pests and diseases that plague other members of the cabbage family. So what are you waiting for? Plant a big patch, and eat hearty, mates!

PART III

FRUIT
Solutions

CHAPTER 8

Tree-Grown Tempters

A lot of folks think that to grow a great (or even edible) crop of tree fruit, you need to all but live with a spray gun in your hands. Well, think again! I'll admit that fruit trees, and nuts, too, can attract big-time trouble. But, armed with my tips, tricks, and terrific tonics, there's not a crafty critter or doggone disease that you can't conquer.

Stricken Saplings

They're Just Standin' There!

You planted your new fruit trees, following the same guidelines you used for your shade trees. The oaks and maples are growing just fine, but the little fruiters aren't doing a thing. What's the trouble?

➡ Fruit trees can be mighty finicky about their home ground. If your younguns are refusing to get up and grow, chances are the blame lies with one—or all—of these factors:

It's the wrong time. Fruit trees prefer to be planted in early spring, when they're completely dormant. If you can't do the job then, or if the nursery can't guarantee delivery before the buds begin to open, wait until next year.

It's the wrong place. Most fruit trees like full sun, and they demand plenty of elbow room. Catalogs list the spacing requirements for full-size, semi-dwarf, and dwarf trees. Choose whichever size you've got room for, and if there's any doubt, go with a smaller version. And, whatever you do, keep new, young trees away from mature ones, because they will compete with each other for water and nutrients.

It's the wrong soil. All but a few

✦ Miracle Mix ✦

TREE PLANTING BOOSTER MIX

Start your trees off on the right root with this powerful powder. It'll help the soil drain well *and* hold moisture—and that's exactly what a fruit tree needs to grow strong and produce well.

4 lbs. of compost
2 lbs. of gypsum
1 lb. of Epsom salts
1 lb. of dry dog food
1 lb. of dry oatmeal

Mix all of these ingredients together in a bucket. Then work a handful or two into the bottom of the planting hole, and sprinkle another handful over the soil after planting.

kinds of fruit trees insist on near-perfect drainage. If the ground is the least bit soggy, they'll just sit in their holes and pout. Or rot. When you plant your new arrivals, mix plenty of compost and manure into the soil, and add a handful or two of my Tree Planting Booster Mix (see page 193).

Do It Their Way

Soil isn't the only thing that can turn promising fruiters into first-class stick-in-the-muds. Fruit trees have their own ideas about the planting process, too.

➡ Here's *my* way to do it *their* way:

Step 1: Dig a hole that's 3 feet deep and 3 feet across. Then, fill it about halfway with soil that has plenty of organic matter added to it. Use some of the soil to make a mound in the center of the planting hole.

Step 2: Take the wrapping and all the strings and wires off the tree. Then prune off any damaged branches and roots.

HAPPY CAMPERS

Not all fruit trees need well-drained, loamy soil. In fact, elderberries (*Sambucus*) thrive with damp roots, and quince (*Cydonia oblonga*) trees, as well as pear (*Pyrus*) trees grafted to quince rootstocks, are happy as clams in clay soil with so-so drainage.

Step 3: Set the tree in the hole, so that the base rests on top of the mound and the roots trail down over the sides. Then check the graft union (the spot where the trunk has been grafted to the rootstock). You want it to be about 2 inches or so above ground level.

Step 4: Remove or add soil until the mound is exactly the right height, then set the tree back in place, and give the roots a nice drink of my Tree Transplanting Tonic (below). It'll help ease the stress of moving into a new home.

Step 5: Fill up the hole with the remaining amended soil, and firm it gently with your foot. That tree will be up and growin' before you can say "Johnny Appleseed!"

Winter Dangerland

For us humans, a crisp, sunny winter day can be heaven on earth. But to a young apple or cherry tree, it's just the opposite. When the sun's warmth hits the southwest side of the trunk, the tree's growth cells spring into action. Then, when the sun disappears and the temperature plummets, the cells rupture and the bark splits wide open. In most parts of the country, January and February are prime times for this nastiness, which in gardening terms is known as sunscald.

➡ Buy some plastic, 4-inch-diameter drainpipe, and cut a 2-foot piece for each of your young trees. Then slit each piece so you can slip it around the tree base. (Be careful you don't ding the bark when you install the collar.) Besides acting as a top-notch sunscreen, the pipe will fend off your trees' four-legged

✦ Miracle Mix ✦

TREE TRANSPLANTING TONIC

For a fruit tree, being transplanted is a shocking experience. This soothing drink will ease the stress of going from a nursery pot, or the bare-root wrappings, to the wide-open spaces of your yard. (It works great for fruit-bearing bushes, too!)

⅓ cup of hydrogen peroxide
¼ cup of instant tea granules
¼ cup of whiskey
¼ cup of baby shampoo
2 tbsp. of fish emulsion
1 gal. of water

Mix all of these ingredients in a bucket, and pour the solution into the hole when you transplant a fruit tree or bush.

wintertime foes: mice, voles, and rabbits. In early spring, when the wild temperature swings even out, remove the pipe. Otherwise, it could give pesky pests a place to hide.

Vamoose, Varmints!

What do you do when your trees are attacked by varmints? Just hope the critters go elsewhere for dinner?

Not at all! Just call on one of these tried-and-true defenses:

✿ Circle the tree trunk with fine-mesh wire or hardware cloth. It'll keep critters' teeth at bay, without giving safe haven to bad-guy bugs.

✿ Drench the area around your young trees (and fruit bushes, too) with my All-Purpose Pest Prevention Potion (at left). It'll make just about any critter turn tail and run!

✿ When you give your lawn its fall feeding, mix some diatomaceous earth and Bon Ami cleansing powder in with the lawn food. You'll clear varmints (especially voles) out of your whole yard and pep up the grass at the same time.

Miracle Mix

ALL-PURPOSE PEST PREVENTION POTION

Voles, rabbits, and just about any other critter I can think of will hightail it away when they get a whiff of this powerful potion.

1 cup of ammonia
½ cup of urine
½ cup of liquid dish soap
¼ cup of castor oil

Mix all of these ingredients in a 20-gallon hose-end sprayer. Then, just before the first snow flies, thoroughly saturate the area around each of your young trees.

Wretched Roots

Gall Darn It!

When you spot tumor-like growths on the roots and crown of a fruit tree, it means just one thing: crown gall. On young trees, the bumps may be soft and spongy; with age, they become brown and woody. The fruit may also be smaller than normal. Eventually, the tree weakens and growth slows. The cause: a bacterium called *Agrobacterium* that invades the plant through open wounds, usually in the summer. It can strike apricot, cherry, peach, and plum trees, as well as blackberries and blueberries. Is it fatal?

➡ Probably not. If you've inherited a tree that's seriously weakened and gall-ridden, you may have to grit your teeth and kiss it good-bye. But if you discover the beastly bumps in the early stages, just cut them off with a clean, sharp knife, and treat the wounds with my Tree Wound Sterilizer Tonic (see page 198). Be sure to cut all the way back into healthy tissue and, between cuts, disinfect your tools with denatured alcohol. When you're finished, seal the cuts with my Liquid Bandage (at right). To prevent damage to the tree from sunburn, perform your surgery early in the morning or on a cloudy day, and when you're finished, mound soil over the affected area.

✦ Miracle Mix ✦

LIQUID BANDAGE

This elixir works just like a bandage to keep germs and pests from moving into newly pruned trees or shrubs.

½ cup of interior latex paint
½ cup of antiseptic mouthwash
1 tsp. of cayenne pepper

Mix all of these ingredients in a small bucket, and paint the solution on pruning wounds to keep bugs and other thugs away from the tender tissue.

Good-bye, Galls!

You've cut off the galls and covered them up, but that doesn't mean you're home free. Another bunch could move in tomorrow. What should you do?

➡ To send *Agrobacterium* to never-never land, follow these guidelines:

✿ When you're shopping for new fruit trees, look for resistant varieties. (Ask your Cooperative Extension Service or garden center to recommend happy campers for your area.)

✿ Give nursery stock the eagle eye, and just say "no" to anything that has suspicious bumps on it.

✿ Control pesky pests that could damage your trees around the soil line.

✿ Be careful! Nicks and scrapes from lawn mowers, weed whackers, or wayward shovels are open doors to crown gall—and other diseases, too.

✦ Miracle Mix ✦

TREE WOUND STERILIZER TONIC

Anytime you cut diseased tissue from a tree or shrub, or even prune healthy branches, kill lingering germs with this powerful potion.

¼ cup of ammonia
¼ cup of liquid dish soap
¼ cup of antiseptic mouthwash
1 gal. of warm water

Mix all of these ingredients, pour the solution into a hand-held mist sprayer, and drench the places where you've pruned trees or shrubs.

Grabby Grubs

Most folks think of white grubs as lawn pests, and most of them are. But one type—the larvae of June beetles—also munches on the roots of young fruit and nut trees. If your tree suddenly wilts, but everything seems fine otherwise, poke around in the ground near the roots. You'll probably find some fat, whitish grubs that are ¾ to 1½ inches long. Now what?

➡ Thanks to the magic of modern science, you've got a simple solution at hand: beneficial nematodes. Just pick some up at the garden center, and apply them according to the directions on the package. The little guys will dive below the soil surface and make short work of the grubby chowhounds. (For more on beneficials, see Chapter 14.)

PLANT THESE at your PERIL!

The roots of black walnut trees secrete a chemical called juglone that's toxic to most other plants. The danger zone isn't small potatoes, either: The roots of a black walnut tree can extend more than three or four times the width of its leafy canopy. Fortunately, juglone doesn't harm turf grass, so your lawn is safe. There's also one happy camper in the fruit community: black cherry trees. Juglone rolls right off their backs or, should I say, roots.

They're Peachy

Peaches are thirsty trees. How can you be sure your peach trees are getting enough to drink?

➡ Here's a simple way to make sure those roots get what they need: Sink a 2-inch-diameter pipe into the ground next to each tree (metal or PVC pipe will do fine). Make sure it's at least 2 feet long. Then, when it rains or you water, the moisture will go down deep where the roots can get at it.

Troubled Trunks 'n Branches

Straighten Down!

Your fruit tree is sending up vertical branches that are churning out shoots galore, but no fruit buds. What should you do?

➡️ Bend those branches down, that's what! In the spring, tie a weight (like a rock, or a mesh bag filled with stones) to each branch that wants to stand at attention. Watch the positioning, though: You want to fasten that weight where it will make each branch as horizontal as possible. If a limb arches, nonfruitful shoots will likely grow from the curve's highest point.

Bored to Tears

Well, not tears exactly. Gummy sawdust is a more accurate description, and it's coming out of holes in the trunk of your peach tree. It's being shed by peachtree borers that are hard at work eating the insides of the tree, making it less resistant to heat and drought, and a prime target for diseases. You'll usually find the villains in the lower 10 inches or so of the trunk, or just below the soil line. In addition to peaches, these nasty caterpillars target apricots, cherries, plums, and almonds.

➡️ You don't have to take this invasion sitting down. Just stick a sturdy wire into each hole, and stir it around to kill the borers. Then spray my All-

Let's Be Buddies

Garlic repels peach-tree borers, but only if it's planted at the same time as the tree, in a circle all the way around the trunk. It sure does work, though!

Season Clean-Up Tonic into the holes (see page 59). If the thought of spearing worms makes you squeamish, or there are just too many to deal with that way, get some parasitic nematodes and a garden syringe, and squirt the good guys into each hole, following the directions on the package. (For more on beneficial bugs, see Chapter 14.) Whichever borer-removal method you use, don't scrape the gummy stuff off the trunk; it'll help seal the openings.

Tired of freezing your fingers pruning your fruit trees in the winter? Well, friends, I've got the solution: Prune 'em in the summer! Contrary to conventional wisdom, fruit trees will not "bleed" to death if you cut into them during the growing season. Wait until late summer, though, when the peak growth period has passed. And make sure you do the job at least two to five weeks before you expect the first frost. That way, the pruning cuts can heal, and any new growth will have time to harden off before Old Man Winter arrives.

Bored No More

If you've gone borer hunting and have wiped out the invaders, what do you do now to keep your trees borer-free?

Follow this two-part process:

Part 1: To fend off the borers, spread a wide band of diatomaceous earth around the tree. Dig it into the top few inches of soil, and renew the supply after every rain. And do all you can to encourage woodpeckers, flickers, and sapsuckers to set up housekeeping—they're the worst enemies a borer ever had.

Part 2: Kill off the adults, which are clear-winged, blue moths that look like wasps. Garden centers and catalogs sell pheromone traps that will get the males. To get the egg-laying females, wrap heavy paper around the tree trunk, from about 2 inches below the soil to about 3 feet up the trunk, and coat it with Tanglefoot or another spray adhesive. The future mothers will get all caught up on their way to lay their eggs, and you'll be home free. (Remember to check your traps every week or so, and replace them with new ones.)

Put Out That Fire!

Fire blight, that is. It's a bacterial disease that strikes apples and pears, and it spreads like (yes) wildfire in warm, moist weather. First, reddish, water-soaked lesions appear on the bark of limbs and branches, and on warm days, an orangy-brown liquid oozes out. Infected shoots look as though they've been scorched (hence the name *fire blight*). Branch tips wilt and turn under at the ends, like a shepherd's crook. Is this stuff as deadly as it sounds?

➡ Not if you're quick on your feet. At the first sign of trouble, prune off all the infected branches at least 12 inches below the wilted section. Then, remove all suckers and water sprouts, where more bacteria could be lurking. After each cut, to avoid spreading the disease, dip your shears or saw in a solution of 1 part bleach to 4 parts water. Finally, spray the tree from top to bottom with a solution of 4 parts vinegar to 6 parts water. Then spray again two weeks later.

Only You Can Prevent Fire Blight

At least you can try. Fire blight is carried by insects, wind, rain, and even dew, and the bacteria sneak into the tree through blossoms or lush, new growth. So there is no guaranteed protec-

tion plan. But that doesn't mean you have to sit there, hoping for the best.

➡ This routine will take you a long way toward a fire-free summer:

❀ Control insects, especially aphids and psylla, which spread the bacterium.

❀ Don't overfeed your trees, and stay away from high-nitrogen fertilizers. They encourage exactly the kind of lush, leafy growth that fire blight bacteria flock to.

❀ When you plant new apple or pear trees, look for resistant varieties. Don't just go by catalog descriptions, though. Ask the folks at your Cooperative Extension Service to recommend good performers for your region—in the case of fire blight, the resistance of any variety can vary greatly from one part of the country to another.

❀ Finally, follow my guidelines for good health in Chapter 14. Your trees—and the fruit-eaters in your family—will thank you!

PLANT THESE at your PERIL!

If fire blight is a problem in your neck of the woods, stay away from 'Bartlett' pears, or any pear that's related to the 'Bartletts'. They attract fire blight like a picnic attracts ants!

They're Goin' Bald!

It's early spring. Your trees are healthy as can be, but they're losing their bark. The reason: Buck deer are using your trees as scratching posts to scrape the velvet off their new antlers.

➡ Your protection plan: Get some plastic-mesh construction fencing, and wrap it loosely around the trunk to a height of about 4 feet. The dear deer will steer clear and go elsewhere for their head rubs.

Lousy Leaves

Aphid Capers

If the leaves on your fruit or nut tree pucker, curl up, and turn yellow, chances are they're being sucked on by aphids. To confirm the diagnosis, look around for ants scurrying up and down the trunk of the tree. They're so crazy about the honeydew the aphids produce—and so smart—that they actually tend herds of aphids so they'll have a steady supply of the sticky stuff.

➡ To round up the aphids *and* the ants and move em' out, give your trees a good blast of water from the garden hose. Then spray twice more, every other day. That'll send most of  the little critters tumbling to the ground. In the case of severe invasion, follow up with my Lethal Weapon Tonic (at right).

Scram, Ants!

You could keep aphids out of your trees by spraying them every 10 days with my Lethal Weapon Tonic, but how do you get rid of all those ants?

➡ If you can keep the ants out of your tree for just a couple of months, good-guy bugs will take over, and your aphid woes will be history. (For more about hero bugs, see Chapter 14.) Here's my favorite ant-removal plan:

❀ First (if necessary), prune your tree so that only the trunk is touching the ground.

❀ Wrap a band of carpet tape or double-sided masking tape around the trunk. The tape won't harm the tree, but it will trap the ants as they try to scamper up.

❀ For added protection, sprinkle bonemeal or diatomaceous earth around the trunk. The ants won't cross the scratchy stuff.

❀ If a colony of ants has set up housekeeping near your tree, spray the nest with water. Then spray again. After being doused a few times, the ants will pack up and move elsewhere.

Miracle Mix

LETHAL WEAPON TONIC

If ants have turned your fruit tree into an aphid ranch, don't pull any punches. Grab your trusty hose-end sprayer out of its holster, and load it with this magic bullet.

3 tbsp. of garlic and onion juice*
3 tbsp. of skim milk
2 tbsp. of baby shampoo
1 tsp. of Tabasco® sauce
1 gal. of water

Mix all of these ingredients in a bucket, and pour the solution into a 20-gallon hose-end sprayer. Then spray your tree every 10 days until the aphids are lyin' 6 feet under Whiskey Boot Hill.

* To make garlic and onion juice, put 2 cloves of garlic, 2 medium onions, and 3 cups of water in a blender and purée. Strain out the solids and pour the remaining liquid into a jar. Use whenever called for in a Miracle Mix. Bury the solids in your garden to repel aphids and other pesky pests.

Silly Psylla

Your pear tree seems to have lost its get-up-and-grow power. What's more, the leaves are turning yellow, and some of them are coated with sooty black stuff that's attracting yellow jackets. Worst of all, the fruit is all scarred and misshapen.

There's only one possible culprit here: pear psylla. These tiny bugs (just 1/10 inch long) attack only pears, mostly in the Eastern and Western states. In addition to the damage their feeding causes, they spread fire blight, one of the most dreaded diseases in all of peardom.

 Your best defense is a no-holds-barred spraying campaign. Here's the plan:

❁ At the first sign of trouble, blast the bugs with Grandma Putt's Simple Soap Spray (see page 94) every two to three days until the vile villains are history. Spray the tree from top to bottom, especially under the leaves, where psylla tend to camp out.

❁ To keep another generation from arriving on the scene, spray with my Basic Oil Mixture (see page 84) several times a year: in autumn, after the leaves have fallen; in early spring, before the leaves emerge; when the first shoots appear (and with them, probably some eggs—look for them with a magnifying glass); one week later; then every seven days until the leaves start to appear. The idea is to keep the tree good and oily, because these bugs don't like to lay their eggs on a slick surface.

All Curled Up

When the leaves of peach or nectarine trees curl, pucker up, and turn red and purple, they've got a common, and potentially dangerous, fungal disease known as (what else?) peach leaf curl. The good news: If you're Johnny-on-the-spot, the solution's a piece of cake.

Here's the program: Remove all the infected leaves, pronto, and burn them or toss them out with the trash. Don't get them anywhere near the compost pile. Then, follow this three-step road back to health:

Step 1: Spray the tree with my Great-Guns Garlic Spray (see page 25) to kill any lingering fungi.

Step 2: Give the tree a generous serving of well-cured manure, and keep those roots well-watered.

Step 3: Hang panty hose pouches filled with mothballs in the tree. The chemicals repel curly fungus.

Dear Jerry, Help! My apple trees look healthy enough, but they seem to have an identity crisis— they think they're evergreens! They keep their leaves all winter long and never bloom in the spring. Should I just give up and plant orange trees? – M.L., Menlo Park, California

Dear M.L., Don't give up! In warm climates like yours, it's common for apple trees to hang on to their leaves when other plants are dropping theirs. (Pears often behave the same way.) Unfortunately, as you've seen, without a period of leafless dormancy, the trees can't bloom and bear fruit. There's a simple solution to the problem, though: Give your apple trees the brush-off! When the other trees and shrubs in your yard start losing their foliage, just take your hand and run it along each branch of your apple trees to strip off the leaves. Then those babies will settle down for a long winter's nap. Come spring, they'll leaf out and bloom to beat the band!

Failing Fruits 'n Nuts

Slim Pickin's

If your fruit trees are blooming, but they're bearing poorly, then the most likely reason is poor pollination (especially if they've produced good crops in past years). This is a predicament I hear about more and more these days. There's a simple reason, too: Fruit trees depend largely on bees to pollinate their blossoms. But in recent years, disease, predatory mites, and pesticides have been killing off honeybees by the millions all over North America. Does this mean the end of home-grown fruit?

➡ Not at all! Just call on the latest good guys for hire: Orchard Mason bees. These gentle little fellas are North American natives, and they've been buzzin' around fruit trees since long before the first colonists brought honeybees to our shores. Unlike most of their relatives, Orchard Masons are solitary nesters; they don't form hives. Furthermore, they don't get all riled up if you surprise them, the way other bees tend to do. They just go on about their business of sipping nectar and pollinating blossoms, so they're safe to have around even if you have youngsters on the scene. Now you can buy your own herd of these wonder bugs at some garden centers and over the Internet. To find out more, just crank up your favorite search engine, and type in "Orchard Mason bees."

It Takes Two to Tango

Besides a slowdown in bee traffic, there could be another reason for a poor fruit crop. If the nonperformer in your yard is a solo act, it may simply need a partner. Most fruit and nut trees can't

pollinate their own blossoms; they need another tree of a differ-
ent variety to deliver the goods. Even trees that are technically
self-pollinating generally produce much more fruit when they
have a little help.

→ The simple solution:
Plant another tree! But
not just *any* tree. A
good fruit-tree catalog
will give you the com-
plete rundown on
which varieties make
the best teammates. If
planting another tree
isn't an option right
now, here's a quick-fix
alternative: Find a
friend or neighbor who
has a compatible vari-
ety, and ask for a few blooming sprigs. Sink the branches into a
bucket of water, set them near your tree, and the birds and
bees will take it from there.

Happy Campers

If you have room for just one
fruit tree, go with a self-pollinating variety of peach, nectarine, or
apricot. The good ones perform
like troupers on their own. Or opt
for a European plum—all varieties are self-pollinating.

It's Not Retirement Time

**Got an old apple tree that just doesn't
want to work anymore? Is there any way
to put life back into an old-timer?**

→ You bet! In the spring, when younger trees have
just put out their blossoms, take a sharp knife, and
carefully strip a ring of bark about $1/4$ inch wide from
around the trunk of your old-timer. Before you can say
"Life begins at 65," that tree will be churnin' out blossoms
that'll knock your socks off—with delicious fruit soon to follow.

The Big Brown Bother

A small, round, brown spot appears on a peach and, in the blink of an eye, that little freckle grows to cover the whole fruit. What have you got? Brown rot, a fungal disease that strikes peaches, plums, cherries, nectarines, and apricots. It gets a toehold when the flowers first start to bloom, but you may not notice symptoms until picking time—and then it's too late.

➡ The key to making sure you get a good crop is to keep your eyes open. If the weather is warm and wet in spring, when blossoms are developing, wait until three weeks before the harvest. Then spray your trees every seven days with my Chive Tea (at right). Don't use any kind of spray when blossoms are forming, or you won't get a crop at all!

Don't Coddle 'Em!

You know the old joke that goes: "What's worse than biting into an apple and finding a worm? Finding half a worm!" Well, the culprit who's responsible for that worm—or half-worm—is the codling moth. And if you've ever grown apples, you know that moth is no joke! Although apples get most of the attention, codling moths also lay their eggs on the branches of pear, quince, and

Miracle Mix

CHIVE TEA

Fruit tree fungi don't stand a chance against this brew!

1 part chive leaves*
4 parts water

Put the chives and water in a pan, and bring the water to a boil. Then remove the pan from the heat, let the tea cool, and strain out the leaves. Pour the remaining liquid into a hand-held mist sprayer. Spray your fruit trees every seven days, and say "Farewell, fungus!"

* Or substitute horseradish leaves.

walnut trees. When the eggs hatch, the larvae burrow into the fruit and feast on the core.

The good news is that stopping codling moths in their tracks is easier than a lot of folks think. Here's my season-by-season battle plan:

In early spring: Scrape off any rough bark from the lower 3 feet of the trunk. Underneath, you'll find cocoons, the winter home of codling moths. Pull off the cocoons, and drop 'em in a bucket of soapy water. Then hang suet in the tree to attract woodpeckers, who'll have a field day feasting on the larvae as they hatch.

In late spring: When the first infected fruit drops, pick up every single piece and destroy it. That way, you'll make a sizable dent in the next generation.

Most bugs have at least one fatal flaw, and codling moths are no exception. Theirs is a sweet tooth the size of Toledo. That's the secret behind my "Drink of Death" Traps. I make a batch of 'em in spring, just as the apple blossoms are beginning to open. All you need are some 1-gallon plastic milk jugs, and a solution that's made of 1 part molasses to 1 part vinegar. Pour 1 to 2 inches of solution into each jug, tie a cord around the handle, and hang the trap from a branch. The moths will belly up (in, rather) for a drink, and that'll be all she wrote! Just one word of caution: Bees like sweet stuff, too, so if some of these good guys are poking around your traps, cover the opening with $\frac{1}{8}$- to $\frac{1}{4}$-inch mesh screen.

In early summer: Wrap a band of corrugated cardboard around the tree trunk, about 3 feet off the ground. As the caterpillars crawl down the trunk to spin their cocoons, they'll be trapped in the paper. Then, you can peel it off and drop it into a bucket of soapy water. Or, if the thought of all those scampering caterpillars makes you squeamish, spray the creepy things with my Garden Cure-All Tonic (see page 212). Either way, when the worms are good and dead, toss 'em on the compost pile, cardboard and all.

The Name's Apple

Apple maggot, that is. But this villain's victim list also includes pears, plums, cherries, and blueberries. Unlike codling moths, which lay their eggs on leaves, twigs, or fruit buds, apple maggots deposit their younguns in the fruit itself, just under the skin.

➡ The best way to control these critters is to wipe out the adults, which are small black-and-yellow flies. Garden centers and catalogs sell red, ball-shaped sticky traps just for this purpose, but I have a better solution. Before the blossoms on your tree turn to fruit, go to the grocery store and buy some red apples with the stems still attached. Spray the apples with Tanglefoot or another commercial adhesive, and hang them in your trees (yes, this works even if the target trees are not apples). You'll need six to eight traps for a full-sized tree; for a dwarf tree (less than 9 feet high), two traps should do the trick. Before you know it, those red orbs will be covered with flies that thought they'd found a nice, cozy maternity ward. As the traps fill up, take them down and replace them with new ones. By the time the real fruit appears, your maggot night-mares will have faded to a dim memory, and it's time to take down your traps for good.

✦ Miracle Mix ✦

GARDEN CURE-ALL TONIC

When you need bad-guy bug relief in a hurry, mix up a batch of this rapid-acting remedy.

**4 cloves of garlic
1 small onion
1 small jalapeño pepper
1 tsp. of Murphy's Oil Soap®
1 tsp. of vegetable oil
Warm water**

Pulverize the garlic, onion, and pepper in a blender, and let them steep in a quart of warm water for two hours. Strain the mixture through cheesecloth or panty hose, and dilute the liquid with 3 parts of warm water. Add the Murphy's Oil Soap and vegetable oil, and pour the solution into a hand-held mist sprayer. Then take aim, and polish off the bugs that are buggin' you!

The Sign of the Crescent

When your plums fall from the tree before their time, pick up one and take a look. If it's misshapen and has a crescent-shaped slit in the skin, it means your tree has been invaded by plum curculios, otherwise known as snout beetles. A mother beetle chews that distinctive opening in the fruit, then lays her eggs inside. When the larvae hatch, they nibble away. While plums are this beetle's favorite target, the hit list also includes apples, apricots, blueberries, cherries, peaches, and pears.

➡️ As in the case of apple maggots, your best strategy here is to get the adult curculios before the fruit appears on your tree. These adults are brown, hard-shelled beetles, about ¼ inch long, with a long snout that curves downward. They spend the winter in the soil and in hedgerows, and wake up when apple trees start blooming. When they're disturbed, plum curculios curl up their legs and antennae and fall to the ground—which makes them prime candidates for handpicking. First, spread old sheets on the ground under your tree. Then wrap a baseball bat or similar weapon in thick padding, and whack the branches. When the beetles rain down, gather up the sheets and shake the culprits into a bucket of kerosene. (Frankly, I never do this job myself. Instead, I put a price on the beetles' heads and hire a posse of bounty-hunting kids as my designated hitters.)

More Curculio Control

You *could* use handpicking as your only curculio-control method, but you'd need to get out there and take batting practice early every morning for about six weeks, starting when you see the first blossoms. So what else can you do?

➡️ I recommend adding these three tactics to your battle plan:

Stick 'em to it. Plum curculios are attracted to anything white. So wrap white paper around the tree trunk, and spray it with Tanglefoot. Then, for good measure, hang white sticky traps from the branches. (Just be sure to take them down after three or four weeks, so you don't trap good guys along with the bad.)

Zap 'em. My Peppermint Soap Spray (see page 135) cuts right through a beetle's hard, waxy shell and deals out death and destruction. So whip up a batch and go get 'em!

Feed 'em to the birds. Curculios are a top menu item for chickens, turkeys, and some of the prettiest songbirds around, including blue-birds, chickadees, flycatchers, and junkos. So invite the gang over for a big lunch!

CHILL OUT!

Apples should keep well in your refrigerator for as long as six weeks, but if you want your crop to last through the winter, it needs temperatures of 30° to 32°F with a relative humidity of 90 percent. An unheated garage or shed would be perfect. Don't worry that you'll wind up with applesicles—the high sugar content will keep the fruit from freezing.

Bye-Bye, Birdies!

Are birds makin' off with your cherries before you can pick enough to make even a single pie?

➡ Here's a trio of ways to say "Mine—*all* mine!"

1. Wind black cotton thread among the branches. It'll confuse the wily wingers: When they see the thread against the sky, they can't judge the distance between strands, so they won't land. Just make sure that you string the thread *before* a bird family builds a nest and fills it with eggs.

HAPPY CAMPERS

Not all cherries grow on trees. Several varieties grow on shrubs that get only about 4 feet tall. Besides being a snap to cover up at fruiting time, cherry bushes are fine-looking flowering shrubs. Look for these winners in fruit and edible landscaping catalogs.

2. Put up a wren house near your cherry trees. Wrens eat no fruit or berries, only insects. And when they've got youngsters in their nests—which is the same time you'll have cherries on your trees—they won't let any other birds within 50 feet of the place. (Don't try this trick in your vegetable garden, because the wrens will chase off all the other insect-eating birds that you need for crop protection.)

3. Instead of full-size cherry trees, grow dwarfs or miniatures. They deliver a full-size, full-flavored crop on plants that are small enough to cover with a sheer curtain or two. The birds won't stand a chance of getting so much as a nibble!

Birds Beware!

Know thine enemy—that's my motto when it comes to bugs, birds, or anything else that's pestering my garden. So what, exactly, do you need to know about our fine feathered friends when it comes to safeguarding your cherry harvest?

 First, you should know that birds target red fruit more than any other color. And given their druthers, birds will go for wild, bitter fruit and leave the cultivated, sweet stuff to us lesser mortals. So put this knowledge to good use:

✿ Instead of red cherries, plant yellow ones. (You'll find some mighty tasty kinds in catalogs.) Unless the birds have no other dining options, they'll fly right on by.

❀ Give 'em other options. Plant one or two of their favorite fruits, such as chokecherry, barberry, wild honeysuckle, mulberry, or Russian olive, and they'll be more likely to bypass your cherries.

Trouble on the Hoof

There's nothing more frustrating than looking out your window and seeing deer helping themselves to your fruit crop. A fence would guarantee protection, but if you can't—or don't want to— fence in your whole yard, you need other muncher-chasing tactics.

➡ Fruit trees are tailor-made for deterrents that can hang from their branches, right alongside the deer's targets. Here are some of my favorite chasers:

❀ Strong deodorant soap

❀ Smelly socks

❀ Athlete's-foot powder or baby powder, sprinkled on a cotton cloth

❀ Dog or human hair

It's a Washout!

Unless deer are on the brink of starvation, any of my aromatic wonders (see "Trouble on the Hoof," above) will send them scurrying. There's just one drawback: Rain or snow will wash away the scent (and in the case of soap, everything else). That

means you can spend a lot of time replacing your deer discouragers. What do you do?

➡️ The simple solution: Before you hang your deterrents in the tree, put each one in a mini-garage. Here's how:

1. Tuck your deterrent of choice into an old panty hose toe or a mesh onion bag, and tie the pouch closed with a string.

2. Poke a hole in the bottom of a 12-ounce foam or wax paper drink cup. (Or use an old plastic flowerpot that has a drainage hole.)

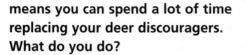

Miracle Mix

DEER BUSTER EGG BREW

To keep the brown-eyed bruisers from even coming close to your fruit trees, lay out the unwelcome mat with this un-tasty drink.

2 eggs
2 cloves of garlic
2 tbsp. of Tabasco® sauce
2 tbsp. of cayenne pepper
2 cups of water

Put all of the ingredients in a blender, and purée. Allow the mixture to sit for two days, then pour or spray it around your trees.

3. Tuck the pouch into the cup, pull the string through the hole, and tie it into a loop. Then fasten the loop to a tree branch, and you're good to go. Your smell emitters should keep their deer-chasing power for about a year, right through rain, sleet, snow, or dark of night!

Aw, Nuts!

It's no secret that squirrels love nuts—any kind of nuts and fruits, too. I'll be the first to admit that it's not easy to foil these clever acrobats, but as one of Grandma Putt's heroes, Winston Churchill, said, "Never, never, never, never give up!"

➡️ Your best defense options depend on what you need to defend. For fruit and nut trees, these are the tactics I use:

❁ Prune your trees so that the lowest branches are at least 6 feet above the ground. Then, about a foot below the lowest branch, circle the trunk with a 2-inch-wide piece of aluminum roof flashing. As the tree grows and the trunk increases in diameter, replace the flashing with a longer piece.

❁ Make sure the squirrels' target is 10 to 12 feet away from other trees, fences, or deck railings. That may mean pruning branches, or even removing trees or shrubs that serve as launching pads.

❁ Spray your trees with my Squirrel Beater Tonic (at left).

⭐ Miracle Mix ⭐

SQUIRREL BEATER TONIC

To keep pesky squirrels from stealing your crop, spray your fruit and nut trees with this spicy potion.

2 tbsp. of cayenne pepper
2 tbsp. of Tabasco® sauce
2 tbsp. of chili powder
1 tbsp. of Murphy's Oil Soap®
1 qt. of warm water

Mix all of these ingredients together. Then pour the mixture into a hand-held mist sprayer, and coat your trees from top to bottom.

Bunny Be Gone!

If the trunks of your young fruit and nut tress show signs of being nibbled at, rabbits may be the culprits.

➡ In the winter, when food is scarce, rabbits may nibble on the trunks of young trees, but they really prefer more tender vittles. So if you set out twiggy branches that you've pruned from trees and shrubs, the bunnies will forget all about your tree trunks. (If those twiggy branches have blossoms on them, so much the better!)

CHAPTER 9

Berry, Berry Good

Are your blueberries just bumbling along? Your raspberries rambling over the whole backyard? Your strawberries succumbing to slugs? Are flying felons fleeing with your fruit? Or are you putting off growing the crops you crave because you've heard that fruit plants are just too much trouble? Well, you've come to the right place. I've got the answers that'll put an end to those berry-bush blues!

Stricken Seeds 'n Seedlings

Rot Got 'Em

You planted some healthy-looking strawberry seedlings, and the next thing you knew, they'd rotted. What went wrong?

 I'll bet my bottom trowel that you planted those baby berries too deep. And it didn't have to be much too deep, either. Strawberries are as picky as the dickens about planting depth: If you set the seedlings in just a little too far, the roots rot; not far enough, and they dry out and shrivel up. The key to success is to plant them so that the crown is right at soil level.

Super Strawberry Send-Off

You planted your strawberry seedlings at the right depth, but they're still not coming up healthy and strong. What went wrong?

Planting depth isn't the only thing you need be concerned about. Here are my four simple secrets to a super start, strawberry style:

Buy the right stuff. Strawberries are prone to viruses, so always buy plants that are certified disease-free. And, when you're shopping at a garden center, give them the old eagle eye. You want to see a healthy neck with no sign of rot, whitish roots, and spotless green leaves.

Get the soil just right. Strawberries need well-drained soil that's slightly acidic (6.0 to 6.5); chock-full of compost, humus, or well-cured manure; and free of weeds. (For the lowdown on soil and my weed wipeout plan, see Chapters 14 and 15.)

Tuck 'em in just right. For each plant, dig a hole that's about

6 inches wide and a few inches deeper than the roots. Then, mound up some soil in the center, set the crown on top, and spread the roots down over the slope. If any of the roots touch bottom, don't bend them to fit. Instead, snip 'em off with scissors. (Folding the roots stresses 'em out.)

THIS IS ONLY A TEST!

Here's my tried-and-true method for planting strawberries at *exactly* the right depth: Set the seedlings into their holes, and water them thoroughly. Then keep an eye on the crowns. If they sink, dig up the plants and add more soil to the bottom of the hole. If the crowns are sticking up, add more soil to the ground surface. Then, just to be extra safe, check your babies again after the first rainfall.

Pinch, then pinch some more. For the first year, pinch off every single blossom that forms. That way, the plants will put all of their energy into forming strong roots, and strong roots = bumper crops in years to come.

It's Berry Confusing

There are lots of strawberry varieties to choose from. How do you know which ones to grow?

➤ There's a strawberry out there for every taste. Here's a rundown of what's available:

June-bearers. If you want a mountain of berries all at once for jam making, freezing, or your annual strawberry social, this is your candidate. The plants form buds in the fall, then produce one big crop of fruit over six weeks or so in late spring. (Up North, that's usually June, but in warmer climates, it's earlier.)

Day-neutrals. These are the plants for folks who just can't get their fill of strawberries. They flower and bear fruit pretty much nonstop for about five months, as long as temperatures stay between 35° and 85°F.

Ever-bearers. Don't be misled by the name. These plants don't keep churning out fruit the way day-neutral strawberries do. Instead, ever-bearers produce one crop in June and another in the fall. They're your best option if you want more than one crop a year, *and* if you live where the weather gets too hot to suit the day-neutral varieties.

STRAWBERRY SUCCESS SOLUTION

Just before you plant your strawberries, give them a bath in this root-rousin' tonic.

1 can of beer
¼ cup of cold coffee
2 tbsp. of liquid dish soap
2 gal. of water

Mix all of these ingredients together in a bucket. Then soak your berries' bare roots in the solution for about 10 minutes before you tuck them into their holes. When you're finished planting, dribble the leftover solution on the soil around your plants.

Puny Plants

Lazy Canes

Last spring, you brought your new raspberry bushes home from the garden center and planted them. They bore a nice crop of summer fruit, but the plants themselves haven't grown much at all since then. Did you do something wrong?

➤ In a word: yes. When you tuck a baby raspberry or blackberry plant into its hole, you need to cut the canes right to the ground, pronto. Otherwise, the plant will use most of its energy producing berries, instead of forming strong roots. It's not too late to make a comeback, though. Just cut back those canes, then cover the soil with an inch or two of good compost. Those babies will be growing on the right root in no time at all.

But They'll Attack Me!

You're craving the taste of home-grown blackberries and raspberries, but just thinking about all those thorns makes you cringe. Don't you wish there were thornless varieties?

Well, there are! Some of the tastiest blackberries are absolutely thornless. And while there aren't any thornless raspberries, they vary greatly in the number of thorns (spines) they do have. Catalogs and comprehensive fruit books list the degree of spininess right along with disease resistance and cold tolerance. So get growin'!

GRANDMA PUTT'S
grow-how

No matter what you do, bramble fruits just won't stay put. New canes are always sneaking out from the base of the plants, and once they get started, they're very difficult to stop. My Grandma Putt always used this rule of thumb when she planted raspberries and blackberries: Plant them at least 12 feet away from the vegetable garden—or any other plants you don't want them to mix with. Then, leave grass growing in the space in between. That way, any wandering canes get mowed down before they can creep very far.

No Takers

If you tried to start raspberries from cuttings, and they refused to form roots, there's one likely reason: You probably took cuttings from canes that bore fruit earlier in the season. Once canes produce berries, they die, and they won't take root no matter what you do.

The simple solution: Try again. Take 4- to 6-inch cuttings from new canes, strip off the bottom leaves, and root them according to "A Healthy Send-Off" on page 41.

Singin' the Blues

A year ago, you planted some blueberries. The instructions that came with the plants said they needed acidic soil, with a pH between 4.5 and 5.5. Your soil measured higher than that, so you added powdered sulfur to bring it into that range. Now the pH test registers 5.0, but the plants aren't growing well at all. And there's no sign of pests or diseases. What could the problem be?

In a nutshell: sulfur. That's the old-time favorite ingredient for increasing soil acidity, and it works—fast. Unfortunately, it combines with water in the soil to form sulfuric acid, which kills off microorganisms that blueberry plants need for good growth. You'll need to dig up those plants, and prepare some raised beds with fresh soil. And this time, instead of using sulfur, add organic matter that's high in acid. Any of these will work like a charm:

❀ Aged sawdust

❀ Coffee grounds

❀ Composted leaves or bark (especially oak, beech, or chestnut)

❀ Pine or hemlock needles

WATCH THE N!

Big doses of pH modifiers can deplete nitrogen from the soil. To head off trouble, combine your acidifiers—or sweeteners—with a snack that's high in the big N, such as cottonseed meal, bloodmeal, or well-cured manure. (For more on soil nutrition, see Chapter 14.)

It's Sweeter Than Candy

If your soil pH registers between 5.6 and 6.0, you should have no trouble getting it down to a blueberry-pleasing level. But anything sweeter than that will be darned near impossible to adjust successfully. So how do you grow blueberries if you've got super-sweet soil?

➧ You grow them in containers. That way, you can give them *exactly* the kind of soil they like best. Choose two different varieties to ensure cross-pollination, and put them in half-whiskey barrels or similar size pots. Fill them to within 6 to 8 inches of the rim with my Blueberry Potting Mix (left), then add a 2-inch layer of mulch to retain moisture. (I use compost or pine needles.) Keep the plants well-watered, and feed them every two to three weeks with an organic fertilizer that's high in nitrogen, such as cottonseed meal or fish emulsion. And, unless you live in a mild climate, move the containers to an unheated garage or enclosed porch for the winter.

✦ Miracle Mix ✦

BLUEBERRY POTTING MIX

You couldn't ask for an easier-to-grow plant than a blueberry bush. Just give it a pot or a raised bed filled with this root-pleasing mix, and get ready for a fine, fruitful feast.

2 parts garden soil
2 parts chopped, composted leaves
2 parts coarse builder's sand*
1 part compost

Mix all of these ingredients together, then fill your containers.

* Don't use beach or "sandbox" sand. It's so fine that it'll harden up if it dries out. It also may contain a lot of ground-up shell fragments, which are highly alkaline.

Wretched Roots

It's an Invasion!

Your new-to-you house came with an out-of-control berry patch, and you want to clear it out and start anew—but you don't want to use an herbicide. Is there any other way to get rid of those galloping roots *before* they take over the whole yard?

➡ You bet there is! In fact, you may have root-free ground faster with my old-fangled method than you'd have if you used an herbicide. Why? Because for those products to be effective, you have to use them in *exactly* the right way, at *exactly* the right time. Even then, when you're up against a hard-charger like blackberries or raspberries, it can take several years to get the pesky things under control. Here's my anytime, once-and-for-all routine:

✿ Grab a pair of pruning shears and a paper bag, and start cutting. Cut each cane into small pieces, and drop them right into the paper bag. When the bag is full, or you stop for the day, get rid of those cuttings. Don't toss 'em on the ground, or the compost pile— they'll take root faster than you can say "Hold on there!"

✿ When you've pruned everything down to the stump, slide a

THEY'RE GRUBBY!

The same white June beetle grubs that go gunnin' for the roots of young apple trees (and your lawn) also target blackberries and strawberries. The evidence: The plants just up and wilt when all else seems fine. Your best response: Douse the soil with milky spore disease or beneficial nematodes to halt the attack. Then for long-term protection, call up the troops, namely, ground beetles, crows, robins, and starlings. (For more on grubs, see page 198; for the lowdown on hit squad hospitality, see Chapter 14.)

sharp hoe under it and cut it off. The key is to sever each little root at the base of the stem. That way, the roots will rot, and those brambles will be history!

The Raspberry Crown Affair

All raspberries and blackberries can fall victim to crown gall, a.k.a. cane gall, a bacterial disease that enters through wounds in the plant. The wart-like growths can appear on either roots or canes. How do you save your plants?

Just cut off the affected plant parts, and destroy them. Then spray the plants from top to bottom with my Compost Tea (see page 20), and lay down about 2 inches of compost mulch. Studies have shown that compost produces fatty acids that kill disease-causing bacteria and fungi, too. (For more on this magic bullet, see Chapter 15.)

The Same Ol' Boring Story

When the canes of your bramble fruits wilt and die in early summer, or simply lack get-up-and-grow power, look below. Most likely, the roots or crowns have been invaded by raspberry root borers, a.k.a. raspberry crown borers.

You could spear the worms with wire, according to the tree-borer guidelines on page 200. But with bramble fruits, I generally take the easy road: Just cut off the infested canes below ground level, and destroy them. Then, in late summer, look for patches of rust-colored eggs on leaves, and destroy them, too. In the case of major infestations, drench the soil in early spring with Bt *(Bacillus thuringiensis)*. Repeat this treatment the following spring, and your borer problems should be history.

Sickly Stems

It's So Complicated!

Confused about how to train and prune your raspberry bushes? I'm not surprised. To hear some folks talk, you'd think the job was more complicated than putting a man on the moon. Well, friends, it's not.

➡ Here are two simple secrets for keeping your raspberries in line and your harvest basket full—without turning berry tending into a second career.

Secret No. 1: Unless you want an ornamental effect, you don't need a trellis. Just let the canes grow naturally.

Secret No. 2. Pruning's a piece of cake. Here's all there is to it:

❀ In the spring, remove all dead or weak-looking canes.

❀ As soon as any cane finishes bearing, cut it off at ground level. That way, the plant will put all its energy into the canes that will produce the next batch of fruit.

❀ If the bed gets too deep to harvest easily, or you get busy and don't prune at all for a year, don't worry about it. Just chop the whole thing to the ground, and let it grow back.

An Upstanding Crop

You'd love to grow raspberries, but you've got no room to let your raspberries sprawl (or even lean). Is it a lost cause?

➡ Not at all. Here's a simple, space-saving solution: Plant a bush on either side of a metal stake that's about 5 feet high. Then, gather up the canes and tie them loosely together with old panty hose. You'll get a full-size crop in a fraction of the space. What's more, the stake and ties will attract static electricity from the air and give your plants a healthy dose of nitrogen (see the electroculture lesson on page 157).

Say When!

You know you should prune your berry plants, but when is the best time?

➥ Too much growth in late summer leaves your berry plants—and next year's harvest—wide open to winter damage. So go ahead and prune, but stop at least a month before you expect the first frost. That way, new canes will have time to harden-off before the cold weather hits.

After you've pruned those old, dry canes from your raspberries, don't toss 'em onto the compost pile. Instead, tuck 'em into a basket beside your fireplace—they make first-class kindling.

It's a Bloody Shame

When deer and rabbits are browsing on your fruit canes, bloodmeal will usually send 'em scurrying. There's just one problem: When it rains, the powder goes right into the soil. Having to replace the stuff is bad enough, but if it happens too often, all that bloodmeal can give the plants an overdose of nitrogen. What's the answer?

➥ It's a simple one: Sink soup cans or plastic cups into the soil among your plants. Then fill each container with a mixture of 1 part bloodmeal to 2 parts water. (Stop about an inch from the top to leave room for rainwater.) As the solution evaporates, add more. The result: Long-term critter control with no nitrogen side effects.

Lousy Leaves

Mitey Bad

At first glance, your berry plants' leaves look as though they've been bleached. But on closer inspection, you see that they're covered with thousands of tiny yellow speckles. Yikes—you've got spider mites!

➡ Most of the time, natural predators like ladybugs keep these tiny guys under control. But sometimes, especially during hot spells, the population explodes. If you don't act fast, these itsy-bitsy, spider-like critters will suck the life out of your plants. So act fast: Hit 'em with my Buttermilk Blast (at right).

Miracle Mix

BUTTERMILK BLAST

When spider mites are draining the juices from your plants, give 'em a drink that'll stop 'em in their tracks.

2 cups of wheat flour
¼ cup of buttermilk
2 gal. of water

Mix all of these ingredients together thoroughly. Then pour the mixture into a hand-held mist sprayer, and douse your mite-plagued plants from top to bottom. The little suckers'll never know what hit 'em!

The Plague from the East

Japanese beetles like raspberries and blackberries almost as much as they like their caney cousins, roses. Now and then, the voracious villains go after the leaves of blueberries, currants, and gooseberries, too. How can you fend off an attack?

➡ Get out there and pick off the rascals! Then, set up some traps to catch any escapees. In the case of a full-scale invasion, reach for my Hot Pepper Spray (see page 88), but *only* if your plants haven't formed fruit yet. It—or any other spray—just might damage the delicate berries, and you don't want that to happen! (See page 87 for my full-scale beetle battle plan.)

Flawed Jewels

Currants and gooseberries are easy-to-grow, carefree shrubs with gorgeous flowers and yummy, jewel-like fruit. Unfortunately, a lot of folks are scared to grow these plants because they're hosts for white-pine blister rust, a fungal disease that produces spots on the plants' leaves. It's not a serious threat to the berries, but it's deadly for white pine trees. As a result, some states (especially those with big pine forests) ban incoming shipment of all currants and gooseberries (Ribes). Others outlaw the planting or possession of the most notorious host, European black currants (Ribes nigrum). Should you just forget about these winners?

Not at all. First, call your Cooperative Extension Service and ask which varieties are legal to grow in your state. Then get recommendations on the best, disease-resistant varieties for your area. When you get your bushes, plant them at least 1,500 feet from any pine tree. That way, you're all but guaranteed to be home free, because in order for the fungus to complete its deadly cycle, both white pine trees and *Ribes* plants must be present. Don't take chances, though: Follow my guidelines for good health in Chapter 14, and spray your fabulous fruiters every two to three weeks with my Compost Tea (see page 20).

SUPER SOLUTION

In the unlikely event that white-pine blister rust does strike your currants or gooseberries, you'll see rust-colored pimples on the undersides of your shrubs' leaves. Dig up the fruit bush and destroy it, pronto. Then drench the surrounding soil with my Fungus Fighter Soil Drench (see page 45).

Miracle Mix

QUASSIA SLUG SPRAY

Stop slugs in their slimy tracks with this potent potion. It helps fend off aphids, too!

4 oz. of quassia chips (available at health food stores)
1 gal. of water

Crush, grind, or chop the chips, add them to the water in a bucket, and let steep for 12 to 24 hours. Strain through cheesecloth, then spray the liquid on strawberries and other slug and aphid targets.

Tuck 'Em In

When a plant has all its vital parts lying right on the ground, as strawberries do, the poor things are targets for every kind of trouble under the sun. So how do you defend your crop?

➡ Just lay down a good, thick mulch of pine, hemlock, or spruce needles. That scratchy blanket will fend off slugs, and keep the leaves and fruit off the ground, away from soil-borne pests and diseases. Plus, something in those evergreen needles actually improves the flavor of the berries. How's that for a triple-threat performance?

Failing Flowers 'n Fruits

Vacuum Up the Villains

When your strawberries are smaller than normal, with dark, sunken patches (a.k.a. catfacing), the problem isn't cats: It's tarnished plant bugs, a.k.a. lygus bugs. The tiny terrors feed on buds and young fruit, injecting them with a toxin that dwarfs and ruins the berries. It's no wonder these villains are Public Enemy

**Number One among commercial strawberry growers. How do
you keep them at bay?**

➡ Take a tip from the pros: Vacuum the pesky pests right off of
your plants. Organic strawberry farmers use a fancy machine
that's especially made for vacuuming up bad-guy bugs. But you
can use the same wet/dry vacuum cleaner that you use in the
garage. Just put an inch or
two of soapy water in the
reservoir first, then get out
there and sweep those beds
clean! Empty the whole
shebang onto the compost
pile. For long-term protection, put out the welcome
mat for minute pirate bugs,
which will gladly gobble up
all the tarnished plant bugs
they can find. (You can read
all about hit squad hospitality in Chapter 14.)

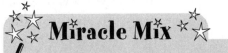

Miracle Mix

WINTERIZING TONIC

To head off trouble next spring,
zap budding bud weevils and
other bugs with this timely tonic.

**1 cup of Murphy's Oil Soap®
1 cup of tobacco tea*
1 cup of antiseptic mouthwash**

Mix all of these ingredients in a
20-gallon hose-end sprayer, filling
the balance of the jar with warm
water. Saturate your berry beds,
and the rest of your garden and
lawn, too. They'll be pest-free
and rarin' to grow come spring.

*To make tobacco tea, wrap half
a handful of chewing tobacco in
a panty hose toe or a piece of
cheesecloth. Soak it in 1 gallon of
hot water until the water turns
dark brown. Pour the liquid into
a glass container with a tight lid
for storage.

Hey, Bud!

**Strawberry bud weevils, or bud
clippers, are so tiny (just $1/12$ to $1/8$
inch long) that you may never
see them, but they can stop your
whole berry crop in its tracks. The
female drills a hole into a flower
bud (strawberry, blackberry, or
raspberry) and inserts one egg.
Then she slices into the stem just
below the bud to halt further growing progress. Sometimes, the
once-and-future flower tumbles to the ground; other times, it**

hangs on the stem. Either way, though, a little grub grows up inside, eating to its heart's content. Now what?

➤ Be prepared to take action when spring temperatures first hit 60° to 65°F. That's when the adults emerge and start doing their dirty work. At the first sign of trouble, get rid of all damaged buds. Then give your plants a once-over with your wet/dry vac to trap any weevils that are left behind (see page 233). To catch any lingerers, douse your plants with my Peppermint Soap Spray (see page 135). In the fall, clean up all plant debris (where the little devils hibernate), and spray the whole bed with my Winterizing Tonic (see page 233). Finally, to make sure the little devils don't come back, invite some weevil-eating birds to join your team. You'll find the roster in Chapter 14.

Handle with Care

It's no secret that raspberries are delicate fruits. They're prime targets for all kinds of mold, rust, and mildew, especially in warm, moist climates. What's the best way to keep them healthy?

➤ There are actually two "best" ways to keep your crop safe from foul fungi:

1. Mulch your plants with compost. It helps guard against both fungal and bacterial diseases.

2. After a rainfall, pick all the ripe fruit ASAP. Then spray the unripened berries with my Chamomile Mildew Chaser (see page 56) to fend off trouble.

SUPER SOLUTION

Birds home in on red more than any other color. So here's a simple way to keep more fruit for yourself: Instead of red varieties, plant yellow raspberries or strawberries, green gooseberries, or white or golden currants. That won't guarantee safe passage for your crop, but it *will* lessen your problems with flying felons!

Goin' for the Blue

If your blueberry bushes have been stripped clean before the berries were even ripe, you can bet pennies to pancakes that our feathered friends have been at work. How can you keep your crops out of danger?

➡️ Birds love blueberries *so* much that I've had real success with only two deterrents:

Tastier fruit. Believe it or not, there *are* fruits that birds like even more than blueberries. Given the chance, they'll zero in on their favorites and leave your baby blues alone—for the most part, anyway. These are the most marvelous morsels: barberry, chokecherry, dogwood, mulberry, Russian olive, and wild honeysuckle.

A good, strong net. Get one that's especially made for deterring birds, and drape it over a framework of wooden stakes or PVC pipe, so that the netting is about a foot away from the blueberry plants. That way, the hungry rascals can't reach through with their beaks and grab the goods.

Are They Done Yet?

As soon as your first blueberries turned blue, you rushed right out and picked them. They tasted good, alright, but not quite as good as you'd expected. Did you just have your hopes set too high?

➡️ Nope, you had your patience level set too low. Blueberries develop their best flavor a few days *after* they've turned blue. To be sure that they've peaked, just "tickle" a cluster with your fingers. If the berries fall right off the branch and into your hand, you've got yourself some winners.

CHAPTER 10

The Best of the Rest

Not all fruit grows on bushes and trees. But whether your crop sprawls across the ground, climbs up a trellis, or sits hunkered down in a garden bed, it can still present you with plenty of perplexing puzzlements. Well, stop fretting—help is at hand. In this chapter, I'll show you how to save your fruit from more fearsome fates than you can shake a flyswatter at!

Stricken Seeds 'n Seedlings

The Cool Side of Melons

Most folks know that melons like it downright steamy—and for a good, long portion of the growing season, too. But what if your climate doesn't live up to those standards? Are your home-grown melon dreams doomed?

➡ Not at all! You just have to know a few tricks of the trade:

1. Start with a variety that matures early and that's been bred to perform in your area. Ask your gardening neighbors or the folks at your Cooperative Extension Service to recommend some winners.

2. Sow your seeds indoors, three weeks before you expect the last frost. And make sure you start those seeds in individual pots that can go right into the ground at planting time, because melons don't like to have their roots disturbed. (See page 146 for more about travelin' pots.)

3. Get the planting bed ready, following my five-step Monster Melon Master Plan on page 238.

4. Move the seedlings to the garden when the soil temperature hits 70°F, and cover the bed with floating row covers, available at garden centers. They'll keep warmth in and bad-guy bugs out. Just make sure to remove the covers as soon as the first blossoms appear—otherwise, bees and other good-guy bugs can't get in to pollinate, and you'll have no crop.

SUPER SOLUTION

When each melon is about half grown, slip a barrier between it and the soil to keep the fruit from rotting. In warm summer climates, a board or a plastic milk jug cut in half will work just fine. In cooler regions, though, use a terra-cotta tile. It'll absorb and hold the sun's heat—and a growing melon needs all the warmth it can get! (To find terra-cotta tiles for next to nothing, check places that sell used or surplus building supplies.)

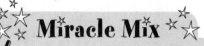

Monster Melon Master Plan

You'd like to grow big, juicy melons. But you don't know where to start. Now what?

➡️ There's really no secret to growing mighty marvelous melons—you just need to give 'em a root-pleasing home. Here's how I do that in five easy steps:

Step 1: Dig a hole about 1 foot deep and 3 feet in diameter. In the center, dig a second hole that's about 1 foot wide and 2 feet deep.

Step 2: Fill the smaller, deeper hole with good, rich compost, and tamp it down firmly. It'll act as a water well that will draw much-needed moisture up to the growing plants.

Step 3: Fill the larger hole with my Marvelous Melon Soil (at right), and mound it up so that the center is about 6 inches above ground level. Then, if you live in a climate that's on the cool side, lay black plastic mulch over the whole bed so the soil can warm up.

Step 4: Several days before planting, remove any plastic and soak each hill thoroughly with my Seed-Starter Tonic (see page 4). When

Miracle Mix

MARVELOUS MELON SOIL

Melons are mighty particular about the ground they call home. This mixture suits 'em to a T.

2 parts coarse builder's sand (not beach or "sandbox" sand)
1 part compost
1 part professional planting mix
1 cup of my Mouthwatering Melon Mix*

Mix all of these ingredients together. Pour the soil mixture into each of your melon planting holes, and get ready to modestly accept your town's Most Mouthwatering Melon award!

*To make melon mix, combine 5 pounds of earthworm castings (available in catalogs), $1/2$ pound of Epsom salts, and $1/4$ cup of instant tea granules.

the soil is dry enough to work, plant your seeds. **Tip:** When you tuck your melon seeds into their beds, put them in pointy end down—they'll sprout faster that way.

Step 5: When the seedlings have their second set of true leaves, thin the plants so that no more than three melon vines will grow from each hill. Then you're off to the races!

The State of the Union

You planted your new grapevines with the graft union above the soil, just as the pot/tag instructions said to do. But nothing ever happened. What went wrong?

My best guess is that the graft union dried out. Like a lot of other fruit trees and bushes, grapevines are usually two plants in one: a vine that produces great-tasting fruit grafted onto hardy, disease-resistant roots. With grapes, the place where those two stems meet is especially sensitive. At planting time, always cover the graft union with a mound of sand to keep it moist while the roots take hold down below. After two months, remove the sandy blanket. Otherwise, roots could sprout from the upper stem, and you'll lose the benefit of your tough-guy rootstock. One more thing: Before you plant your vines, soak them for about an hour in a bucket of my manure tea (see page 20) with a handful of bonemeal stirred in. Those grapes'll be scrambling up their trellis faster than you can say "A glass of Chardonnay, please."

Warm Fuzzies

Back in Grandma Putt's day, almost nobody outside of New Zealand had ever heard of a kiwi, much less grown one. Nowadays, these sweet, fuzzy fruits are almost as common in supermarkets as apples and pears. In fact, maybe you're hankering to grow your own, but your winters get too cold. Are there any options?

➡️ Actually, there are two:

❁ Grow a fuzzy kiwi *(Actinidia deliciosa)* in a pot, and bring it inside when the temperature plummets. Besides their portability, potted kiwis have another feather in their cap: They actually bear fruit faster than their in-ground counterparts.

❁ Grow hardy kiwis (either *A. arguta* or *A. kolomikta*). They taste like their more sensitive cousins, only a tad sweeter. The fruits are fuzzless and about the size of grapes—so you can just pop 'em in your mouth, no peeling needed. Like the fuzzy kinds, they perform like champs in containers, but they'll also stand right up in the ground and say "boo" to Old Man Winter. *A. arguta* is hardy to -25°F; *A. kolomikta* can take a bone-chilling -40°F.

For the best selection of plants—and expert advice on growing them—contact a company that specializes in out-of-the-ordinary fruits. Your favorite Internet search engine will find many listed under "edible landscaping" or "exotic fruit."

BOYS AND GIRLS TOGETHER

Or sometimes apart. Some kiwi varieties produce both male and female flowers on a single plant. Other varieties come only in single-sex versions. In that case, of course, you'll need a boy plant and a girl plant to produce fruit. If you come across a catalog or garden center that doesn't tell you which category a plant falls into, take your business elsewhere.

Wretched Roots

The Crowning Unglory

When rhubarb leaves turn yellow and collapse, and the whole plant wilts, there's just one possible cause: Phytophthora crown rot, a fungal disease that destroys the crown and the main roots. The foul stuff can attack kiwis, too. In that case, you'll see yellow leaves and stunted plants.

➡ There is no cure for crown rot, so you'll have to dig up the victims, and destroy them. It's easy to keep the deadly disease out of your garden, though: When you replace your plants, fill the new holes with a mixture of 2 parts good topsoil, 1 part compost, and 1 part shredded pine bark, a.k.a. pine bark fines. They release turtanical acid, a chemical that fights rot-causing fungi. Then, every spring, spread an inch or so of the bark on the bed. As it rains or you pull weeds, the shreds will work their way into the soil and deliver long-term protection. Shredded pine bark works like magic in containers and perennial flowerbeds, too. Just make sure you get the real thing and not hardwood chips—they don't produce the same chemical reaction.

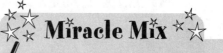

Miracle Mix

ROBUST RHUBARB TONIC

Grandma Putt served this nutritious slop to her rhubarb plants twice a year. I still feed it to her grandplants.

1 cup of tea
1 tbsp. of Epsom salts
Vegetable table scraps (all that you have on hand—but no meat or fats)
1 qt. of water

Mash all of these ingredients together until you've got a sort of slurry. (Or do the job in a blender or food processor.) Then pour the mushy mix over the soil in your rhubarb bed. Serve up one meal in spring and another in fall. Then stand back, and watch those plants go!

Easy Does It

Grape roots are a mighty unthirsty bunch. If your vines are doing poorly, or even rotting away, the problem may be overwatering.

➡ Like all plants, grape vines need watering until they've hunkered in. But it's easy to give them more H_2O than they can handle. When you plant new vines, water them according to this rule of root:

✿ Once a day for a week.

✿ Once a week for a month.

✿ Once a month for the rest of the growing season—but only if the weather is drier than usual.

✿ After the first year, let Mother Nature quench their thirst.

Wired for Inaction

If your otherwise healthy melon vines wilt and die, suspect wireworms. For a positive I.D., poke around in the soil. If you see shiny, orange worms, you've found your villain.

➡ The simple solution: Spear chunks of potato on sticks that are about 8 inches long, and bury them so that about 3 inches of the stick shows above ground. Then, every day or two, pull up the tater bits, toss 'em in a pail of soapy water to kill the worms, then toss the whole thing on the compost pile. For more about wireworms, including instructions for can-o'-worms traps, see page 153.

PULL, DON'T CUT

When you harvest your rhubarb, grab each stalk near the base, and pull it off with a slight twisting motion. Don't cut the stalks: The stubs that remain will ooze sap, thereby inviting rot to drop in and polish off your plants.

Sickly Stems

You're Boring Me

Your melons were doing fine, then your turned your back for two seconds (or so it seemed). When you looked again, they'd wilted from stem to stern. The cause: squash vine borers—little fat, white caterpillars with white heads. If you look closely, you'll see small holes in the stems, with stuff that looks like gooey sawdust piled up beside them.

 Your mission—blot out those borers. Here's how:

> ❖ For fast-acting relief, slit the stem at each hole, then reach in with a bent wire and pull out the borer. (Grandma Putt always used a crochet hook for this procedure.) Drown the culprit in a bucket of soapy water laced with ¼ cup of alcohol, and heap soil over the opening in the stem.

> ❖ Or, if you can get to a garden center quickly, buy some Bt *(Bacillus thuringiensis)*, and inject it into each hole, following the directions on the package.

ALL FOR ONE

Melons, squash, and cucumbers belong to the same big (mostly) happy family. And they all share the same arch-enemies, the worst of which are squash vine borers, cucumber beetles, and squash bugs. (For the lowdown on the beetles and bugs, see Chapter 6.)

Keep 'Em Under Cover

You can head off borer problems by covering your melon, squash, and cucumber plants in the early spring. That way, the adult moths can't get in to lay their eggs. But if you don't get the

covers off in time, good-guy bugs can't pollinate the flowers. Is there another way to go?

➡ Here's a trick that'll keep the borers at bay without the need for a full-scale cover-up: Just wrap panty hose or row cover fabric around the base of each plant. That's where these villains generally strike, and if they find the door closed, they'll probably go elsewhere. Don't take chances, though: Keep a lookout for clusters of bright red eggs, and wipe them off, pronto. For added protection, adopt a toad or two. They eat squash-borer moths by the bucket-load. (You'll find the full adoption procedure in Chapter 14.)

Miracle Mix

SCAT CAT SOLUTION

Surround your prized plants with this pungent potion, and pussycats will go elsewhere for munchies.

5 tbsp. of flour
4 tbsp. of powdered mustard
3 tbsp. of cayenne pepper
2 tbsp. of chili powder
2 qts. of warm water

Mix all of these ingredients together. Then sprinkle the solution around target plants that are in the ground or in containers.

Holy Cats!

If some rascal is munching on your young kiwi vines, and you confront the suspect with the evidence, I'll bet dollars to donuts she'll say "meow." How can I be so sure? Because, believe it or not, cats love kiwis as much as they love catnip. (Don't ask me why—my family felines aren't talking.)

➡ Fortunately, you don't need to know why kitties crave kiwi. You just need the recipe for my Scat Cat Solution (above). It'll surround your prize plants with an, um, aromatic fence that no cat worth her nose will cross!

Think Thirds

The way some folks carry on about pruning grapes, you'd think it was open-heart surgery. If you've been denying yourself all this good eatin' (and maybe drinkin') because you thought you could never get the system down, think again.

➥ The fact is, if you plant grapevines, you're gonna get grapes. Just choose the best, disease-resistant varieties for your region, then cut the vines back by a third of their length every year in late winter. (For the latest and greatest in grapes, call your closest Cooperative Extension Service office.)

Lousy Leaves

Look Twice

At first glance, the damage to your grape leaves looks like the work of Japanese beetles. But if your vines are at the edge of a lawn, it's a good bet the culprits are rose chafer beetles. Once you've seen them, there's no chance of mistaken identity: Chafers are lighter in color and smaller than their Japanese cousins, and they have much longer legs. They're just as lethal, though. Left unchecked, chafers can destroy your whole grape crop.

➥ Shout "Checkmate!" and get to work. If you spot the invasion in its early

Let's Be Buddies

Japanese beetles—those rampaging roughriders from the East—are wild about grapes and kiwis. Keep the rascals at bay by growing pots of geraniums *(Pelargonium)* near your fruit vines. (For more ways to battle these big, bad beetles, see page 87.)

stages, just pick the chafers off the plants, drop them into a jar of soapy water, and screw on the lid. When you're sure the no-goodniks are dead, remove the lid, and set the jar on the ground among your grapes. The smell of their decomposing comrades will make the chafers go elsewhere for dinner. In the case of a full-scale attack, though, don't waste a minute: Blend those chafers into a batch of my So Long, Sucker Spray (see page 71), and spray the grapevines from top to bottom.

Miracle Mix

TOODLE-OO TERRORS TONIC

Our ancestors thought tomatoes were poisonous, so they avoided them like the plague. Flea beetles still do. Just spray your plants' leaves with this timely tonic, and kiss your flea-beetle battles good-bye!

2 cups of tomato leaves, chopped
¹/₂ tsp. of liquid dish soap
1 qt. of water

Put the leaves and water in a pan, and bring the water to a simmer. Then turn off the heat and let the mixture cool. Strain out the leaves, and add the dish soap to the water. Pour the solution into a hand-held mist sprayer, and spritz your plants from top to bottom. This potent potion also repels whiteflies, asparagus beetles, and cabbageworms. (Like all repellent sprays, though, you need to renew the supply after every rain.)

Up the Creek *with* a Paddle

Flea beetles are some of the tiniest bad guys on the planet, but they do whale-size damage to melons (and plenty of other plants, too). The trouble isn't so much the itty-bitty holes they chew in the leaves—it's the nasty and incurable diseases they spread in the process. Is there any cure?

➡ Well, the varmints may have you outnumbered, but you've got them outsmarted, so hop to it! There are more ways to outwit flea beetles than you can shake a dog collar at, and you can read about a lot of them on page 152. But if you get a real kick out of stalking tiny game, as I do, go at 'em with my favorite low-tech weaponry: a pair of sticky paddles. Just get two 2-inch wooden strips about 3 feet long, and staple a sheet of 10- by 12-inch cardboard to one end of each. (In this case, the color doesn't matter.) Spray the cardboard with Tanglefoot, or coat it with petroleum jelly, so that it's good and sticky. Then, hold a paddle on each side of a beetle-ridden plant, and gently jiggle the plant with your foot. As the flea beetles leap off the leaves, they'll land on the paddles.

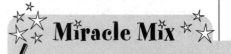

Miracle Mix

MAGICAL MILDEW CONTROL TONIC

At the first sign of mildew—or whenever the weather is damp and humid—spray your mildew magnet plants with this timely tonic.

4 tbsp. of baking soda
2 tbsp. of Murphy's Oil Soap®
1 gal. of warm water

Mix all of these ingredients together. Then pour the solution into a hand-held mist sprayer and thoroughly douse your plants when you see telltale signs of mildew.

Take a Powder and Duck Down

Melons and all their cucumber clan relatives are prime targets for two kinds of mildew: powdery and downy. Powdery mildew first appears as circular, whitish spots on the lower leaf surfaces. Left unchecked, the nastiness spreads until the whole leaf is covered in white powder. Leaves attacked by downy mildew sport yellowish brown spots on the upper surfaces. In damp weather, purple spots appear on the undersides.

➡ Whichever mildew you're dealing with, the solution is the same: Cut off the afflicted plant parts, and destroy (don't compost) them. Then, spray your plants from top to bottom with my Magical Mildew Control Tonic (above).

Failing Flowers 'n Fruits

Blasted Bandits!

Your ripe melons have been disappearing in the night, and you suspect raccoons. You don't want to set traps, so how else can you stop these midnight raiders?

→ Get the felons by the foot! Just lay a 3-foot-wide strip of black plastic all the way around your melon patch. Raccoons have hairless and very sensitive feet, and they don't like to walk on anything that feels strange. One step onto that slippery-slidey stuff and those 'coons'll clear out!

SUPER SOLUTION When you thin out your young melons, slip a panty hose foot over each fruit that's staying on the vine, and tie the end closed. That way, you'll fend off more pesky pests and dastardly diseases than you will ever know. (This terrific trick works just as well with clusters of grapes.)

Less Is More

You say your melon vines are offering up a whole lot of fruit, but the quality is, well, not quite what you'd hoped for?

→ To rectify the situation, when the melons are about the size of a walnut, cut off all but four or five fruits on each vine. The plant will direct all of its energy to the survivors, and they'll grow up big, sweet, and juicy. And don't feel bad about sacrificing all those baby melons—just rush 'em into the kitchen, peel 'em, and pickle 'em in your favorite sweet brine recipe.

When, Oh, When?

With melons, what you pick is what you get: They don't ripen off the vine, the way a lot of other fruits and vegetables do. So how do you know when to say when?

It depends on what kind of melon you've got. Here's the rundown on when to harvest your crop:

Honeydews, casabas, Crenshaws, and true cantaloupes are ready when their skin turns either white or creamy gold, depending on the variety. Don't pull the fruits; cut them from the vine using a sharp knife.

Muskmelons, the kind most commonly grown in home gardens, are ripe when it takes just a little pressure to pull the fruit from its stem. If you wait just a tad longer, they'll separate, or "slip," from the vine all by themselves. By that time, they could be overripe.

Watermelons are tricky, and it seems everybody's got a different theory. My advice is to note the time the plants come into bloom. Then, about 35 days later, start looking for one or more of these clues:

❀ The part of the melon that sits on the ground is yellow.

❀ The tendril closest to the melon has turned brown.

❀ When you tap the fruit lightly, instead of a ping, you hear a lower-pitched thump or thunk.

SAY IT ISN'T SO!

If you think that cantaloupe is your favorite fruit in the whole world, you may be in for a surprise. The melons that go by the name of cantaloupe in grocery stores—and the ones most home gardeners grow—are not cantaloupes at all: They're muskmelons. True cantaloupes have a hard, warty rind. They're grown a lot in Europe, but almost never in North America.

Block That Rot!

To grape growers in humid climates, black rot is Public Enemy Number One. The fungus turns plump, pretty grapes into ugly, black, dried-up berries called mummies. Don't let this happen to your crop!

➤ To stop black rot dead in its tracks, you just need to understand how it operates. The fungus sleeps through the winter in the mummies, then wakes up in spring and produces spores galore. When it rains, the spores burst loose from the mummies, land on the new foliage, and the cycle starts all over again. So get out there and get rid of those mummies! Pluck 'em off the plants, pick 'em up off the ground, and send 'em off with the trash. When you prune the vines, destroy all the clippings, too.

Let's Be Buddies

After you've cleaned up all your fungus-filled grape mummies, plant crimson clover (*Trifolium incarnatum*) under your grapevines, and keep it about 5 inches high. The clover will block any spores that are left on the ground and keep them from leaping up on to your grapes.

Patience Pays Off

A healthy clump of rhubarb will supply you with pie, chutney, and cobbler makings for two decades or more—if you handle your plants the right way in the beginning.

➤ With rhubarb, the key to long-term performance is short-term restraint. During its first year in your garden, rhubarb is just for show, so don't harvest any leafstalks, a.k.a. "petioles." The plant needs them to make food for the roots. Do clip off any flower stalks as soon as they appear, though, because they'll drain nourishment from the plant. In early spring of the second year, you can harvest a few leafstalks, but leave most of them on the plant. From the third year on, pick to your heart's (and tummy's) content.

PART IV

HERBAL
Helpers

CHAPTER 11

Kitchen Companions

B y and large, herbs are so easy to please that some folks think they can just sow the seeds and sail home free. Then—BINGO—trouble strikes! Roots rot, leaves mildew, pesky pests ride in from out of nowhere, and Jack Frost flattens whole beds with a single puff. Well, don't you worry. Here are the answers to those problems and a whole lot more of your herbal woes!

Stricken Seeds 'n Seedlings

Ready, Set, Grow!

But your herb seeds didn't—at least not the way you'd expected them to. And you thought herbs were so easy to please!

➤ If your seeds didn't come up at all, they could have fallen victim to the same disasters that can plague annual flower seeds (see page 4). Or, the problem could lie with your choice of plants. Some herbs either don't come true from seed or take forever to germinate. My advice: Get out there and try again. And this time, handle your growing stock according to my tips below.

SENSATIONAL SEEDERS

These great-tasting herbs are as easy as pie to start from seed sown right in the ground. Or, if you want to get a jump on the growing season, start 'em indoors according to the simple guidelines on page 255.

Basil *(Ocimum basilicum)*: Annual.

Chervil, a.k.a. French parsley *(Anthriscus cerefolium)*: Annual.*

Chives *(Allium schoenoprasum)*: Perennial, Zones 3 to 10.

Cilantro, a.k.a. coriander *(Coriandrum sativum)*: Annual.*

Dill *(Anethum graveolens)*: Annual.*

Fennel *(Foeniculum vulgare)*: Perennial, Zones 4 to 10.*

Garlic *(Allium sativum)*: Grown from bulbs.

Marjoram *(Origanum majorana)*: Perennial, Zones 5 to 10.

Parsley *(Petroselinum crispum)*: Perennial, Zones 6 to 10.*

* These herbs resent having their roots disturbed. Sow the seeds directly in the garden when the soil has warmed up, or start them in individual travelin' pots. For how to make your own supply, see page 146.

Potted Perfectionists

You'd like to grow perennial herbs for cooking, but you're not sure which ones will do best under your growing conditions.

➡ Try the perennial herbs listed below. But don't even bother trying to start them from seed. Buy seedlings from a garden center or catalog, and you'll be off to the races. If some of the zone numbers don't match up with your climate, don't fret: Just treat the plants as annuals, and replace them every year. Better yet, grow them in containers, and let them bask in a sunny window all winter long.

Bay (*Laurus nobilis*): Zones 8 to 10.

French tarragon (*Artemisia dracunculus*): Zones 4 to 8.

Garden sage (*Salvia officinalis*): Zones 5 to 9.

Mints (*Mentha*): Zones 4 to 10.

Oreganos (*Origanum*): Zones 5 to 10.

Rosemary (*Rosmarinus officinalis*): Zones 7 to 10.

Thymes (*Thymus*): Zones 4 to 9.

SUPER SOLUTION

If you want to be sure of getting the biggest bang for your buck, buy your plants from small growers who specialize in herbs. And always ask how the stock was propagated. The good growers will be delighted to tell you!

What You Smell Is What You Get

The baby culinary herb plants you find in a garden center or big home-store chain may have no fragrance at all, or the aroma may be only a faint whiff. How can you be sure you get fragrant herbs?

➡ You need to shop with your nose. Rub a leaf between your fingers, then bring it up to your nose and smell it. If you don't get

Miracle Mix

HERB SOIL BOOSTER MIX

When you plant your herbs, add some of this marvelous mix to the soil. Those youngsters will be sure to get off to a rip-roarin' start.

**5 lbs. of lime
5 lbs. of gypsum
1 lb. of 5-10-5 garden food
½ cup of Epsom salts**

Mix all of these ingredients together, and work the formula into each 50-sq.-ft. area of herb garden to a depth of 12 to 18 inches. Then let it sit for 7 to 10 days before planting.

a concentrated whiff of scent, put that plant right back where you found it. Don't take it home, thinking that it'll develop fragrance and flavor as it grows, because it won't. What you smell and taste now is as good as it gets.

It's a Date

When you're starting herbs indoors, you need to sow the seeds anywhere from 4 to 12 weeks before your last expected frost. And if you've got even a handful of different kinds, how do you remember what to sow when?

When you send off your seed order, check the catalog for each plant's indoor start time. You'll generally see it given as the number of weeks before the last expected frost. Then, figure out what that date is in your area, mark it on your calendar, *and* write it on an envelope. When the seed packets arrive, tuck each one into the appropriate envelope. Then, when the calendar says, "Today's the day," just grab the right package, and get to plantin'!

Cool It!

Most grown-up herbs are gung-ho sun worshipers. Seedlings, though, do better with a little shade. Out West or down South, Ol' Sol can make them go belly-up faster than you can say

HAPPY CAMPERS

Even up North, not all herbs demand a full day of Ol' Sol's time. These popular winners will all perform well in four to six hours of sunlight (what gardening books generally describe as either "partial shade" or "partial sun"). Beware, though: The flavor and aroma won't be as intense as they would be if the plants grew in full sun.

Basil (*Ocimum basilicum*)

Chives (*Allium schoenoprasum*)

Cilantro, a.k.a. coriander (*Coriandrum sativum*)

Mints (*Mentha*)*

Parsley (*Petroselinum crispum*)

* Mint will thrive in just three to four hours of sun a day.

"Please pass the sunscreen." If your direct-sown herbs are keeling over, the reason is probably sunstroke.

➡ Here's a simple way to give them shelter: When you sow your seeds, cut some fresh, feathery fern fronds, and stick them in the soil so they shade the bed. (Bracken or wood ferns are perfect; steer clear of heavier-leaved plants like sword ferns.) When the seedlings germinate and stick their heads above ground, they'll bask in the shade. But as those young plants grow bigger and tougher, the ferns will keep pace, dying back and gradually letting in more of the sun's rays.

Fudge the Numbers!

To perform their best, most of the herbs that folks grow for kitchen use need 8 to 10 hours of direct sun a day—what the garden books and catalogs call "full sun." But in a hot climate, that much sun will cook your herbs before you ever get them into the kitchen. What's the solution?

➡ Simple: Fudge the numbers. In the South, Southwest, or at high altitudes, full sun translates into a maximum of four hours—preferably in the morning.

The Usual Suspects

Like all other seedlings, baby herbs have two big-time enemies: cutworms and damping-off fungi. What do you do to combat these foes?

 To foil cutworms, give your outdoor seedlings protective collars and a carpet of wood ashes or diatomaceous earth. (See page 146 for more on cutworm control.) Fend off fungi by following my damping-off prevention guidelines on page 7.

Wretched Roots

Foul Fungi

When herbs fall prey to a root rot fungus, it's all but guaranteed that you have one of two problems. Either your plants are getting too much water, or they're sitting in poorly drained soil. Both conditions are fairly easy to remedy.

➡ Here are two ways to deal with water woes:

✿ If you catch the problem when the plants are just turning yellow—a sure sign of overwatering—ease off on the hose trigger. How do you know when to water again? Stick your index finger in the ground. If it's dry from the tip up, reach for the hose.

✿ When drainage is poor, even if you're keeping a tight rein on the water supply, the water will hang around the roots too long and cause trouble. In that case, you need to improve the soil pronto (for the lowdown on that, see Chapter 14), or grow your herbs in containers.

Rhizoctonia Rides Again

Rhizoctonia root and stem rot is a disease that attacks herbs as well as leafy greens and other vegetables—even in loose, well-drained soil (see page 181). In later stages, the stems, lower leaves, and roots turn to black, rotten messes. If that happens, your only option is to pull up the plants, and destroy them. But don't panic! If you reach the scene early, you can save the day.

➡ Just cut off the droopy leaves, and saturate the soil with my Fungus Fighter Soil Drench (see page 45). Then, mulch the soil with compost or shredded pine bark to fend off further attacks.

Invasion of the Ground Snatchers

If you've ever shared space with so much as a single mint plant, you know that its roots travel faster than a race car at the Indy 500. The same holds true for mint's relatives, such as catnip, lemon balm, and pennyroyal (to name only a few). So how do you keep these hard-chargers in their place?

PLANT THESE at your PERIL!

Mint may be the most notorious of the herbal wanderers, but this crew also has mighty itchy feet, er, roots:

Artemisias (*Artemisia*), especially 'Silver King' and 'Silver Queen'

Bee balms (*Monarda*)

Sweet woodruff (*Galium odoratum*)

Thymes (*Thymus*)

Wild oregano (*Origanum vulgare*)

To keep these ground snatchers in check, follow the tips at left.

➡ The surest way to foil a takeover bid is to plant the mint family in pots. That way, their roots can't possibly escape. But that's not the only containment policy. Here's a quartet of other ways to keep roving rooters from rambling too far:

Fence 'em in below ground. Sink terra-cotta flue tiles or other bottomless containers into the soil, and plant your mints inside. You won't have to fuss with special potting soil, and the roots will lose most of their wanderlust.

Put 'em where they're not happiest. For instance, most mints will grow just about anywhere, but their ideal home is rich, moist soil in full sun to partial shade. So give your plants average soil that's on the dry side. They'll still thrive, but they'll be more likely to stay within bounds.

Give 'em tight quarters. Potential ramblers can't get far if you put them in a small, hemmed-in plot of ground—say, between a walkway and the walls of your house or garage.

Let 'em duke it out. When you plant two different aggressors side by side (catnip and peppermint, for instance) they seem to keep each other under control—at least to some degree!

Sickly Stems

Not Here, Kitty!

There they go again! Your neighbors' cats are digging up your herb garden, and leaving, um, aromatic souvenirs behind. You've talked to your neighbors, but they haven't done anything to corral Fluffy and Puffy. And you don't want to mask the scent of your herbs with smelly deterrents. What else can you do?

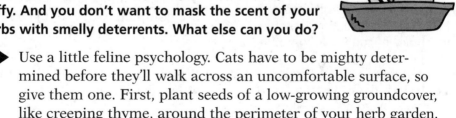

➡ Use a little feline psychology. Cats have to be mighty determined before they'll walk across an uncomfortable surface, so give them one. First, plant seeds of a low-growing groundcover, like creeping thyme, around the perimeter of your herb garden. Then, on top of the seedbed, lay 2- to 3-foot-wide strips of chicken wire. When the plants grow up, they'll cover the ugly, flat fencing, so you won't notice it. But when the kitties' paws touch that wire, they'll be outta there faster than you can say "I tought I taw a puddytat."

Quack! Quack!

Slugs are on the rampage in your herb garden, devouring the stems and leaves of your basil and sage! What to do?

➡ Go cut some quackgrass *(Agropyron repens)*. Scientists at the U.S. Department of Agriculture have proven that this perennial pain-in-the-grass has a big plus going for it: It kills slugs, without harming earthworms or other good-guy garden helpers. To put these magical powers to work in your herb garden (or any other slug-menaced places), just cut off the grass blades, and let them dry out in the sun. Then chop them into small pieces, and sprinkle them in a thin layer around your mature plants. Just be aware that an overdose of dry (or any size dose of fresh) quackgrass can damage some plants. So make sure the blades are completely dry and keep the layer light. Test it first on a few plants of each kind you want to protect *before* you mulch your entire garden.

To protect seedlings, entice slugs to their death with a batch of my Quack-Up Slug Cookies (at left).

✫ Miracle Mix ✫

QUACK-UP SLUG COOKIES

Slugs will think it's time to party when they get a yeasty whiff of these tasty treats. But after a couple of bites, they'll have a killer of a hangover!

1 part dried quackgrass blades, finely chopped
1 part wheat bran*
1 can of beer

Mix the quackgrass and bran in a bowl, then slowly add the beer, stirring until the mixture has the consistency of cookie dough. Run the dough through a meat grinder, or chop it into small bits (roughly $1/8$ to $1/4$ inch thick). Let the "cookies" air-dry overnight, sprinkle them on the ground among your plants, and let the good times roll!

*Available in supermarkets and health food stores.

It's Too Darn Hot

Even heat-loving herbs call it quits when both the temperature and humidity sky-rocket. Especially in the steamy South, plants' stems, leaves, and roots are all sitting ducks for fungal diseases—not to mention simple heatstroke. So how do you keep your savory-seasoning crops from keeling over?

➡ These simple tricks will keep your herbs fit as a fiddle down South, or anywhere else that Mother Nature opens the steam vents:

❀ Grow all your herbs in raised beds. That will improve both drainage and air circulation—and that's crucial for fending off fungal diseases.

❀ Add heaps of manure and compost to the soil. Besides giving off chemicals that destroy fungi, this duo provides steady, balanced nutrition that keeps plants free of stress. And in brutal heat, a stressed plant can become a dead plant mighty fast.

❀ Cast shade on the scene. Down South, all herbs need shade from 2:00 p.m. on, and some—including chives, parsley, sorrel, and the mint clan—require permanent shelter. Grow them in the shade of taller plants, or cover their bed with a lattice roof or an awning made of greenhouse shade cloth.

❀ Juggle your calendar. Some herbs won't survive a Southern

Miracle Mix

HAPPY HERB TONIC

No matter what temperatures your climate delivers, keep all of your herbs healthy and chipper with this nifty elixir.

1 cup of tea
½ tbsp. of bourbon
½ tbsp. of ammonia
½ tbsp. of hydrogen peroxide
1 gal. of warm water

Mix all of the ingredients together in a bucket. Then dish up hearty helpings every six weeks throughout the growing season.

summer no matter how much you baby them. If you're not sure what grows when in your neck of the woods, check with gardening friends, your local garden club or herb society, or the closest Cooperative Extension Service.

Lousy Leaves

Keep 'Em Close at Hand

We humans aren't the only beings who love the taste of fresh herbs. Other critters, including rabbits and deer, go for some of them in a big way, too. So how do you keep the culprits from eating you out of house and garden?

➡ Reach for any one of my critter-chasing Miracle Mixes, located throughout this book (or see Jerry's Mixers 'n Elixirs on page 335). Or, you can just plant your herbs right up close to your house. I grow most of mine in containers on my deck. Four-legged diners have to be awfully hungry—and have no other alternatives—before they'll venture to within a few feet of a house. There's another plus to this planting scheme: You can just step out the door and clip whatever you're hankerin' to cook with.

A Dilly of a Duo

What dastardly demon is defoliating your dill? The culpable culprit could be one of two caterpillars: the tomato hornworm or the parsleyworm.

➡ **Tomato hornworms** can be anywhere from 3 to 5 inches long. They're green with white stripes on their bodies and a fearsome-looking horn projecting from the rear (hence the name *hornworm*). It's a fake weapon, though. The only harm these guys cause is to plants—specifically, dill, eggplant, peppers, potatoes, and tomatoes. Your best response: Pick the varmints off your plants, drown them in a bucket of soapy water, and empty it onto the compost pile. In the case of a major invasion, blast the bad guys with my Orange Aid (see page 170).

Parsleyworms are about 2 inches long and green, with a yellow-dotted black band over each body segment. When they're disturbed, they send out a pair of orange horns to scare the enemy. (These guys are paper tigers, though, so don't worry!) Your best response: Leave 'em be. Parsleyworms almost never eat enough to cause real damage, and they grow up into swallowtail butterflies, which will flit around your garden, sipping nectar and pollinating your posies. If the parsleyworms are causing more destruction than you want to put up with, gently pick them off your dill and move them to another dining area (see "Dining Disasters," above). Better yet, keep a patch of food growing just for them, and chances are, they'll never give your dill another thought.

DINING DISASTERS

When chow time arrives, parsleyworms keep their dining in the family—the carrot family (*Apiaceae* in botanical lingo), that is. In addition to carrots, dill, and (of course) parsley, the clan includes these cousins:

Anise (*Pimpinella anisum*)
Celery (*Apium graveolens*)
Cilantro (*Coriandrum sativum*)
Fennel (*Foeniculum vulgare*)
Parsnip (*Pastinaca sativa*)
Queen Anne's lace (*Daucus carota*)
Water hemlock (*Cicuta maculata*)
Yarrows (*Achillea*)

Don't Hurt That Hornworm!

What if you spot a tomato hornworm with little papery cocoons on his back. Is this some kind of mutant breed?

 There's nothing mutant about this guy. As a matter of fact, his days are numbered—those baubles are the eggs of braconid wasps, the natural parasites of tomato hornworms. Move the worm away from your garden, but let him live so the wasps can reproduce and continue their good work. Tomato hornworms have hordes of other natural enemies, too. See Chapter 15 for the full roster.

Two Tiny Terrors

Even herbs can't always escape the clutches of aphids and spider mites—that dastardly delinquent duo. You'll see the pear-shaped aphids clustered on the undersides of leaves. Spider mites are so tiny that you could waste hours looking for them, but there's no mistaking their damage: dry, yellow, stippled leaves, often covered with little white dots.

No matter which minute marauders are makin' merry with your herbs, just spray your plants with a blast of water from the garden hose, three times, every other day. Nine times out of ten, that'll solve the problem. If that doesn't do the trick, whip up a batch of Grandma

---

SUPER SOLUTION

Here's a one-word solution to some of your biggest herbal woes: kelp. This sensational seaweed provides essential plant nutrients, helps plants absorb water better, and keeps all manner of pesky pests at bay. Outdoors, hardy perennials that get regular sprayings of kelp tolerate cold temperatures better than their unsprayed counterparts. And tender perennials spending the winter indoors hold up better under the low light and dry air that most homes offer up. So how do you deliver this wonder drug? Just spray your herbs and all your perennial plants with my Winter Wonder Drug (at right) every two to three weeks throughout the growing season.

Putt's Simple Soap Spray (see page 94), and let 'er rip. Just remember to rinse off the soap *before* you toss the herbs into anything you plan to eat!

Battered Basil

Dark spots on basil leaves can mean one of two things: Either those plants caught a chill, or there's a fungus among us. Just by eye-balling the spots, it's hard to tell cold injury from a fungal disease. Fortunately, though, the weather is a dead giveaway.

➥ The first thing you need to do is pluck off all of the spotty leaves. Then follow this action plan:

✿ If the temperature is below 40°F, your culprit is cold. Just toss the plucked leaves on the compost pile. In the case of a late spring cold snap, cover your plants pronto, and keep blankets (or bottomless soda bottles) in place until the temperature rises. If the dip in the mercury comes at the end of the growing season, harvest your crop, and rush it into the kitchen. Don't dawdle—even a light freeze will turn basil black in a flash.

✿ When spots appear in warmer weather, it signals a fungal attack. Most likely, it's not deadly. First, destroy the infected leaves. Then spray your basil with my Compost Tea (see page 20), and repeat every two weeks for the rest of the growing season.

Miracle Mix

WINTER WONDER DRUG

To keep your herbs and other perennial plants happy and healthy all winter long, douse them with this terrific tonic throughout the growing season.

1 tbsp. of liquid kelp, a.k.a. seaweed extract
⅛ tsp. of liquid dish soap
1 gal. of water

Mix all of these ingredients together, and mist-spray your herbs from top to bottom every two to three weeks throughout the growing season.

This Mosaic Ain't Pretty

Basil leaves that are splotched or mottled in yellow, with turned-down edges, *do* have a serious problem: cucumber mosaic virus. Will you have to kiss this year's pesto good-bye?

➡ If the infection is advanced and widespread, the answer is yes. But in the earlier stages, there is hope. First, pluck off and destroy all of the infected foliage. Then follow up with my Flower and Foliage Flu Shot (see page 64). To head off any more attacks, control the culprits that spread the virus: cucumber beetles. (See page 159 for my cuke beetle battle plan.)

Failing Flowers

What's with All the Flowers?

You started your herb seeds in flats, then moved them along to individual pots. When the time came, you hardened them off and planted them in the garden. Then, in what seemed the blink of an eye, the plants were flowering to beat the band. And the bushels of tasty leaves that you'd been banking on never showed up. How come?

➡ The problem is that some herbs hate to have their roots disturbed. And they tend to show it by producing flowers prematurely, before they've had a chance to develop a good crop of leaves. If a short growing season makes direct sowing all but impossible, start your seeds indoors in pots that can go right into the ground at transplanting time. (You'll find some of these cantankerous customers on page 253. To learn how to make my favorite travelin' pots, see page 146.)

Early Bloomers

If your dill flowers before its time, that's not a problem—that's a solution for all kinds of garden variety troubles. How so?

➡ Dill blossoms attract and support beneficial bugs by the bucketload, including bees, good-guy wasps, and parasites that control tent caterpillars and codling moths. These super plants also help repel aphids and spider mites, draw caterpillars from cabbages, and protect corn from diseases. And according to Grandma Putt, dill improves the flavor of cole crops and is generally good for lettuce and onions. So don't just sit there—go get yourself a big sack of dill seeds!

GRANDMA PUTT'S
grow-how

Unfortunately, dill does have its dark side. Grandma Putt never planted it near tomatoes or carrots because she said it would reduce their growth. Hey—nobody's perfect!

Time It Right

If you're anything like me, harvesting herbs is an ongoing process—you just clip whatever you're planning to cook with that day, or whatever strikes your fancy as you're strolling through the garden. It's another matter, though, when you want larger quantities, either to use fresh or to store for the winter. So when's the best time to harvest?

➡ To get the biggest flavor bang for your buck, follow these simple guidelines:

Beat the flowers to the finish line. Most herbs reach their peak of flavor, fragrance, and quantity just before the flower buds open. If you cut them way back then, the plants will often regrow and give you a second harvest.

Make it morning. Try to harvest your herbs early, after the dew has dried, but before the sun gets hot. That's when the volatile oils that give herbs their flavor and aroma reach their highest levels. The plants are also cool then, so they'll stay fresh longer. If early morning isn't possible, aim for an overcast day.

Don't overdo it. Once they're cut, herbs go downhill fast, so harvest only as much as you're sure you can handle before the cuttings start to wilt. (You can always go back for more the next day.)

Whoops! I Missed

You went away on vacation, and missed the peak harvest season. Does that mean you just have to pack it in for the year?

➡ Not at all—just shift your sights. For instance:

✿ Instead of leaves, harvest the seeds.

✿ Clip the flowers. Then, use them in salads or desserts, add them to homemade herbal vinegars, or dry them for use in craft projects (for some dandy ones, see Chapter 13).

✿ Leave some of the seed to self-sow and give you plants for next year.

SUPER SOLUTION

The more you clip your herbs, the more leaves they'll churn out—and the longer you'll keep their flowers at bay. That's important, because once most herbs form flowers, the leaves have passed their prime for good eatin'. On the flip side, the flowers of all herbs attract many kinds of beneficial bugs. The simple solution: Plant a few more of each herb than you intend to eat at the leafy stage. Then, let those extra plants go on to flower. That way, you'll keep those good-guy bugs on the job, solving pest problems not only in your herb garden, but also all over your outdoor green scene.

TASTE MAKERS

With this versatile crew, you get more than just tasty leaves.

Herb	Zesty Seeds	Flavorful Flowers	Volunteer Plants
Anise (*Pimpinella anisum*)	Yes		
Basil (*Ocimum basilicum*)		Yes	Yes (some varieties)
Borage (*Borago officinalis*)		Yes	Yes
Caraway (*Carum carvi*)	Yes		Yes
Chervil (*Anthriscus cerefolium*)		Yes	
Chives (*Allium schoenoprasum*)		Yes	Yes
Cilantro, **a.k.a. coriander** (*Coriandrum sativum*)	Yes		Yes
Dill (*Anethum graveolens*)	Yes	Yes	Yes
Marjoram (*Origanum majorana*)		Yes	
Mint (*Mentha*)		Yes	
Mustard (*Brassica*)	Yes		Yes
Rosemary (*Rosmarinus officinalis*)		Yes	
Thyme (*Thymus*)		Yes	

That's Not Italian!

You sowed a big patch of oregano seeds so you could use the pungent herb in homemade spaghetti and pizza sauce, just like the kind you get at your neighborhood Italian restaurant. But when you plucked your first crop of leaves, you could hardly smell them. And the flavor…well, it might as well have been dried grass. Are your taste buds failing, or does the restaurant have a hot line to Italy?

➡️ Neither! You just planted the wrong kind of oregano. The type that's generally sold as seeds is wild oregano *(Origanum vulgare)*, and it's one of the most fickle plants on the planet. Scent and flavor can vary from none at all to pretty darn good, depending on climate and growing conditions. Even individual plants differ in their taste and aroma. The stuff you want—and that's generally used in Italian cooking—is Greek or Italian oregano *(O. heracleoticum)*. It delivers what most folks think of as good, down-home Italian flavor every time. You need to grow it from started plants, though, and not seeds.

GRANDMA PUTT'S
grow-how

Want sweeter flavor from your garlic? Then do what Grandma Putt did: When she planted her garlic, she always crushed the cloves a little to bruise them, and she tucked a couple of olive pits into each planting hole. Talk about sweet! When you harvest those bulbs, roast 'em, and spread 'em on toasted Italian bread—your taste buds will think they've died and gone to heaven!

Less-Than-Gorgeous Garlic

Not many plants are easier to please than garlic, but you may notice a couple of problems at harvest time: split husks and undersized cloves.

➡️ You can't send the bulbs back and exchange them for new ones, but you can head off trouble next time around. Here's how:

Split husks indicate that you waited too long to harvest your crop, and the cloves outgrew their skin. Next time, dig up the bulbs when most of the leaves have yellowed. That's generally by late August.

Cloves grow smaller than they should when the ground is compacted. When you plant your next crop, work at least an inch of compost into the soil to make it nice and loose—and don't let anybody step on the bed!

Let's Be Buddies

Borage has more going for it than good looks and great flavor: Planted with strawberries, it helps the fruits grow stronger and tastier.

Super Stand-Ins

Do you love the taste of fresh cucumbers, but lack the space to grow them? Or maybe you just don't want to fuss with all of the cucurbit clan's pesky pest problems. Is there a way to enjoy the cucumber flavor without the drawbacks?

There sure is. Plant one (or both) of these cucumber taste-alikes:

Borage *(Borago officinalis)*. An easy-seeding annual with long, fuzzy leaves, floppy stems, and pretty blue flowers—and every bit of this plant tastes just like cukes. (If you don't care for the texture of the leaves, use them to flavor your recipe, then take them out before you serve the dish.)

Salad burnet *(Sanguisorba minor)*. An old-time, rough-and-ready perennial that's hardy to Zone 3 and thrives in just four to six hours of sun a day. It's easy to grow from seed, and forms neat little clumps that stay evergreen in all but the coldest climates. In this case, it's the leaves you want, so keep a steady supply coming by clipping off the flowers and old foliage.

Dried Is Dandy,
But Frozen Is Finer

You say the basil you harvested, dried, and stored so carefully has about as much flavor as chopped-up newspaper? I'm not surprised. It *is* possible that something went wrong in the drying process (see Chapter 13 for my dandy drying routine). More likely, though, it's just business as usual for basil. Along with chives, mint, and parsley, basil naturally retains little flavor when it's dried. So how do you keep that just-picked taste all winter long—or even longer?

➡ Freeze those leaves! Even pungent herbs, such as thyme, rosemary, sage, and bay, fare better when they're frozen. They don't keep their fresh-from-the-garden good looks, of course, but they do pack almost the same flavor wallop they had the day you picked them. Here are some of the easy-as-pie methods I use. Just pull out whatever quantity you want to cook with, and put the rest back in the freezer:

SUPER SOLUTION

Basil turns black when it's frozen. The color change doesn't affect the flavor, but who wants to eat black leaves? To keep them green, blanch them before freezing: Just put the leaves in a strainer, and pour boiling water over them for a second. Then, lay the leaves on paper towels, and let them cool naturally. Don't dip basil into ice water, as you do when you blanch vegetables—that will only dilute the flavor.

✿ Wrap bunches of herb sprigs (one kind per bunch) in aluminum foil.

✿ Chop fresh herbs, and freeze them in plastic containers.

✿ Purée chopped herbs with water, butter, or olive oil. Then pour the mixture into ice cube trays. When the cubes are frozen, pop them out of the trays, and store them in plastic containers or freezer bags.

Help—We're Buried in Herbs!

You know the old saying, "When life hands you a lemon, make lemonade"? Well, what do you do when Mother Nature (or your own misjudgment at seed shopping time) hands you more herbs than you can possibly use—fresh, dried, *or* frozen?

➡ Make herbal vinegar, that's what! It packs a flavor punch you'll never find in store bought vinegars, and it's as easy to make as a pot of tea. Why, in just a few hours, you can whip up a year's worth of Christmas, birthday, and hostess gifts. What's more, the final product looks as elegant as anything you'd pay megabucks for at a fancy-food boutique (see "Jerry's Easy Herbal Vinegar," below).

✦ Miracle Mix ✦

JERRY'S EASY HERBAL VINEGAR

Grandma Putt had a term for anything that was a snap to make, but knocked folks' socks off when you served or gave it to them as a present. She said those recipes had a "high glory factor." Well, if you want to bask in glory out of all proportion to your efforts, tuck this formula into your recipe book.

6 to 8 fresh herb sprigs
1 qt. of good quality vinegar

Wash and dry the herbs, then pack them into a clean, quart-sized glass canning jar. Heat the vinegar until it's warm (don't let it boil!), and pour it over the herbs. Cover the jar opening with plastic wrap or waxed paper,* and screw on the top. Put the jar in a dark place at room temperature, and let it sit for a couple of weeks. Then open the lid and sniff. You'll know the vinegar is ready when you get a strong fragrance of herbs. Strain out the solids, pour the flavored vinegar into a pretty bottle, and tuck in a fresh herb sprig or two. Then get ready for all the oohs and ahs!

*If the jar lid is plastic, you can dispense with this step. The inner wrap simply keeps metal lids from reacting with the vinegar.

CHAPTER 12

Healthy Herbs

The home-grown herbal remedies Grandma Putt reached for way back when are all the rage now. But, just like any other plants, herbs have their own share of woes from time to time. Those troubles won't last long, though. Whether it's crafty critters or awful ailments that are after your plants, or you're simply confused about what to do with your health-giving harvest, here's some super solutions.

Stricken Seeds 'n Seedlings

Easy Does It!

You're hankering to grow some health-giving herbs, but you're looking for some that are extra easy to please. Where do you start?

➡️ The winners in the chart below are a snap to grow from seed sown right in the garden, and besides curing what ails you (or helping to), they'll add real pizzazz to your green scene. What's more, this crew couldn't be simpler to use: In each case, you can just brew a cup of tea, and drink to your good health.

Herb	How It Helps
Angelica (*Angelica archangelica*), Zones 4 to 9. Grows to 8 feet tall, with fragrant, white, umbrella-shaped flower clusters on 6-foot stalks in summer.	Aids digestion, reduces gas, eases menstrual cramps, relieves cold and flu symptoms.
Anise hyssop (*Agastache foeniculum*), Zones 4 to 8. A bushy, 4-foot plant with spikes of lavender-blue flowers in summer and fall. Flowers and leaves smell and taste like licorice.	Clears up sore throats and congestion, fights indigestion.
Bee balms, a.k.a. bergamot or Oswego tea (*Monarda*), Zones 3 to 9. An upright 2- to 3-footer, with sweet-smelling leaves and red flowers that attract butterflies, hummers, and bees.	Helps ease nausea, vomiting, and flatulence.
Feverfew (*Tanacetum parthenium*), Zones 5 to 9. A beautiful, 2-foot-tall plant with lacy, light green leaves and delicate, daisy-like flowers from early summer to early fall.	Zaps headaches; eases dizziness, tinnitus, and arthritis pain; relieves menstrual cramps.
Roman chamomile (*Chamaemelum nobile*), Zones 3 to 8. Grows 4 to 6 inches tall, and spreads out to 1 foot or more, with sweet-scented, lacy leaves and white, daisy-like flowers in summer.	Relieves muscle spasms, soothes stomachaches, kills germs that produce gingivitis, relaxes nerves.

The Seeds Are Fine—*You're* Stricken!

It's time to sow your herb seeds, and your bad back is kicking up a fuss. How can you get your garden planted if you can't bend over?

➥ Sow standing up, that's how! Just get a piece of PVC pipe that reaches approximately from your waist to the ground. Then, send the seeds down through the pipe and onto the prepared seedbed. When the seeds are where you want them, use your foot or a hoe to firm the soil over them.

Double-Duty Herbs

So, you say you'd like to try some medicinal herbs, but you don't want to fuss with a whole separate garden?

➥ This one's easy. Most of the same plants that spice up your cooking do double duty as health-care workers. Here's a few of my favorites:

Basil fights cold and flu infections, sharpens mental alertness, and even cures warts.

Bay contains chemicals that fight tooth decay and ease the pain of headaches and stomachaches.

Dill soothes upset stomachs, eases muscle spasms, freshens breath, and (for all you nursing moms) stimulates the flow of breast milk.

Garlic kills bacteria, clears lung congestion, lowers blood sugar and cholesterol levels, boosts circulation, and acts as an antihistamine.

Sage restores vitality and strength, fights fevers, and soothes mucous membrane tissue—curing mouth ulcers, sore gums and throats, and even laryngitis, in the process.

Put 'Em There

It's early spring, and your self-sowing herbs are popping up, just as you hoped they would. The only trouble is, they're coming up in all the wrong places.

➡ This year, you have only one choice. As soon as those younguns have their second set of true leaves, dig up the seedlings, and put them where you want them to grow. Then, in the fall, try this trick:

❧ Get your planting bed ready. Pound two stakes in the ground, and run a string between them, a foot or so above the soil surface.

❧ Wait until the seeds are almost ripe on the plants, then cut the flowers from the plants, leaving 6 inches or so of stem.

❧ Tie the flower stalks to the string, so that the seedheads are hanging upside down, a few inches above the ground. When the seeds are ready, they'll drop onto the soil, exactly where you want them—and you won't have to fuss with gathering the seeds from the flowers.

Too Darn Damp

You had a feeling that your site was a little too moist and shady to grow herbs, but you tried anyway. Now, your little seedlings have keeled over and died. Is there any way to grow herbs in these conditions?

➡ You're in luck. While it's true that most herbs need well-drained soil and plenty of sunshine, there are exceptions. When you

THEY'LL BUZZ OFF

Bees won't go near feverfew, so keep it far away from fruits or vegetables that depend on insects to pollinate their blossoms. On the flip side, feverfew's bee repelling talent makes it a perfect choice for poolside planters, children's play areas, or any other place where you'd rather not have buzzers on parade.

replant your bed, reach for these moisture- and shade-lovers:

Angelica (*Angelica archangelica*)

Bee balms (*Monarda*)

Mints (*Mentha*)

Parsley (*Petroselinum crispum*)

Sweet woodruff (*Galium odoratum*)

The Old Home Ground

If you've tried growing herbs in containers, and the results have been, well, not what you'd hoped for, there's a good chance that the problem was in the soil. To grow their best, herb plants need soil that lets their roots spread easily, picking up exactly the right balance of water, air, and nutrients. Too little or too much of any of that trio will leave plants unhealthy, or even dead.

➡ Here's my simple formula for an herb-pleasing potting mix: equal parts of coarse perlite, coarse sand, top quality topsoil, and good compost. You can buy all of them at garden centers. (Of course, you can also make your own compost following any of my easy recipes in Chapter 15.)

Miracle Mix

HERB BOOSTER TONIC

Even herbs enjoy a nice, cool drink when the going gets hot. Quench their thirst with this summertime pick-me-up.

**1 can of beer
1 cup of ammonia
½ cup of Murphy's Oil Soap®
½ cup of corn syrup**

Mix all of these ingredients in a 20-gallon hose-end sprayer. Then spray your herbs every six weeks during the growing season.

How Dry It Is

There are few containers finer-looking than a terra-cotta strawberry jar with lush, healthy herbs spilling out of its pockets. There's just one problem: Those tall pots dry out fast, and when you water, it's hard to get the soil evenly wet.

To solve that little dilemma, get a piece of 2-inch-diameter PVC pipe that's just long enough to reach from the bottom of the pot to the top of the soil surface. Drill holes through the sides (make sure some of them line up with the pockets in the jar). Then, before you fill the container with soil, insert the pipe in the center so that the top will be just at the soil surface. When you water, pour that H_2O directly into the pipe. It'll seep through the holes and spread out in all directions.

Wretched Roots

What Rotten Luck!

If your herbs are looking a tad too soft and lush above ground, and pests are traveling from near and far to get at them, then the trouble lies below ground. In short, the roots are getting too much to eat. They're getting an overdose of nitrogen, which encourages mountains of leafy growth. That, in turn, makes the plants sitting ducks for slugs, snails, rot, and other diseases. But you *can* save the day.

First, clip away the lush foliage, and lay down a blanket of compost. It'll help balance the nitrogen overload, and fight off pests and diseases. Then put those plants on a diet and always remember: Most herbs are light to moderate feeders.

Feed 'Em Right

Okay, you've administered dietary first aid. Now you need to feed your herbs for the rest of the growing season. Exactly what does a light to moderate feeder eat—and when?

➤ Give your herbs a light meal two or three times during the growing season, but stop feeding them at least a month before you expect the first frost. Feeding too late in the fall tends to weaken plants and make them more susceptible to winter's cold. As for what kind of chow to serve, my upright, bushy herbs perform their best on what Grandma Putt called punched-up compost. By that, she meant a mixture of good-quality compost and either rabbit, chicken, or sheep manure. Why those three? Because those critters' waste material has a higher concentration of the nutrients that herbs need than either horse or cow manure has. I use about 2 parts compost to 1 part manure. I let it sit for about a week, so the hot compost can kill any lingering weed seeds. Then I spread it around my plants, and gently work it into the top inch or so of soil. I can almost hear those herbs say "Yum, yum!"

Miracle Mix

SLUGWEISER

Beer is the classic bait for slug and snail traps. But what attracts the slimy thugs isn't the alcohol in the beer, or even the hops and malt—it's the yeast. So fill up your traps with this potion. After all, why waste a good brewski on the enemy?

1 lb. of brown sugar
½ package (1½ tsp.) of dry yeast

Pour these ingredients into a 1-gallon jug, fill it with warm water, and let the mixture sit for two days, uncovered. Then pour it into your slug traps, and watch the culprits belly up to the bar!

So Long, Slugger!

Slugs and snails zero in on unhealthy herbs the way ants throng to a picnic. Of course, there are a jillion good baits you can use, but what if you've

got kids or pets on the scene? Even if your bait is harmless to the good guys, you don't want it disappearing into the mouths of your family and friends!

➡ I've got a nifty trick for serving up bait in a way that *only* slugs and snails can get to it: First, find some wide-mouthed pint bottles, like the kind many juices come in. Pour about an inch of my Slugweiser (at left) into each bottle, then sink the traps in the ground so the top of the bottle is just at ground level. The slimers will slither up to the edge, and dive right in, but the beverage at the bottom will be beyond the reach of small human hands and long canine tongues.

Sickly Stems

Whiteflies on the Wing

You brushed up against your herb plants, and a white cloud rose up from the stems and leaves. It can be only one thing: white-flies on the wing. So how do you shoot 'em down?

➡ Whiteflies have so many natural predators that outdoors, they're usually more of a nuisance than a threat to your plants. Still, things can get out of hand now and then. When that happens, try this trick: Staple a 24- by 36-inch sheet of yellow posterboard to a wooden stake, and coat the paper with petroleum jelly or commercial sticky stuff. Shove the stake into the ground so that the sticky trap is behind your stricken herbs. Then, spray the plants with water from the garden hose. You'll blast the culprits off the plants and right onto the sticky trap.

Unwanted House Guests

It's one thing to do battle with whiteflies outdoors, but once they come indoors, they can do big-time damage to your herbs and other houseplants. Don't panic, though: Help is as close as your broom closet.

➥ Just grab your vacuum cleaner, and vacuum those pests right up. To make the job even easier, wrap some yellow electrical tape around the vacuum hose nozzle. The tiny terrors will flock to the scene. When you've made a clean sweep, tuck the vacuum cleaner bag into the freezer to kill the flies. Then, dump the whole thing onto your compost pile.

Is Their Diet Off-Balance?

Whiteflies seem to target plants that aren't getting enough phosphorus or magnesium in their diet. So test your soil. Then...

➥ If the results show a deficiency of either nutrient, or both, reach for one of the following healthy snacks:

Phosphorus: bonemeal, fish emulsion, poultry manure, seaweed

Magnesium: dolomitic limestone, Epsom salts

A GREENHOUSE HELPER

If your indoor herbs live in their own sunroom or greenhouse, you're in luck: A teeny-tiny hired gun can charge to your rescue. An almost invisible parasitic wasp, *Encarsia formosa*, a.k.a. whitefly parasite, lays its eggs in whitefly nymphs—thereby keeping the population to a minimum. You can order your own posse from garden catalogs.

Lousy Leaves

Pesky Powder

You've seen this grayish white powder before, and here it is again, all over your herb leaves. Just about any herb can be the target for powdery mildew, but bee balm, lemon balm, and rosemary are especially vulnerable. What's the cure?

If you catch the nasty stuff in its early stages, just clip off the affected leaves, and spray your plants from top to bottom with my Magical Mildew Control Tonic (see page 247). Once the mildew has really taken hold, though, your best bet is to cut the plants back to the ground. They'll resprout, clean as a whistle. Then, to fend off further trouble, follow the healthy plant guidelines and the disease prevention tips in Chapter 14.

That's *Not* Cat Food!

Is Puffy nibbling on the leaves of your indoor herbs? Or, even worse, using the potting soil as a litter box?

➡ This trick will make her scurry in a hurry: Just moisten a cotton ball with lemon-oil furniture polish, and set it on the soil in the pot. For extra large plants, such as bay trees or mature rosemary shrubs, use two or three cotton balls per pot.

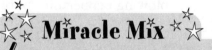

Miracle Mix

TEA TIME FOR APHIDS

Aphids start showing up near the end of spring, and they love tasty new herb leaves. If the pesky pests are making a mess of your future medicine, give them a sip of this tantalizing tea.

½ cup of parsley flakes
2 tbsp. of minced garlic
3 cups of water

Mix all of these ingredients together, and boil down to 2 cups. Strain and cool. Put 2 cups of the tea in a 20-gallon hose-end sprayer, and drench your herbs until the aphids are history.

There Goes My Cough Medicine!

Your anise hyssop is wilting, shoots are curling, new leaves are dying, and you're mad as the dickens—you'd been planning to use that crop to make throat-soothing tea all winter long. Who's depleting your medicine chest?

 Tarnished plant bugs, that's who! These tiny tricksters *love* anise hyssop. On the downside, you probably have a lot more rascals on the scene than you think you have. Tarnished plant bugs are both small (less than 1/4 inch long) and shy, and they tend to duck out of sight when they're disturbed. On the upside, you have several potent weapons at your beck and call. My favorite: a vacuum cleaner. If vacuuming bugs off plants isn't your style, give the rascals a taste of my Peppermint Soap Spray (see page 135). Just make sure you rinse it off the leaves before you make your anise hyssop tea, or you might end up blowing peppermint bubbles!

Failing Flowers

Okay, Now What?

Now that you've got your herbal medical team churning out health-giving leaves and flowers galore, what do you do with them? Should you dry everything?

 Of course, you *can* dry your herbs, and most likely, you'll want to dry some of them. (For my simple drying directions, see Chapter 13.) The fact is, though, that most herbs lose some of their healing potency when they're dried. To capture the biggest punch, I like to freeze my herbs, or preserve them in vinegar or tinctures. (For my favorite freezing and vinegar-making methods, see Chapter 11.)

The Truth about Tinctures

If you've never made an herbal tincture, you might think you need a degree in pharmacy just to understand the procedure.

The fact is, though, it's as easy as 1-2-3-4. Here's all you need:

- ½ cup or so of fresh herbs (leaves, flowers, or both)
- Vodka, gin, or brandy (80 to 100 proof)*
- A clean glass jar with a screw-on top

Then, follow this routine:

1. Harvest your herbs, rinse, towel them dry, and chop finely.

2. Put the herbs in the jar, and pour in the alcohol until it reaches 2 to 3 inches above the top of the herb layer.

3. Cover the jar with a tight-fitting lid, and put it in a warm, dark place. Let the mixture sit for at least four to six weeks—the longer, the better. During that period, shake the jar now and then to keep the herbs from packing down on the bottom.

4. Strain out the solids, and pour the liquid into clean, fresh bottles. Label them, and store them in a cool, dark place out of reach of children. Then, take the tincture for whatever ails you. How you take it is your call: You can sip it straight from a spoon, or mix it in warm water or fruit juice.

* If you're sensitive to alcohol, or you're making the tincture for children, substitute warmed (not boiled!) vinegar or a half-and-half mixture of glycerin and distilled water.

NOT FOR PEOPLE ONLY

We all know that herbal teas can be good for what ails us humans. But did you know that your plants can benefit from these healthy brews, too? Here's a trio of tasty examples:

Chamomile strengthens young seedlings, helps protect them from damping-off fungus, and fights mildew.

Comfrey spurs the development of seedlings (especially tomatoes), controls blackflies, and fends off diseases.

Valerian root attracts and energizes the local earthworm population.

CHAPTER 13

Crafter's Crops

G randma Putt always said that there's no finer gift than one you've made with your own two hands—especially when you've grown the makings in your garden. And there are few greater frustrations than watching your home-grown, herbal craft supplies fall prey to varmints or your own beginner's unluckiness. Well, here's a gift for you: solutions to more problems than you can shake a wreath at.

Stricken Seeds 'n Seedlings

Lousy Lavender

You planted a whole bed of lavender seeds and all you got were a couple of scrawny plants. What happened?

There could be a couple of reasons for that show of non-strength. Either you chose the wrong kind of lavender to grow from seed, or you failed to give the seeds the preplanting treatment they needed. Here's what could've gone wrong:

The wrong stuff. Most varieties of lavender don't come true from seed. You need to buy started plants, or grow them from cuttings or root divisions. (See "A Healthy Send-Off" on page 41.)

The wrong routine. If you're really itchin' to sow seeds, there are a few lavenders you could try, including the English types 'Hidcote', 'Munstead', and 'Lady'. But be forewarned: The seeds tend to be slow, erratic germinators, and the plants vary in height, growth habit, and flower color. If you're determined, you can do it—*if* you first perform a minor surgical procedure called "scarifying." Before you plant the seed, you need to nick its hard outer coat with a sharp knife or razor blade. Once you've done that, the little seedlings will spring right up, and you'll get...what you get!

HAPPY CAMPERS

These perennial herbs perform best when you sow their seed (or, in the case of garlic, bulbs) in the fall, rather than spring:

Angelica (*Angelica archangelica*)
Caraway (*Carum carvi*)
Dill (*Anethum graveolens*)
Garlic (*Allium*)
Mustards (*Brassica*)
Parsley (*Petroselinum crispum*)
Soapwort (*Saponaria officinalis*)
Sweet cicely (*Myrrhis odorata*)

It's All in the Timing

Lavender isn't the only herb with reluctant seeds. Some other herbs can be pretty darned stubborn, too. Does that mean you should avoid growing from seeds altogether?

 No. Instead, sow the seeds in the fall. Some herbs break out of their shells much faster when they're exposed to alternating spells of freezing and thawing, wet and dry soil, and wild temperature swings (in other words, Old Man Winter's usual shenanigans).

They Won't Give Up!

You thought you'd routed all the weeds before you planted your herbs. Now, though, some tough customers are popping up among the little seedlings. You don't want to start digging and pulling, because sure as shootin', you'll destroy some of your baby plants' roots in the process. How can you get rid of the intruders without hurting your young plants?

It's simple: Give those weeds a lethal shower—in their own stalls. Here's my four-step process.

Step 1: Cut each weed back to ground level.

Step 2: Slice the bottom off a 1-quart plastic bottle that has a screw-on top. (You'll need one bottle for each troublesome weed.) Set the bottle over the weed, and push it about 2 inches into the ground.

Step 3: Mix up a batch of my Weed Wipeout (at right), stick your sprayer head into the top of the sunken bottle, and pull the trigger. Drench that weed stub until the potion is running off in streams. Then screw the top back on the bottle.

Step 4: Leave the bottle in place for a couple of weeks, then inspect your handiwork. Chances are, your weed woes will be history. But if any extra-tough guys are still showing signs of life, give them another dose of the tonic. Before long, they, too, will go belly-up!

Doesn't Seem Like Old Times

You want to plant some of your herb seedlings in containers, and you've found some great-looking, terra-cotta pots at the garden center. There's just one problem: They look a little too *new* to be holding old-time crafting herbs. Your little seedlings will soon be ready to leave their starter flats and move into more grown-up quarters. Is there any way you can age those pots fast?

➡️ There sure is! Just "paint" the containers with plain yogurt, and set them outside in the shade. As the yogurt dries, moss and lichen will grow on the terra-cotta surface. Keep an eye on the pots, and when they've aged enough to suit you, hose them off gently. Generally, it takes a week or so to produce an authentic-looking "antique."

Thyme for Fun

Common thyme *(Thymus vulgaris)* can give your food a tasty kick, alright, but when you're trying to jazz up craft projects, you want more than zesty flavor—you want thyme that looks great, too.

➡️ Expand your thyme frame. Plant any of this quartet,

⭐ Miracle Mix ⭐

WEED WIPEOUT

When you've got weeds that won't take no for an answer, knock 'em flat on their backs with this potent potion.

1 tbsp. of gin
1 tbsp. of vinegar
1 tsp. of liquid dish soap
1 qt. of very warm water

Mix all of these ingredients together, and pour the solution into a hand-held mist sprayer. Then, drench the weeds to the point of run-off, taking care not to spray any nearby plants.

and your wreaths, potpourri, and dried arrangements will be the talk of the town:

Caraway thyme (*T. herba-barona*) has tiny, dark green leaves that smell exactly like (you guessed it) caraway seeds, with clusters of rose-pink flowers in midsummer.

Creeping thyme, a.k.a. mother-of-thyme (*T. serpyllum*) forms flat, dense mats of green or gray leaves, and churns out masses of flowers in late spring and summer, in white, red, lilac, or pink.

Lemon-scented thyme (*T. x citriodorus*) has just the aroma you'd expect, along with pretty pink or purple flowers, and leaves in shades of yellow, gold, or silvery green (depending on the variety).

Woolly thyme (*T. pseudolanuginosus*) has tiny flowers in shades of pink or mauve, and gray, furry foliage that makes you want to reach down and pet it.

Wretched Roots

Toughen Up

You say you just can't grow lavender for love nor money—even though you've given it prime space in your fertile, well-tended perennial border? Well, you hit the problem right on the head, pal: Your lavender is being coddled to death!

 To make your lavender happy, move it to a place where its roots can strut their stuff. Where is that? The driest, rockiest spot you've got, that's where! This old-time herb might produce blossoms that take you right back to your grandma's cozy parlor, but take it from me: Lavender is one tough cookie! It performs best in spots that leave other plants gasping "Water! Water!"

Valerian Vandalism

Your valerian is in full bloom, and you stroll out to admire the flowers. You look down...and see roots! Some critter has been digging them up and chewing on them! And the telltale footprints left behind indicate that the culprit is a cat. What do you do to keep the kitty away?

Cats like nothing better than chewing on valerian roots. But as much as they love valerian, they hate another great-looking herb: rue. That gives you a defense strategy that couldn't be simpler—or better looking. Just plant rue among your valerian, and Fluffy will flee, *fast*!

YOU MIGHT RUE THE DAY

Rue can solve your cat problems, alright, and other garden-variety woes besides. But this old-time charmer does have its dark side. Here's a closer look at this herb:

Good points. Besides keeping ornery cats at bay, rue repels Japanese beetles, fleas, and both houseflies and horseflies. It also happens to be a great looking, easy-to-grow perennial, with blue-green leaves, small, greenish yellow flowers, and decorative brown seedheads that look great tucked into wreaths and swags.

Bad points. Rue has an absolutely drop-dead effect on basil and sage—so don't put it anywhere near that duo! Also, some folks are allergic to the sap in rue's foliage. If you're one of those unlucky folks, make sure you wear gloves and long sleeves whenever you work with the plants.

Sickly Stems

Trouble in the Middle

You've just moved to the sunny South, and you've planted the same herbs you loved up North. Now your artemisia, woolly thyme, and gray santolina are giving you nothing but trouble. After a heavy rain the other day, they all started rotting in the center, at the base of the stems. You've planted your herbs in raised beds with well-drained soil, and you're not overwatering. So what gives with the gray guys?

 They're just carrying on business as usual. Herbs that have white, gray, or silvery leaves are the dickens to grow in a hot, humid climate—and when they get rained on in those conditions, they generally *do* rot. To these plants, heaven on earth is a place with plenty of sunshine, low humidity, and hot, dry winds. My best advice: Get rid of those weather wimps, and stick with herbs that are happy on your new home turf.

GIVE IT YOUR BEST SHOT

If you really have your heart set on using some beautiful silvery leaves in your craft projects, and you live where the weather is hot and damp, you can still give it your best shot. Here's how:

Say "no" to organic mulch. It encourages moisture retention, which you *don't* want in this situation. Instead, mulch your gray and silver plants with pebbles, gravel, or coarse sand. That way, you'll keep the leaves and stems dry at soil level, and allow for air circulation.

Lift 'em up. If you want to grow low, spreading plants, such as creeping thyme, plant them in tall containers to keep stems and foliage off the ground. (A strawberry jar or a tall clay flue tile is perfect.)

Give 'em shelter. When a rainstorm threatens, whisk your container-grown herbs under a roof, and cover in-ground plants. Remove the topcoats the minute the rain stops, so that fresh air can circulate.

Sprawling Stems

The stems of your southernwood are long, lanky, and sprawling across the bed like kids at a slumber party. Do you have a major problem on your hands?

 No, just a minor inconvenience. From the sound of it, the plants are just getting a little more shade than they like. As long as the plants are healthy, you don't need to move them. Just shear the stems back almost to the ground in late spring or early summer to encourage bushier growth.

Lousy Leaves

They're So Small!

You planted lemon balm in your sunny herb garden, thinking you'd get bushels and bushels of big, lemon-scented leaves to use in your potpourri. You got lots of lemony leaves, alright, but they're anything but big. How come?

 Although lemon balm will grow beautifully in full sun, it produces its biggest, most succulent leaves in partial shade. So, either move your plants to shadier territory, or keep them where they are, and live with the diminutive foliage.

Changing Colors

You moved your potted woolly thyme into a shady area because you were afraid it was suffering in the sun. But the beautiful silver leaves turned green! What went wrong?

 In a word, nothing. If you move silver-leaved herbs into the shade, in any climate, the foliage will turn green. It's not a permanent change, though; when they're back in the sun, the leaves will revert to their normal silvery gray.

Mitey Troubling

Your herbs have sailed through the summer without a care in the world. Now you've brought them indoors for the winter, and suddenly, they're under attack. They've got dry, yellow, stippled leaves, covered with little white dots.

To fend off spider mites, add humidity to the air with this simple trick: Fill some trays with pebbles, and set your pots on top of them. Then, pour water into the tray to within about ½ inch of the stones' surface. Add more water as the level goes down, but don't let it touch the bottom of the pots—you want your plants to be sitting *over*, not *in*, the water.

The marauders are spider mites. These invaders are so tiny that you could waste hours looking for them, but there's no mistaking their damage. For some reason, dry indoor air seems to call out to these terrible tykes. But you can fight back.

➡ Here's how to thwart a mite attack:

✿ Spray your herbs with water or, if the plants are small enough, set them in the bathtub, and turn on the shower. Just be sure to cover the pot with a plastic bag first, so the soil doesn't wash out.

✿ If good ol' H_2O doesn't do the trick, kill the culprits with Grandma Putt's Simple Soap Spray (see page 94).

It's Gone Bald!

When the weather turned cold, you moved your lemon verbena indoors, and the next thing you knew, it had lost all of its leaves. Is it dead?

No, just dormant. Lemon verbena tends to drop its leaves when you move it indoors. Just keep the plant dry and cool until it resprouts, then start to water and feed it again.

Give 'Em A Pinch

Your herbs are healthy and pest-free as can be, but they're not giving you the full, leafy growth that you'd like. What can you do about that?

Pinch 'em. Then pinch 'em again and again. Every week throughout the growing season, pluck or cut off the growing tip of every single shoot. If you can't do the job every week, just do the best you can. The more you pinch, the more new leaves (or fresh flowers) the plants will churn out.

What'll I Do with 'Em All?

You've got your pinching routine down pat. Now what can you do with all the little growing tips?

 A big supply of herb prunings can provide some top-notch health food for your compost pile. In particular, yarrow, valerian, and comfrey will jump-start the breakdown process for other plant ingredients. (For more on making "black gold," see Chapter 15.)

Plenty—there's gold in them thar tips! Depending on what kind of herbs they are, here are examples of how I handle my bonus leaves (or flowers):

✿ Toss basil, parsley, rosemary, or salad burnet in salads, casseroles, or stir-fries.

✿ Dry santolina, lavender, or artemisia to use in craft projects.

✿ Freeze mint, lemon balm, or scented geraniums in ice cube trays, and then use the cubes in drinks.

✿ Scatter rue, tansy, or mint around wherever you need to repel pesky pests, such as mice, moths, or fleas.

Failing Flowers

They Just Don't Look Good

Your herbs are ready to be harvested, and you're itchin' to spend the winter using them in all sorts of projects. There's just one problem: They don't have the clear color and vibrant good looks you'd been hoping for. You know the plants are healthy, though, and all season long, you've fed them with a good, balanced chemical fertilizer from the garden center. What's the problem?

➡ Their diet, that's what! Chemical fertilizer will supply all the nutrients any plant needs to grow on. But, for reasons of their own, herbs produce their best-looking show and their most potent, volatile oils when they're on an organic diet. So next year, give your plants either punched-up compost (see page 329), a commercial organic fertilizer, or one of my mix-it-yourself versions in Chapter 15.

Here's a super-simple way to dry stems that you plan to use for wreath-making: As you cut each one from the plant, lay it inside a bushel basket, and press it up against the side. As the stems dry, they'll take on the curved shape of the basket—exactly what you need for your wreaths.

It's Grimy Gray!

You cut stacks of artemisia to use in herbal wreaths. But as the stalks dried, the beautiful silvery foliage turned an ugly gray. What went wrong?

➡ My hunch is that you rushed the season a bit. If you cut artemisia too soon, it does turn gray (don't ask me why, though—I have no idea). But I do know that if you wait until after September 1 to harvest your sprays, they'll keep their silver color.

Yikes—They Look Like Ghosts!

You tied your cut herbs into bundles and hung them from your kitchen rafters to dry. It made the room look just like the pictures in country decorating magazines. Now, though, the leaves, stems, and flowers are pale reminders of their former, living selves. And, if there's any aroma left, it would take a beagle to find it. What went wrong?

➤ You forgot to turn out the lights (so to speak). Sunlight bleaches most herbs (except basil, which turns black in the sun), and strips out much of their flavor and scent. For first-class drying, you want a space that has three things going for it: low humidity, good air circulation, and near-total darkness.

High Tech or Low?

When it comes to drying herbs, there are folks who hang bunches in the attic, just like their grandmothers did, and folks who swear by microwave drying. Who's right?

➤ Everyone is—the choice is yours. Here's a rundown of some simple drying methods that even *I* can follow:

In a dark room. Set some old window screens or hardware cloth on bricks or other supports, and spread the herb stalks on top. Leave a door or window open a crack, and unless you live in a dry climate, turn on a fan or two for air circulation.

In a room where light penetrates. Gather the sprays into bunches of five or six stems each, and tie the stems together with twine. Then put each bunch upside down in a brown paper bag (making sure the herbs clear the bottom), fasten the top with a rubber band, and hang the bundles from anything that'll hold them.

In a microwave oven. Put a single layer of herbs between two paper towels, and nuke 'em for two to three minutes. Give them additional 30-second jolts as necessary until they're dry.

In a gas oven. Spread your herbs in a single layer on a baking sheet. Then, turn the oven to its lowest setting, and heat it, with the door open, for two to three minutes at the lowest temperature that will keep the pilot light on. (This will get rid of any moisture.) Turn off the oven, set the tray of herbs inside, and close the door.

About an hour before you plan to harvest your herbs, hose them off with a light spray of water to remove any lingering soil, bugs, or soap film. The leaves and stems will retain more of their fresh color and fragrance if you perform this necessary chore before cutting the plants (and you won't have the mess indoors, either). Then, as soon as the leaves are dry, grab your shears, and start clippin'.

Make Some Moth-Chasers

You've heard that moths steer clear of herbs, and you'd like to put them to the test, but which herbs do you use?

Use any combination that pleases your nose—moths hate 'em all. The best way to repel them is to make some moth-chasing sachets. They work every bit as well as those smelly old mothballs, and they're a snap to make. Just sew up some little cotton bags or buy them at a craft store (the size and shape are your call). Then fill the bags with some of these dried herbs:

Lavenders (*Lavandula*)

Santolinas (*Santolina*)

Southernwood (*Artemisia abrotanum*)

Tansies (*Tanacetum*)

Thymes (*Thymus*)

Wormwood (*Artemisia absinthium*)

PART V

NIP IT
in the Bud

CHAPTER 14

Great Groundwork

Wen it comes to garden-variety problem solving (as with so many other aspects of life), the best defense is a good offense. In this chapter, I'll let you in on some of my tried-and-true secrets for defeating trouble *before* it starts. How? By building strong, healthy soil, fending off dastardly diseases, and—last, but certainly not least—enlisting powerful allies in the war on plague and pestilence.

Super Soil Secrets

Soil Lingo 101

Confused by some of the terms gardeners use when they talk about soil? I don't blame you. But you don't have to stay in the dark.

➡ Here's a brief language lesson. After all, it's hard to solve a problem when you're not even sure what to call it!

Texture and structure refer to the relative amounts of sand, silt, and clay particles the soil contains. Sandy, or light, soil drains quickly and doesn't hold nutrients very well. Clay, or heavy, soil holds nutrients like a dream, but it also holds water all too well. When it gets wet, it sticks together like two sides of a peanut butter sandwich. A gardener's (and your average plant's) dream soil is loam: a nicely balanced mix of sand, silt, clay, and organic matter. Loam holds a good supply of nutrients, doesn't dry out too fast, and doesn't stay soggy, either.

pH (short for potential of hydrogen) measures acidity and alkalinity on a scale that runs from 0 (pure acid) to 14 (pure alkaline), with 7 being neutral. While there are many exceptions, most garden plants tend to perform best when the pH is close to neutral, because that's when nutrients in the soil are most available to the roots. Beneficial soil bacteria also seem to be most active in the 6.0 to 7.0 pH range.

Rich and lean have to do with fertility. Rich soil is chock-full of all the nutrients, including trace elements, that plants need for healthy growth. Soil that's lean has a low supply of nutrients.

It's Test Time!

The first secret to making super soil is to know what you're starting off with. So, you've tested your soil, and added the nutrients that the results called for, but your plants still don't seem happy. What's the problem?

➡ It could be that your soil sample was less than first-rate. Next time, have the job done by a professional testing lab. A good one can give you the full scoop on nutrients (major and minor), as well as soil texture. The lab will send you instructions for taking your samples, but here are some other pointers to keep in mind:

Don't take just one. Order separate tests for areas where you'll grow plants that have very different requirements—for instance, tomatoes in the vegetable garden and azaleas in the shrub border.

Give them a hint. When you send in your soil sample, include a list of everything you intend to grow. That way, the lab folks can provide you with specific recommendations for giving each plant the nutrients and pH range it needs.

Keep it clean. A stick, stone, or scrap of mulch can skew the test results. Even using a trowel that has iron in it can throw off the nutrient reading. So, work with a non-iron tool, fish out all foreign objects before you pack up your samples, and don't take your sample until at least 30 days after you've added fertilizer or any soil amendments.

Think "roots." You want to know what's in the soil that your plants' roots will be feeding from, so don't dig any deeper than that. For vegetables and flowers, stay within the top 5 to 6 inches of soil.

Think "normal." Don't take a sample from an atypical spot, like the site of a former compost pile, or a low area where puddles form after a rain.

For super-simple soil sampling, use a bulb planter. You'll pull up a neat, clean chunk of soil every time.

Sweet and Sour

Your soil test results are back, and they say that you need to alter your pH. You've been told to add sulfur to make your alkaline soil more acidic (below 7), or ground limestone to make your acidic soil more alkaline (above 7). But you've also heard that these are just quick fixes. Is this true?

Yep, you've heard right. Although sulfur and limestone are good, quick fixes, they don't last forever. Eventually, you'll have to crank up the old spreader all over again. And neither of these minerals does a thing for the soil structure. I've got a better plan: Add the right kind of organic matter in the first place. You'll get longer-lasting results and improve the structure of your soil at the same time. The chart on page 92 lists some of my favorite sweet-and-sour condiments.

Hard-Hearted Hardpan

You were digging a hole for a new tree, when your shovel hit what felt like a concrete sidewalk. It wasn't, though. It was hardpan, a layer of soil that's so compacted, it can take a pickaxe to break through it. Water just sits on top of the layer, rotting any roots that happen to come along. So, what should you do—go at it with a jackhammer, or rent a pricey, high-powered tiller, and let 'er rip?

You could, but it won't really solve the problem, and it might make matters worse. Tilling the soil can compact the pores, so that air and water can't move through. Repeated tilling, especially in clay soil, can actually cause hardpan to form. But there's a simple way to get rid of this nasty stuff, or keep it from forming in the first place: Just reach for my favorite magic bullet—organic matter.

Hit the Road, Jack!

If tilling is a no-no (see "Hard-Hearted Hardpan," page 303), how *do* you get organic matter into hard-as-rock soil?

 If you want to start a whole new planting bed, whip up one of my super soil sandwiches (at right). To soften up the hardpan in your whole yard over time, go at it piece by piece: Every time you have some organic matter on hand, dig a hole, toss in your stash, and refill the hole. It's best if the hole reaches down to the hardpan layer, but if you don't have time to dig that far, don't bother; just go deep enough to cover whatever material you're planning to bury. The depth could range from an inch or so for a couple of tea bags, to a foot or more for tree and shrub prunings. As the material decomposes, it will eventually break up the hard stuff—and keep it broken up.

WE'LL HAVE A BALL!

Although a professional lab test will tell you the texture of your soil, it's easy—and fun—to try this do-it-yourself version. Simply roll a handful of moist (not wet, and not dry) soil into a ball, just like a snowball. Then squeeze it hard. If it crumbles into a pile that looks like left-over cake crumbs, congratulations! You've got loam. If the ball just packs more solidly, like a billiard ball, your soil is mostly clay. And if you can't even form a ball with your soil, it's too sandy.

It's Not So Hard

What if you don't have a hardpan problem, or even clay soil? Maybe your home ground is sandy, rocky, or chock-full of big-city grit. Is tilling a no-no for *all* soil types?

Unless you've got a major hardpan problem, it's fine to add a large quantity of organic matter to the soil, and till it in deeply. It's the fastest, most efficient way to improve your soil. Just don't do any more tilling than you have to, and never work when the ground is wet—that will give you compacted soil faster than you can say "Step on it!"

A Super Soil Sandwich

Your soil isn't fit to grow much of anything. You know that big doses of organic matter would help, but you don't have the time or the inclination to get out there and dig for hours on end. Should you just pave your yard and grow everything in pots?

➡ Well, you *could* do that, but there's an easier road to a great-looking green scene. In fact, you can turn that no-good ground into fertile, fluffy beds without lifting a shovel—or renting a tiller. It's best to start the action in the spring, a year before you intend to plant. Here's what you should do:

Step 1: Mark off your planting beds. If you want straight-sided plots, use stakes and string. For curvy shapes, lay a rope or garden hose on the ground.

Step 2: If you have

HOLEY MOLEY!

My hole improvement method isn't just for soil with hardpan. It's a simple way to add get-up-and-grow power to any kind of soil. Best of all, any kind of organic matter will work, in virtually any combination. You don't even need to think about carbon-to-nitrogen ratios as you do with a serious compost pile. (For the lowdown on that, see Chapter 15.) What can you toss into your holes? Grass clippings, leaves, and vegetable scraps are obvious choices, but here are some hole fillers that you might not think of:

- Coffee grounds
- Dirty paper birdcage liners
- Feathers
- Hair from your (or your pets') brushes
- Leftover rice or pasta (minus sauces)
- Newspaper (worms love it!)
- Old pieces of cotton, linen, or wool (no synthetic fabrics)
- Paper egg cartons
- Paper towel and toilet paper rolls
- Peanut shells
- Shredded junk mail (just skip the glossy paper)
- Tea bags
- Used vacuum cleaner bags, complete with contents
- Wine corks
- Wood chips

hardpan, puncture the layer in a few places, using a garden fork, or even a hammer and metal rod. That way, earthworms can penetrate the nasty stuff and eventually soften it.

Step 3: Lay a 1- to 2-inch-thick layer of newspapers over the bed, overlapping the edges and trampling tall weeds as you go. (Just ignore the turf grass and short weeds.) Then soak the papers thoroughly with water.

Step 4: Spread 1 to 2 inches of compost over the papers. Then cover the compost with 4 to 6 inches of whatever organic matter you can come by easily. Leaves, pine needles, dried grass clippings, seaweed, and shredded paper will all work like a charm.

Step 5: Add alternate layers of compost and organic matter until the stack reaches 12 to 24 inches high.

Step 6: Saturate the bed-to-be with my Super Soil Sandwich Dressing (at left), then go about your business. Meanwhile, the "sandwich" will cook, and by the following spring, you'll have 6 or 8 inches of loose, rich, super soil, ready for planting.

Step 7: Set in your seedlings, or sow your seeds, and mulch with compost, dried grass clippings, or finely shredded pine bark. As the plants grow, keep mulching. As time goes by, and the mulch breaks down, the layer of super soil will reach deeper and deeper into the ground (thanks to earthworms, beneficial bacteria, and other helpful soil dwellers).

Miracle Mix

SUPER SOIL SANDWICH DRESSING

When you've got your ingredients all stacked up, top off your "super soil sandwich" with this zesty condiment. It'll kick-start the cooking process, and by the following spring, your super soil will be rarin' to grow!

1 can of beer
1 can of regular cola (not diet)
1/2 cup of ammonia
1/4 cup of instant tea granules

Mix all of these ingredients in a bucket, and pour the solution into a 20-gallon hose-end sprayer. Then spray your "sandwich" until all the layers are saturated.

But I Want to Plant *Now!*

Spring has sprung, and you don't want to wait months for this sandwich to cook—you want (and need) to get some plants in the ground, pronto!

No problem! Just make the top layer with 4 to 6 inches of good-quality topsoil, or a half-and-half mix of compost and topsoil. Then, saturate it with my Super Soil Sandwich Dressing (at left), wait two weeks, and plant to your heart's content.

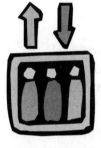

Up or Down?

It seems that every time you turn around, you hear somebody (including yours truly) raving about raised beds as the answer to all kinds of garden-variety soil problems. Well, these elevated planting sites can work wonders, alright, but there actually are times when you want to sink your beds, not raise them. So, how do you make the call?

You just need to understand how each type works. Here's a rundown:

Raised beds improve both drainage and air circulation, and make the soil warm up faster in the spring. This is the way to go if you have heavy, damp soil; you live in a humid climate; or you want to grow plants that

PAPER OR PLASTIC?

The next time the supermarket checkout clerk asks you that all-too-familiar question, say "Paper, please." Then, rush right home with those bags, tear them up, and add them to your super soil sandwich, toss them onto the compost pile (they're a first-class source of carbon), or just bury them in the ground. If you can run the sacks through a paper shredder, so much the better—the smaller the pieces are, the faster they'll break down into plant-pleasing soil.

need all the warmth they can get for as long as they can get it.

Sunken beds capture and hold moisture, and provide some protection from the wind. They're your answer if you have very sandy soil, or your climate is hot, dry, and windy.

Diseases: The Defensive Line

Stop Stressing

If your plants are getting sick for no apparent reason, it just might be that they're stressed out. Like people, plants tend to get out of sorts, or even fall ill, when the weather turns sticky and sweltering, or when a drought hits. So, what do you do?

➡ Nothing—just give your plants their own space. Don't spray or prune them, and don't pick any flowers or veggies unless they're about to go over the hill. Just give your garden a good drink of water, and let it rest awhile.

Cool It!

Are fungal and bacterial diseases getting out of hand in your garden?

➡ Here's good news: Scientists have proven that compost produces chemicals that are toxic to both kinds of dis-

GRANDMA PUTT'S
grow-how

Every time I emptied yet another bottle of milk, Grandma Putt always filled it up with water, shook it, and poured the solution onto some plant or other. She said that it acted like gentle liquid manure. Now scientists tell us that milk also helps protect plants against viruses. So don't you dare throw out another milk (or cream) container without sharing the contents with your garden!

eases. But that's not all! Researchers in British Columbia have recently discovered that compost produced in the easy, low-temperature way (like the stuff you get with my hole improvement method on page 305) is even more effective at germ warfare than high-maintenance hot compost. Maybe it pays to be lazy after all!

There's a Fungus Among Us—Again

If you live down South, where the climate is hot and humid, chances are you have more than your share of fungal woes. Can you get any relief?

➡ One way to clear out soil-dwelling fungi is to solarize your soil (heat it up to 150°F, or so). As a bonus, you'll also kill off pests like Colorado potato beetles and root-knot nematodes. For this process to work, you and Ol' Sol need to get cookin' during the hottest part of the year, which in most places is July and August. Here's my simple four-step plan:

Step 1: Dig up a plot of soil that's about 10 feet square. Then spread a 1- to 2-inch layer of fresh manure on top, and work it in well.

Step 2: Rake the soil into planting beds or rows (because you

Miracle Mix

ALL-AROUND DISEASE DEFENSE TONIC

Wet, rainy weather can mean diseases on the rampage, especially in late winter and early spring. Keep your outdoor scene healthy and happy with this timely tonic.

1 cup of chamomile tea
1 tsp. of liquid dish soap
½ tsp. of vegetable oil
½ tsp. of peppermint oil
1 gal. of warm water

Mix all of the ingredients together in a bucket. Mist-spray your plants every week or two until the really hot weather (75°F and higher) sets in. This elixir is strong stuff, so test it on a few leaves before totally spraying any plant.

won't be able to cultivate after the soil has been solarized).
Water well, then let the ground settle overnight.

Step 3: The next day, cover the plot with a sheet of clear, 3- to
6-mil plastic, and pile rocks or soil around the edges to keep it
in place. Patch any holes or tears that you find. Make sure the
plastic has some slack in it, so it can puff up (instead of blowing away or even bursting) when the heat starts rising.

Step 4: Wait about six weeks—longer if the weather's cool.
Then take off the plastic, water the soil, and plant your crops.
Don't dig any deeper than 6 inches, or you'll bring up untreated
soil—fungi, nematodes, and all.

Katie, Bar the Door!

**Once fungal diseases start romping through your
garden, they're a royal pain in the grass. Instead of
spending all that time doing battle, stop the foul
things before they get started. How?**

➡ Just follow these guidelines for first-class
fungus fighting—they'll help ward off
bacteria and viruses, too:

Plant smart. Look for plants that naturally thrive where you
live. They'll be stronger, and better able to fend off diseases and
pests. (For more on defensive planting, see Chapter 15.)

Keep it clean. Get rid of dead plant debris the minute you
spot it, especially at the base of plants, where fungal spores
thrive. And, every two weeks during the growing season, wash
down your whole yard and garden with my All-Season Clean-
Up Tonic (see page 59).

Mulch often. A blanket of fresh organic mulch will keep fungi
in the soil from splashing up on your plants when it rains or
when you water. It will also fend off disease-spreading weeds.

Aim low. When you water, point your hose at the ground. Better yet, install a drip irrigation system or a soaker hose. Wet foliage—especially after dark—is an open invitation to fungus.

Encourage allies. Good-guy bugs and other predators will polish off boatloads of disease-spreading insects. For more on enlisting your own troops, see page 314.

Search and destroy. Inspect your plants at least every couple of days, and if something doesn't look right, deal with it *now*. Tomorrow could be too late.

Go on the offensive. Every week during high fungus season, spray your plants—especially prime targets like roses—with my Fungus Fighter Tonic (see page 110).

Dear Jerry, I ordered what the catalog claimed were disease-resistant plants, but they still came down with the fungus I wanted to avoid. Was I taken for a ride? Or is this whole disease-resistance business just marketing hype? – P.B., New Orleans, Louisiana

Dear P.B., No, it's not marketing hype at all, just a misunderstanding of terminology. The word <u>resistant</u> simply means that a plant is less likely to fall victim to a particular disease (or pest) than its non-resistant counterparts are. But no plant is guaranteed to be completely immune to trouble. Also, the degree of resistance can vary greatly from one part of the country to another. In your case, you need to remember that fungi multiply like crazy in a humid climate, so any plant will be more prone to problems in New Orleans than the same variety would be in, say, Santa Fe or Las Vegas.

Hit Squad Hospitality

Help Wanted

All through this book, I've been telling you to call up an army of good guys to do your pest-control dirty work. But exactly how do you do that?

➡ Well, I'm glad you asked. Here's a look at my simple recruitment policy:

Lay off the pesticides. I know that's a frightening thought if you've been using them for a long time, but a couple of weeks after you quit cold turkey, throngs of good guys will show up and start chowing down on the bad guys.

Give 'em a drink. All living things need water, but you don't need to install a fancy pond. Just sink plant saucers into the ground, set some pebbles inside, and pour in water, letting some of the stones stick up above the surface. It gives insects— and insect eaters like toads, frogs, birds, and bats—a bar to belly up to.

Mix it up. Do what Grandma Putt and her pals did: Plant a mixed bag of flowers, herbs, veggies, trees, and shrubs. The more menu and shelter options you offer up, the more kinds of helpers will come calling—and the more kinds of pests they'll polish off.

Go native. If you want a first-class dream team on your side, look for plants that are native to your neck of the woods. Local heroes will flock to your doorstep.

That Was No Lady!

You ordered some ladybugs from a catalog, and set them out in your garden, according to the instructions on the package. But the next thing you knew, they'd flown the coop. What went wrong?

➤ Nothing went wrong—at least from the bugs' point of view. The ladybugs most often sold commercially are collected while they're hibernating, and when they wake up, their standard operating procedure is to move on to fresh territory. Instead of purchasing these beneficials, plant a floral welcome mat using some of the winners on page 315, especially morning glories and yarrow. Native ladybugs will flock to your side, and they'll stay on the job as long as you don't kill off their bad-bug food supply by other means.

GLOW, LITTLE GLOWWORM

The glowworms that my favorite songwriter, Johnny Mercer, wrote about are actually the larvae of fireflies, a.k.a. lightning bugs. The grown-ups don't do any pest-control work (they feed on flower pollen and nectar), but the babies gobble up some of the vilest villains around, including slugs, snails, maggots, and caterpillars.

Bad Buys on Good Guys

If it's not a good idea to buy ladybugs, does the same go for other beneficial insects?

➤ As far as I'm concerned, it goes double in spades for three of the most commonly sold hero bugs, and I'll tell you why:

Lacewings are a waste of money because they frequently die in shipment, and they're a snap to lure to your garden by planting morning glories, or anything in the mint, carrot, or sunflower family.

Praying mantises can be fun for kids to watch, but they eat as many good guys as they do pests. So who needs 'em?

Parasitic wasps send a passel of pests to their just reward and, unlike lacewings, they do ship well. What makes a cheapskate like me cringe is paying good money for critters that, just like lacewings, flock to the mint, carrot, and sunflower clans.

Good Buys on Good Guys

Are there any good-guy bugs worth buying? Or is hired help just too tough to find?

Just like Jeeves, this tiny quartet gives you plenty of satisfaction—and then some:

Beneficial nematodes are worth their weight in gold. In addition to killing off their own villainous relatives, these almost-microscopic critters demolish some of the most feared felons in all of gardendom, including seedcorn and onion maggots, Japanese beetle grubs, black vine weevils, wireworms, and strawberry root weevils. And that's just the tip of the iceberg!

Predatory mites are bigtime enemies of spider mites and thrips. Some are hardy and will stay on in any garden year-round; others survive winters only in the South. Garden centers and catalogs usually sell a premixed blend of types, so you're almost guaranteed protection from one year to the next.

Bt (*Bacillus thuringiensis*) is a beneficial bacterium that controls pests galore, including a number of leaf-eating beetles and

SUPER SOLUTION

Want to find flowers that will make great drawing cards for hero bugs? Here's a clue: Look at a vase of cut flowers. If you spot one that's dropped a lot of pollen on the table, you've found a winner!

weevils, mosquito and blackfly larvae, and scores of caterpillars. There are close to three dozen varieties of Bt, and each one is a specialist, so you need to read the label *very* carefully.

Milky spore disease is a combination insecticide that consists of two bacteria, *Bacillus popilliae* and *B. lentimorbus*. Its big—and well-deserved—claim to fame is that it kills the grubs of Japanese beetles and several of their relatives, but doesn't hurt other living things. This stuff doesn't come cheap, but if grubs and their parents are demolishing your lawn and garden, I say go for it—you'll be glad you did!

Say It with Flowers

You know that you need to plant flowers to entice good-guy bugs to your home ground, but how do you know who likes what?

➡ While it is true that a few bugs have very definite tastes, most of the troops are pleased as punch with any flower that's rich in pollen and nectar. The key to keeping beneficials on duty is to have *something* in bloom throughout the growing season, and plant a mixed bag of flowers that are rich in pollen and nectar. Here's a small sampling of proven enticements:

Asters (*Aster*)
Black-eyed Susans (*Rudbeckia*)
Boltonia (*Boltonia asteroides*)
Coreopsis (*Coreopsis*)
Cosmos (*Cosmos*)
Dill (*Anethum graveolens*)
English daisy (*Bellis perennis*)
Lavenders (*Lavandula*)

Mints (*Mentha*)
Morning glories (*Ipomoea*)
Pinks (*Dianthus*)
Purple coneflower (*Echinacea purpurea*)
Shasta daisy (*Leucanthemum* **x** *superbum*)
Sunflowers (*Helianthus*)
Yarrows (*Achillea*)

Not Just for Show

Hummingbirds are famous as nectar sippers—and hovering showboats. But here's something you might not know: These colorful little guys also eat hordes of insects. In fact, often when they seem to be drinking nectar from a flower, they're really snatching up tiny bugs. So how do you let the hummers know that you've got a pest-control job open?

➡ Plant bright red flowers that are tubular or trumpet-shaped. Once the little guys have taken up residence, they'll go for other colors, too, but it's red that draws them initially. Some of their favorite flowers (and mine, too) are fuchsias, bee balms, daylilies, snapdragons, lilies, and trumpet vines.

Let's Be Buddies

Bats and toads won't win many beauty contests, but when it comes to playing the pest-control game, you definitely want these guys on your team (and in your garden)! Just look at the stats:

• Every single night, an adult bat can put away 500 to 600 pests an hour, and its prime targets are mosquitoes, beetles, and the flying (and egg-laying) forms of cutworms, cabbageworms, and corn earworms.

• The average toad consumes 15,000 bad-guy bugs in a single year and—for reasons I don't understand and the experts probably don't either—almost none of the good guys. The menu includes armyworms, gypsy moth larvae, mosquitoes, and all kinds of beetles, but the specials of the day, every day, are slugs and cutworms.

For big-league players, these guys don't ask for much of a signing bonus. You can lure bats to your team simply by hanging bat houses in trees, at least 15 feet above the ground. (Most garden centers and catalogs sell sturdy, inexpensive ones.) All toads ask for is some shallow water, like a birdbath sunk into the ground, and a place to hide from noise, predators, and the midday sun. You can buy some pretty fancy "toad abodes," but an upside-down clay flowerpot with a gap broken out of the rim works just fine.

Varmint or Volunteer?

If you're used to thinking of birds as garden-variety thieves, think again. Sure, some of them will help themselves to your fruits and vegetables if they have the chance. But most birds eat bad bugs by the bucketload. Wingers that hang around for the winter also chow down on hibernating insects, grubs, and bug eggs. Still, if you've planted a brand-new veggie or annual flower garden, you don't want seed-eaters robbing you blind. So how do you tell friend from foe?

➡ Look at the beak. If a bird has a short, thick, cone-shaped beak, it's a seed-eater, and you want it to steer clear of newly sown beds until your plants are past the seedling stage. But, if it's got one of the following kinds of beaks, lay out the welcome mat—that bird's worth its weight in raspberries!

Short, wide, and gaping. Birds with this kind of schnoz grab food on the fly. Swifts, swallows, nighthawks, purple martins, and whippoorwills fit this bill.

Thin and pointy. A bird with this kind of beak downs more bugs than you can shake a row cover at. This team includes wrens, warblers, kingbirds, phoebes, and all sorts of flycatchers.

Hi, Hi, Birdie

A family of birds has set up nestkeeping in your favorite tree, and the winged warriors are polishing off pests galore. The trouble is, your neighbor's cat is trying to polish off your fine feathered friends. How can you make that cat scat?

➡ Here's a great-looking solution: Plant a climbing rose at the base of the tree on the sunny side, and train the thorny canes up the trunk. The birds-on-the-brain feline will get her kicks elsewhere.

CHAPTER 15

Planting for Success

Grandma Putt always said, "You can avoid an awful lot of yard trouble simply by putting the right plant in the right place." In this chapter, I'll tell you how to do just that. Then we'll look at nutrition secrets, because a well-balanced diet is as vital to a plant's health as it is to ours. Finally, I'll give you some timely troubleshooting tips, so you can spot small problems before they turn into great big ones.

Power Planting

Low-Maintenance, My Foot!

You don't want your yard and garden chores to take more time than you have to spend on them. So you played it smart: You read some books on low-maintenance landscaping, then filled your yard with the authors' four-star picks for easy-care plants. But you're still running from pillar to post, dawn to dusk, trying to keep everything shipshape. Are these uppity garden writers trying to pull the wool over your eyes?

➡️ Nope—nobody's trying to mislead you. While it's true that some plants tend to require less upkeep than others, "easy care" does not mean "no care." There are two possible reasons for your dilemma: Either you simply bit off more than you could chew, or you chose plants that might be as easy as pie to care for in somebody else's yard—but not in yours. Or, it could be a little of both. Here's my two-step route to a truly low(er)-maintenance yard and garden:

Step 1: Decide on a garden size that you're sure you can handle comfortably and cheerfully, then reduce it by a third. You can always expand it later on if you want to. In the meantime, dig up your excess plants and give them to friends, or pack them off to a charity plant sale.

Step 2: Choose plants that thrive in the growing conditions you have now. Don't struggle to make a home for whatever strikes your fancy in a catalog. It'll only be an exercise in frustration for you *and* the plants.

The Numbers Game

Choosing plants to suit your growing conditions means looking up your zone number, and then matching it to the ones in the catalog descriptions, right?

Not quite. The USDA's Plant Hardiness Zone Map will tell you the lowest temperature that strikes your region in an average winter. But there are a few more weather-related numbers that will help you plant for success:

How hot it gets, and for how long. That's crucial information, because some plants need all the heat they can get for as long as they can get it. Others turn into pest and disease magnets when the temperature climbs much above 80°F—or stop producing flowers, fruits, or vegetables. To find these figures, check out the American Horticultural Society's Heat Zone Map. It's based on the average number of days in a year with temperatures above 86°F. You can find it on the society's Web site at **www.AHS.org.**

 Plant hardiness zone numbers are based on the coldest temperature in an *average* winter. So why take chances? Go with plants that are hardy to at least one zone colder than yours. That way, you won't have to panic if the weatherman says, "We'll have a record low tonight, folks!"

The length of your growing season. It begins with the last frost in the spring and ends with the first frost in the fall. Those dates tell you a lot more than simply when to sow seeds or stand by with warm covers. Your allotment of frost-free days determines whether flowers will have time to bloom, or fruits and veggies will have time to ripen in your climate. Often, the answer is a clear-cut yes or no. At other times, it's "maybe." You may or may not decide to gamble with marginal plants, but beware: Chances are you'll have to do a lot of coddling—and still risk failure—during the growing season.

You Did the Math, But...

Your plants still aren't happy. Why not? Because, although frost dates and zone numbers are important guidelines, plenty of other factors, such as wind, rainfall, altitude, humidity, and even air quality affect a plant's health and well-being. Those details vary like night and day within both hardiness and heat zones. Even within your own yard, growing conditions are different from one place to the next. So what's the secret to winning the planting game?

➡ The same as it was for acing an exam in school: Do your homework! Before you even start perusing catalogs or strolling through a garden center, study your yard, and take notes. Here are some things to jot down:

Places sheltered by walls or buildings. Most likely, they're warmer than the open space only a few feet away.

Strips of ground beside busy streets. They'll receive more pollution than parts that are away from the street or blocked by the house or a solid fence.

Low spots where frost gathers. They'll get cold earlier in the fall, and stay cold later in the spring. Low spots also tend to stay moist longer, even if the soil is well-drained.

Areas that warm up early in the day. They'll also warm up early in the spring.

The direction of slopes. A north-facing slope gets less sunshine, and stays cooler than one that faces south.

LET IT SNOW

A plant with the wind blowing on it is a plant that's under stress. But before you can put up an effective windbreak, you need to know where the winds come from. Here's an easy way to find out: Just look out the window during a snowstorm. Those blowing and piling flakes will show you exactly which direction the wind is coming from, and what walls, fences, or other obstacles stop it in its tracks.

Made in the Shade

Does your garden bask in more shade than you'd like? If so, you're not alone. It sometimes seems that half the letters in my mailbag start out with "Jerry, I've got a shade problem."

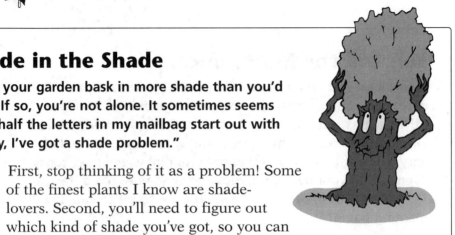

First, stop thinking of it as a problem! Some of the finest plants I know are shade-lovers. Second, you'll need to figure out which kind of shade you've got, so you can find the shady characters that like it. Here's the rundown:

Dense shade: Cast by north-facing walls, or low, dense branches of evergreen trees; good for a shade-loving vine, such as trumpet honeysuckle, Dutchman's pipe, climbing hydrangea, or English ivy.

Dappled shade: Cast by foliage of oaks, maples, or elms; good for hostas, ferns, and early-blooming bulbs and wildflowers such as Jack-in-the-pulpit.

Filtered light: Falls through the openings in an arbor, the small leaves of willows or birches, or a translucent structure like a fiberglass overhang; good for lamiums, bleeding hearts, hostas, astilbes, and goatsbeards. A word to the wise: When catalogs say that a plant likes "shade," what they often mean is filtered light.

A SHADE OF DIFFERENCE

In northern regions, like Alaska and the Pacific Northwest, you can grow real sun worshippers in shady spots. That's because during those long summer days, the extra hours of light make up for the lack of direct sunshine. And in the South and Southwest, or at high altitudes, Ol' Sol is so intense that most sun-lovers not only tolerate shade—they need it, at least during the hottest part of the day.

Walk on the Wild Side

Doing all of this plant research sounds like a *lot* of work. Isn't there an easier way to find happy campers?

➡ Yes and no. Before you try to grow any plant, you need to know what kind of hospitality you can offer it. Otherwise, you're taking a stab in the dark, and could wind up throwing time and money down the drain. But once you know what your growing conditions are, it gets easy—just look for plants that are native to your area. That's not half as hard as it might sound. There are nurseries that specialize in breeding flowers, herbs, trees, shrubs, and even fruits and vegetables that grow, or once grew, naturally in a given area. To find a native-plant nursery near you, just crank up your favorite Internet search engine and type in "native plants."

GRANDMA PUTT'S
grow-how

When most folks think of companion planting, they think of the vegetable garden. But for Grandma Putt, the idea went way beyond that. She tucked every single plant among the ones it would help in some way, or be helped *by*. Those good buddies fended off pests, improved the flavor or aroma of their neighbors, or simply helped each other grow bigger and stronger—or, often, all of the above. Here's a handful of her favorite combos:

Columbines (*Aquilegia*) and rhubarb

Morning glories (*Ipomoea*) and corn

Petunias (*Petunia*) and beans

Wallflowers (*Erysimum cheiri*) and apple trees

Wild mustard (*Brassica kaber*) and grapevines or fruit trees

A Little Latin Goes a Long Way

How many times have you ordered a plant from a catalog, or taken a young one home from the garden center—then watched it grow up into something you hadn't bargained for at all? Or worse, watched it go straight downhill because it just wasn't

suited to your turf? If you're like most folks, the answer is "way too often."

➡ That's why it's mighty helpful to know a little botanical Latin—or at least know where to look it up. Among other things, a plant's Latin name can tell you what it looks like, where it came from, or under what conditions it grows in the wild. For instance, a plant with *alpinus* in its name hails from a mountain region. So it might be right at home on your range in the Rockies. *Altus* means tall, and that's probably not what you want for a container on your breezy deck. Plants from the hot, dry Mediterranean region often sport the word *mediterraneus* in their names. They can be your best friends if your weather is hot and dry, or if you need to conserve water. On the other hand, those plants are likely to need some serious TLC if you live in a cold, rainy, or humid climate.

Fabulous Food and Drink

Two for the Road

Are you confused by those shelves and miles of aisles at the garden center? They carry enough kinds of fertilizers to make your head spin! How do you choose the right one for your garden?

➡ Deciding which one to buy isn't so hard, once you understand the choices. Every fertilizer on the market falls into one of two categories: chemical/inorganic or natural/organic.

Chemical/inorganic fertilizers are made from synthetic substances containing highly concentrated amounts of nutrients, primarily nitrogen, phosphorus, and potassium (see "Diagnosing

Diet Deficiencies" on page 334). When you apply a chemical fertilizer, you see almost instant results, because the nutrients are immediately available to your plants. But this quick fix adds nothing to the soil itself. In fact, those potent chemicals actually destroy the beneficial organisms, including earthworms, which create the soil's natural nutrients and keep it in good shape. When used over time, the chemicals build up in the soil and can hinder plant growth.

Natural/organic fertilizers don't feed your plants at all. Rather, they add essential nutrients to the soil, where they become available to the plants. They also improve the soil structure, which strengthens living conditions for your underground hit squad. Organic fertilizers are made of naturally occurring substances, just like the ones I use in my Miracle Mixes. There are some excellent commercial brands, but it's easy to make your own (see the chart on page 327).

The Big Three

You've seen the triple-digit numbers, like 12–4–8, on fertilizer labels, and you know they stand for nitrogen (N), phosphorus (P), and potassium (K). But what do those substances do for your plants exactly?

➡ I'm glad you asked. Here's your basic chemistry lesson for the day:

Nitrogen supplies the grow power for leaves and stems. That's why lawn fertilizers are so high in nitrogen—and why an overdose of the stuff can make other plants grow too lush and leafy.

Phosphorus promotes the growth of strong, vigorous roots and the formation of flowers, fruits, vegetables, and seeds.

Potassium supports all phases of growth, and helps plants stand up and fight back when pests and diseases strike.

I'll Drink to That!

Solid food is fine for a routine diet, but plants like a little liquid refreshment now and then, too. What, besides tap water, is fit for them to drink?

 Water of another sort, that's what! When you change the water in your fish tank, or toss an over-the-hill floral arrangement onto the compost pile, don't send the used H_2O down the drain. Serve it to a plant instead. That liquid is chock-full of health-giving nutrients. So is the water that you've used to cook eggs, vegetables, or pasta, or to rinse out glasses or bottles that held any of these beverages:

Almost everyone enjoys a can of soda now and then, but for your plants, soda is more than just a refreshing treat—it's super chow. It's not the sugar or the yummy flavor that does the trick: It's the carbon dioxide, which plants need to turn the sun's energy into food. To serve up this power lunch, first surround your plants with a 3-inch layer of mulch, like bark chips, gravel, or pine needles. Then, twice a week during the growing season, pour a can of soda right through the mulch. The chunky covering will keep the gas under wraps long enough for the plants' roots to drink it up.

- ❁ Beer
- ❁ Coffee
- ❁ Juice
- ❁ Milk
- ❁ Soda pop
- ❁ Tea
- ❁ Whiskey
- ❁ Wine

Thanks, Rover!

Need to give your plants a snack, but you're plum out of plant food?

Borrow some chow from your pup. Dry dog food contains some of the same ingredients found in organic fertilizers. Just add a handful to the hole at planting time, or sprinkle it on the soil around established plants, and work it in gently. To play it extra-safe, though, before you use dog food on a newly planted seedbed, read the label. Many brands contain corn gluten, which is a great source of nitrogen—but also a popular pre-emergent herbicide (that means it stops seeds from germinating). Chances are, the concentration won't be strong enough to hurt your seeds, but then again, why take chances?

BUILDING STRONG PLANTS EIGHT WAYS

To grow up strong and healthy, plants need a diet with each of these eight basic food groups in it. Usually, a well-balanced blend of organic matter fills the bill just fine. Once in a while, though, your plants may be running a nutrient deficit (see "Diagnosing Diet Deficiencies" on page 334). When that happens, I choose from the smorgasbord below.

Food Group	Sources	Food Group	Sources
Nitrogen	Alfalfa meal Bloodmeal Coffee grounds Corn gluten Fish emulsion Legume crops Manure	Magnesium	Dolomitic limestone Epsom salts
		Manganese	Manganese sulfate
Phosphorus	Bonemeal Fish emulsion Poultry manure Seaweed	Sulfur	Epsom salts Ground sulfur Gypsum Manure
Potassium	Bananas (peels and fruit) Cow manure Greensand Wood ashes	Micronutrients	Alfalfa hay Compost Eggshells Grass clippings Hair Leaves Wood ashes Worm castings
Calcium	Bonemeal Clam shells Eggshells Gypsum Limestone		

Weed Woes

A few weeds here and there won't hurt anything, but when they get out of control, they rob your plants of nutrients and give shelter to disease-spreading pests. So how do you boot these tough customers off your turf?

➡ How you wage war on weeds depends on where they're growing, what you want to grow in their place, and how long they've been there. Here's my basic weed management policy:

Smother 'em. If you're starting a new planting bed, or a whole series of them, use my Super Soil Sandwich recipe on page 305. For unpaved walkways or paths between beds, use a variation on the theme: Just lay cardboard, brown paper bags, or newspapers over the soil, then spread on whatever kind of topping suits your fancy. Shredded bark, pea gravel, and pine needles, for instance, are all easy on the feet and the eyes.

Procrastinate. Don't rush to get warmth-craving plants into the ground. When heat-lovers have to struggle to grow in cold soil, weeds can do them in fast.

Seed heavily. Weeds pop up in any bare soil they find. When you're direct-sowing flowers, vegetables, or herbs, cover the space with the plants you want in your garden. Later, you can thin the seedlings to the right distance.

Use transplants. Young plants take off the minute you set them into the ground. That means they can start shading out weeds right from the get-go. Plus, when something green does pop up, you'll know it's a weed, and you can pull it without worrying that you're ousting a future friend.

Get 'em when they're down. Perennial weeds are at their weakest just before they flower. That's the time to give 'em a lethal dose of my Weed Wipeout tonic (see page 289).

Here, There, and Everywhere

Maybe the weeds that drive you wacky are not the ones in your planting beds, but the ones that spring up in cracks in your driveway and the gaps between the stones in your terrace. What do you do about those little nuisances?

➡ Give 'em a dose of my Brussels Sprouts Brush-Off Soup (below). Brussels sprouts and their cole-crop cousins, cabbage, broccoli, and kale, all contain thiocyanate, a chemical that's toxic to newly germinated seeds, especially small ones. The whole *Brassica* clan has the stuff, but Brussels sprouts pack the biggest dose. Just pour the soup on the ground in early spring, and you'll soon bid those weeds good-bye. But be careful where you use this potent stuff: Although thiocyanate won't hurt established plants, it can't tell the difference between the seeds you've sown—or the volunteers you're hoping for—and the weeds you want to get rid of!

⭐ Miracle Mix ⭐

BRUSSELS SPROUTS BRUSH-OFF SOUP

Brussels sprouts are one of the healthiest veggies we can eat, but this marvelous mix delivers a knockout punch to weeds. Serve it up in early spring, before the seeds germinate.

1 cup of Brussels sprouts*
1/2 tsp. of liquid dish soap
Water

In a blender, combine the Brussels sprouts with just enough water to make a thick mush. Then add the dish soap, and pour the mixture into cracks in your sidewalk or driveway, or anyplace you want to stop weeds before they pop up. (Just don't use it in places where you want flower, herb, or veggie seeds to grow.)

* Or substitute cabbage leaves.

Black Gold

Hands down, good compost is the healthiest diet a plant could ask for. Chances are you already know that. But, maybe you're buying your supply of "black gold" at the garden center because you think that making it is just too messy or complicated. Is it?

➤ Actually, the process is a lot simpler than some folks make it out to be. And if appearance matters, just get yourself a commercial compost bin. Every month or so, open the door and spritz your future treasure with my Compost Booster (at right). As for what to put inside, you want roughly three high-carbon ingredients (the "browns") for every one that's high in nitrogen (the "greens"). That's important, because if you have too much carbon, the compost could take years to cook. Too much nitrogen, and it'll give off an odor that would make a skunk turn green with envy. Here's the menu:

The Browns

✿ Chipped twigs and branches

✿ Dead flower and vegetable stalks

✿ Dry leaves and plant stalks

✿ Hay

✿ Pine needles

✿ Sawdust

✿ Shredded paper

✿ Straw

The Greens

✿ Coffee grounds

✿ Eggshells

✿ Feathers

✿ Flowers

✿ Fruit and vegetable scraps

✿ Grass clippings

✿ Green leaves and stems

✿ Hair (pet or human)

✿ Manure

✿ Seaweed

✿ Tea bags

Cool and Easy Composting

You say that balancing ingredients and spinning a compost bin is not your idea of fun, even if the end product is worth its weight in gold, silver, *and* platinum?

➤ Then try cold composting. In this method, anaerobic bacteria break down the organic material without the help of oxygen, so there's no turning required. And there's no need to worry about the ratio of browns to greens. Just one word of warning: When you open the bags, you'll be hit with a potent odor, but it will disappear as soon as the compost is exposed to the open air. Here's my three-step method:

Step 1: Fill a large plastic garbage bag with a mixture of chopped leaves, grass clippings, and vegetable scraps. For every couple of shovelfuls of bulky, carbon-rich material (see the browns and greens list on page at left), add a few cupfuls of my Compost Booster (above).

★ Miracle Mix ★

COMPOST BOOSTER

Just like your plants, your compost needs a boost now and then. Once a month, spray it with this energizing elixir.

1 can of beer
1 can of regular cola (not diet)
1 cup of ammonia
1/2 cup of weak tea water*
2 tbsp. of baby shampoo

Mix all of these ingredients together in a 20-gallon hose-end sprayer, and saturate your compost with the solution. This'll really keep things cookin'!

*Soak a used tea bag in a mix of 1 gallon of warm water and 1 tsp. of liquid dish soap until the mix is light brown.

Step 2: When the bag is nearly full, sprinkle a couple of quarts of water over the contents, and mix until all of the ingredients are moist. To do that, just shake small or light bags; roll large or heavy ones.

Step 3: Tie the bag shut, and leave it in an out-of-the-way place where the temperature will stay above 45°F for a few months. For faster results, roll or shake the bag every few days. That's all there is to it!

When Bad Bugs Do Good Things

Your compost pile is crawling with thugs! You've found slugs, ants, grubs, pill bugs, and centipedes all over the place. How do you get rid of them?

 You can't get all those critters out of an open compost pile—and furthermore, you don't want to. Those little guys might do damage to your plants, but in the compost pile, they're on your side. They, along with earthworms and beneficial bacteria, are helping turn all that yard and kitchen waste into black gold. Just make sure you keep your compost pile well-separated from your flower and vegetable gardens, so your helpers don't meander on over for a midnight snack!

Timely Troubleshooting

They're Sick—Now What?

Your plants look as though they've been clobbered by disease or pesky pests, but your usual get-well treatments haven't worked. Now what?

Sometimes a plant problem can be hard to diagnose. That's when it's time to call in the pros. Clip off a few affected leaves, stems, or both, and send them to your closest Cooperative Extension Service. Include a note giving as much information as you can about the problem, as well as the plant's location and growing conditions. If you can take a snapshot of the plant and send it along, so much the better. Your friendly neighborhood scientists will examine the evidence and get back to you with a diagnosis and a prescription.

SPOT THE SYMPTOMS

If you'd rather treat plant problems on your own, use this chart to help you make the right diagnosis.

Symptom	Possible Cause	What to Do
Dead buds, shoots, and/or leaves	Cold damage	Cover up plants that are in the ground; move container plants to protected spots; harden off young plants before setting them outdoors in spring.
Pale, spindly growth; variegated leaves turning all green; gray leaves turning all green	Too much shade	Prune or remove trees or shrubs to let in more light, or move plants to brighter spot.
Dropping, wilted, or scorched leaves	Too little water	Soak soil thoroughly, then mulch to keep soil moist.
Leaves wilted or turning brown; top growth dying; general decline in appearance and vigor	Poor drainage	Either move plant to better site or improve drainage.
Wilting and greenish yellow foliage	Too much water	Don't water until soil dries out. Then, take it easier!
General decline in appearance and vigor (especially in fruit trees, roses, and fruit bushes)	Compacted soil	Reroute foot and vehicle traffic; add organic matter to soil.
Branches dying; leaves silvery, mottled, or speckled tan or white	Air or ground pollution, or damage from road salt	Avoid using salt to melt snow; instead, use sand, cinders, or clay cat litter to provide traction; feed and water plant thoroughly, or move it to new location.

Diagnosing Diet Deficiencies

Discolored leaves on your plants can mean that something's lacking in their diet. Here's how to recognize the hunger pangs. For comfort food that will ease their pain, see "Building Strong Plants Eight Ways" on page 327.

 Nitrogen deficiency. Leaves are small and yellow; on some plants, they may turn red or purple as green pigment levels drop; severe stunting or dwarfing soon follows.

Phosphorus deficiency. Leaves are small and may fall early; edges may be scorched, purplish, or blue-green; plant growth is generally reduced and weak; flower and fruit production plummets.

Potassium deficiency. Leaf tips and edges are yellow and scorched-looking, with brownish purple spotting underneath. This is most common in light, sandy soils.

Calcium deficiency. Leaf tissue turns dark from the base outward and dies because feeder roots have died.

Iron deficiency. Leaves turn yellow between the veins; veins stay green or faintly yellow.

Magnesium deficiency. Leaf centers turn yellow or reddish; dead spots appear between the veins.

Manganese deficiency. Leaves at the top of the plant turn yellow in the center and between the veins, but there's no sign of red.

Sulfur deficiency. Leaf veins are lighter in color than the tissue in between.

Miracle Mix

NETTLE TEA

Stinging nettles pack a load of nitrogen that's as potent as manure. They also give off pest-repelling chemicals. So what are you waiting for? Brew a pot of this powerful tea, and double your firepower!

1 lb. of stinging nettle leaves
1 gal. of water

Put the nettles in a bucket, pour in the water, and let the mixture steep for at least a week. Strain out the leaves, and water your plants with the brew. Then toss the leaves on the compost pile, or bury them in the garden.

PART VI

JERRY'S
Mixers 'n Elixirs

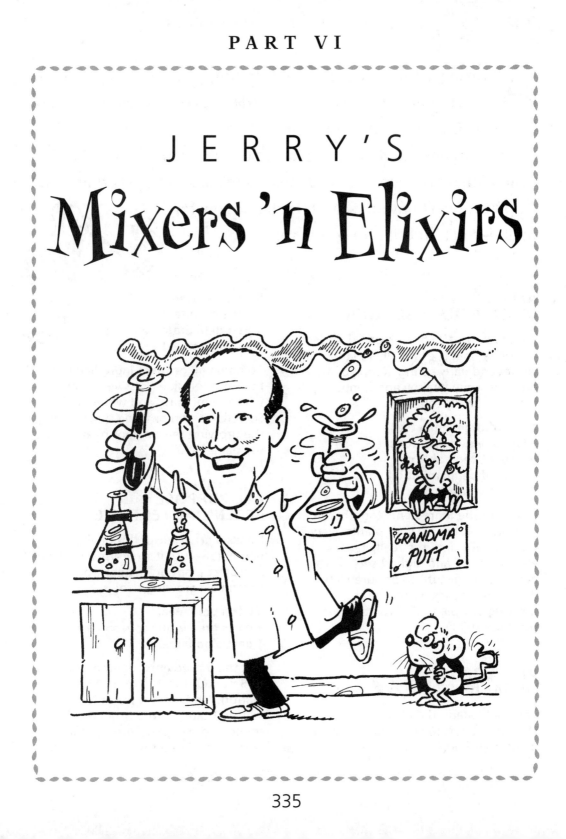

GRANDMA PUTT

All through this book, I've been telling you about my Miracle Mixes that can solve more garden-variety woes than there is tea in China. In this section, I've gathered all those recipes together in one handy-dandy place. So when you do come head to head with a problem like seeds that won't start or pests that won't stop, you won't have to search high and low for relief—you'll find it all right here!

ALL-AROUND DISEASE DEFENSE TONIC

Wet, rainy weather can mean diseases on the rampage, especially in late winter and early spring. Keep your outdoor scene healthy and happy with this timely tonic.

1 cup of chamomile tea
1 tsp. of liquid dish soap
½ tsp. of vegetable oil
½ tsp. of peppermint oil
1 gal. of warm water

Mix all of the ingredients together in a bucket. Mist-spray your plants every week or two until the really hot weather (75°F and higher) sets in. This elixir is strong stuff, so be sure to test it on a few leaves before totally spraying any plant. (For related text, see page 309.)

ALL-PURPOSE ORGANIC FERTILIZER

This well-balanced diet is the best stuff your beets (or any other veggie plant) ever had.

5 parts seaweed meal
3 parts granite dust
1 part dehydrated manure
1 part bonemeal

Combine all of these ingredients in a bucket, then side-dress your plants with the mixture, and water well. Serve it up two or three times during the growing season. (For related text, see page 139.)

ALL-PURPOSE PERENNIAL FERTILIZER

Here's a great recipe for healthy perennials—use it to boost soil before *and* after planting to keep your perennials growing strong.

3 parts bonemeal
3 parts greensand or wood ashes
1 part bloodmeal

Mix the ingredients together. Apply 3 to 5 pounds per 100 sq. ft. before planting and work it into the soil, or scatter 2 tablespoons around each clump and scratch it into the soil surface. (For related text, see page 63.)

ALL-PURPOSE PEST PREVENTION POTION

Voles, rabbits, and just about any other critter I can think of will high-tail it away when they get a whiff of this powerful potion.

1 cup of ammonia
1/2 cup of urine
1/2 cup of liquid dish soap
1/4 cup of castor oil

Mix all of these ingredients in a 20-gallon hose-end sprayer. Then, just before the first snow flies, thoroughly saturate the area around each of your young trees. (For related text, see page 196.)

ALL-SEASON CLEAN-UP TONIC

This fantastic fixer will keep your whole yard and garden squeaky clean—which is just what pesky pests and dastardly disease germs hate more than anything!

1 cup of liquid dish soap
1 cup of antiseptic mouthwash
1 cup of tobacco tea*

Mix all of these ingredients in a 20-gallon hose-end sprayer, and give your plants a good shower. Repeat the process every two weeks through-out the growing season. (For related text, see page 59.)

*To make tobacco tea, wrap half a handful of chewing tobacco in a panty hose toe or a piece of cheese-cloth. Soak it in 1 gallon of hot water until the water turns dark brown. Pour the liquid into a glass container with a tight lid for storage.

ALL-SEASON GREEN-UP TONIC

This excellent elixir will supercharge your veggies—and the rest of your green scene—all summer long.

1 can of beer
1 cup of ammonia
1/2 cup of liquid dish soap
1/2 cup of liquid lawn food
1/2 cup of molasses or corn syrup

Mix all of the ingredients together in a large bucket, pour the mixture into a 20-gallon hose-end sprayer, and spray your vegetable plants to the point of run-off every three weeks throughout the growing season. Then mix up another batch to use on your lawn and all of the other plants in your yard! (For related text, see page 121.)

BLACK SPOT REMOVER TONIC

At the first sign of black spots on your rose leaves, rush to the rescue with this terrific tonic.

15 tomato leaves
2 small onions
1/4 cup of rubbing alcohol

Chop the tomato leaves and the onions into fine pieces, and steep them in the alcohol overnight. Then, use a small, sponge-type paintbrush to apply the mix to both the tops and bottoms of any infected rose leaves. (For related text, see page 90.)

BLIGHT BUSTER TONIC

At the first sign of blight on your potatoes, tomatoes, or celery, haul out this powerful weapon.

1 tbsp. of light horticultural oil
    (available at garden centers)
1 tbsp. of baking soda
1 gal. of water

Mix all of these ingredients together, pour the solution into a hand-held mist sprayer, and spray your plants to the point of run-off. (For related text, see page 137.)

BLUEBERRY POTTING MIX

You couldn't ask for an easier-to-grow plant than a blueberry bush. Just give it a pot or a raised bed filled with this root-pleasing mix, and get ready for a fine, fruitful feast.

2 parts garden soil
2 parts chopped, composted leaves
2 parts coarse builder's sand*
1 part compost

Mix all of these ingredients together, then fill your containers. (For related text, see page 225.)

*Don't use beach or "sandbox" sand. It's so fine that it'll harden up if it dries out. It also may contain a lot of ground-up shell fragments, which are highly alkaline.

BRUSSELS SPROUTS BRUSH-OFF SOUP

Brussels sprouts are one of the health-iest veggies we can eat, but this mar-velous mix delivers a knockout punch to weeds. Serve it up in early spring, before the seeds germinate.

1 cup of Brussels sprouts*
1/2 tsp. of liquid dish soap
Water

In a blender, combine the Brussels sprouts with just enough water to make a thick mush. Then add the dish soap, and pour the mixture into cracks in your sidewalk or driveway, or anyplace you want to stop weeds before they pop up—just don't use it in places where you want flower, herb, or veggie seeds to grow. (For related text, see page 329.)

*Or substitute cabbage leaves.

BUG-OFF BULB BATH

This spa treatment will help your spring- or summer-blooming bulbs fend off disease germs and pesky insect pests.

2 tsp. of baby shampoo
1 tsp. of antiseptic mouthwash
1/4 tsp. of instant tea granules
2 gal. of hot water (120°F)

Mix these ingredients together in a bucket. Then drop in your bulbs, and let them soak for two to three hours (longer for larger bulbs). Don't peel off the papery skins! The bulbs use them as a defense against pests. Plant the bulbs immediately or let them air-dry for several days before you store them—otherwise, rot could set in. (For related text, see page 103.)

BULB BREAKFAST

When you plant your bulbs, get the show on the road with this nutritious first meal.

10 lbs. of compost
5 lbs. of bonemeal
2 lbs. of bloodmeal
1 lb. of Epsom salts

Mix all of these ingredients together in a wheelbarrow. Then, before you set your bulbs into the ground, work the mixture into every 100 sq. ft. of soil. If you're planting on a smaller scale, just work a handful of compost and a teaspoon of bonemeal into the soil in each planting hole before you tuck in the bulb. (For related text, see page 100.)

BULB CLEANING TONIC

When you take your tender bulbs, corms, and tubers from the ground in the fall, wash them in this timely tonic. It'll keep pests and diseases from moving in over the winter.

2 tbsp. of baby shampoo
1 tsp. of hydrogen peroxide
1 qt. of warm water

Combine all of these ingredients in a bucket, and bathe your bulbs in the mixture. Just be sure to let them dry thoroughly before you put them away for the winter— or you'll end up with rotted bulbs! (For related text, see page 105.)

BUTTERMILK BLAST

When spider mites are draining the juices from your plants, give 'em a drink that'll stop 'em in their tracks.

2 cups of wheat flour
¼ cup of buttermilk
2 gal. of water

Mix all of these ingredients together thoroughly. Then pour the mixture into a hand-held mist sprayer, and douse your mite-plagued plants from top to bottom. The little suckers'll never know what hit 'em! (For related text, see page 230.)

BYE-BYE BLACK SPOT SPRAY

This simple formula works like a charm to head off ugly black spot on roses.

1 tbsp. of baking soda
1 tsp. of liquid dish soap
1 gal. of water

Mix these ingredients together, pour the solution into a hand-held mist sprayer, and spray your roses every three days during the growing season. There'll be no more singin' the black spot blues! (For related text, see page 90.)

CABBAGEWORM WIPE-OUT TONIC

Whip up a batch of this terrific tonic for all the cabbage family plants in your garden.

1 cup of flour
2 tbsp. of cayenne pepper

Mix the ingredients together, and sprinkle the results on young cabbage family plants. The flour swells up inside the cabbageworms and bursts their insides, while the hot pepper keeps other critters away. (For related text, see page 188.)

CATERPILLAR KILLER TONIC

No matter what kind of caterpillars are buggin' your plants, a jolt of this aromatic blend will do 'em in.

½ lb. of wormwood leaves
2 tbsp. of Murphy's Oil Soap®
4 cups of water

Simmer the wormwood leaves in 2 cups of water for 30 minutes. Strain out the leaves, then add the Murphy's Oil Soap and 2 more cups of water. Pour the solution into a 6-gallon hand-held sprayer, and apply to your plants to the point of run-off. Repeat as often as necessary until the caterpillars are history. (For related text, see page 57.)

CHAMOMILE MILDEW CHASER

To help keep powdery mildew from pounding your plants, serve them this tea once a week, especially in late summer and early fall.

4 chamomile tea bags
2 tbsp. of Murphy's Oil Soap®
1 qt. of boiling water

Put the tea bags in a pot, pour the boiling water over them, and let it steep for an hour or so, 'til the brew is good and strong. Let it cool, then mix in the Murphy's Oil Soap. Pour the tea into a 6-gallon hose-end sprayer, and fire away! Try to apply this elixir early in the day, so your plants' leaves can dry by nightfall. (For related text, see page 56.)

CHIVE TEA

Fruit tree fungi don't stand a chance against this brew!

1 part chive leaves*
4 parts water

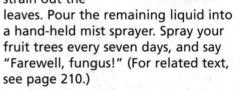

Put the chives and water in a pan, and bring the water to a boil. Then remove the pan from the heat, let the tea cool, and strain out the leaves. Pour the remaining liquid into a hand-held mist sprayer. Spray your fruit trees every seven days, and say "Farewell, fungus!" (For related text, see page 210.)

*Or substitute horseradish leaves.

COMPOST BOOSTER

Just like your plants, your compost
needs a boost now and then.
Once a month, spray it with this
energizing elixir.

1 can of beer
1 can of regular cola (not diet)
1 cup of ammonia
$\frac{1}{2}$ cup of weak tea water*
2 tbsp. of baby shampoo

Mix all of these ingredients together
in a 20-gallon hose-end sprayer, and
saturate your compost with the solution. This'll really keep things cookin'!
(For related text, see page 331.)

*Soak a used tea bag in a mix of 1
gallon of warm water and 1 teaspoon
of liquid dish soap until
the mix is light brown.

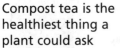

COMPOST TEA

Compost tea is the
healthiest thing a
plant could ask
for. It delivers a well-balanced supply
of all those important nutrients—
major and minor—and fends off
diseases at the same time.

1 gal. of fresh compost
4 gal. of warm water

Pour the water into a large bucket.
Scoop the compost into a cotton,
burlap, or panty hose sack, tie the
sack closed, and put it in the water.
Cover the bucket, and let the mix
steep for three to seven days. Pour
the solution into a watering can or
hand-held mist sprayer, and give your
plants a good spritzing with it every
two to three weeks. *Note:* You can

make manure tea (another wonderful
mixer) using this same recipe. Just
substitute 1 gallon of well-cured
manure for the compost, and use the
finished product the same way. (For
related text, see page 20.)

DAMPING-OFF PREVENTION TONIC

This wonder drink will say a loud
and clear "No way!" to those foul
damping-off fungi.

4 tsp. of chamomile tea
1 tsp. of liquid dish soap
1 qt. of boiling water

Mix the tea and soap with the water,
and let the mixture steep for at least
an hour (the longer, the better). Let it
cool to room temperature, then mist-
spray your seedlings as soon as their
little heads appear above the starter
mix. (For related text, see page 7.)

DEER BUSTER EGG BREW

To keep the brown-eyed bruisers from
even coming close to your fruit trees,
lay out the unwelcome mat with this
un-tasty spritzer!

2 eggs
2 cloves of garlic
2 tbsp. of Tabasco® sauce
2 tbsp. of cayenne pepper
2 cups of water

Put all of the ingredients in a blender,
and purée. Allow the mixture to sit
for two days, then pour or spray it
around your trees. (For related text,
see page 217.)

FLOWER AND FOLIAGE FLU SHOT

There's no cure for plant viruses, but this "vaccine" *could* help plants fend off attacks.

2 cups of leaves
  from a healthy green pepper plant
1/2 tsp. of liquid dish soap
2 cups of water

Put the leaves and the water in a blender and liquefy. Then dilute the mixture with an equal amount of water, add the dish soap, and pour the solution into a hand-held mist sprayer. Drench your plants from top to bottom. (For related text, see page 64.)

FLOWER FEEDER TONIC

Once your plants are churnin' out flowers again, put them back on a well-balanced diet.

1 can of beer
2 tbsp. of fish emulsion
2 tbsp. of liquid dish soap
2 tbsp. of ammonia
2 tbsp. of hydrogen peroxide
2 tbsp. of whiskey
1 tbsp. of clear corn syrup
1 tbsp. of unflavored gelatin
4 tsp. of instant tea granules
2 gal. of warm water

Mix all of the ingredients together. Feed all of your perennials (and bulbs) every two weeks in the morning, and you'll have glorious blooms all season long! (For related text, see page 66.)

FLOWER POWER TONIC

A dose of this tonic will get your flowers up and growing in no time!

1 cup of beer
2 tbsp. of fish emulsion
2 tbsp. of liquid dish soap
2 tbsp. of ammonia
2 tbsp. of whiskey
1 tbsp. of corn syrup
1 tbsp. of instant tea granules
2 gal. of warm water

Mix all of these ingredients together in a watering can. Drench your annuals every three weeks during the growing season to keep them blooming all summer long. (For related text, see page 30.)

FLOWER SAVER SOLUTION

This recipe makes 1 quart of solution.

1 cup of lemon-lime
  soda (not diet)
1/4 tsp. of household
  bleach
3 cups of warm water
  (110°F)

Mix all of these ingredients together, and pour the solution into a clean vase. It'll make those posies perk right up! Use it from the get-go for all of your cut flowers. (For related text, see page 72.)

FUNGUS FIGHTER SOIL DRENCH

When foul fungi are fussin' around in your soil, polish 'em off with this potent potion.

4 garlic bulbs, crushed
1/2 cup of baking soda
1 gal. of water

Combine these ingredients in a big pot, and bring the water to a boil. Then turn off the heat, and let it cool to room temperature. Strain the liquid into a watering can, and soak the ground around fungus-prone plants. (There's nothin' fungi hate more than garlic!) Go *very slowly*, so the elixir goes deep into the soil. Then, dump the strained-out garlic bits onto the soil, and work them in gently, so as not to disturb plant roots. (For related text, see page 45.)

FUNGUS FIGHTER TONIC

This terrific tonic works like magic to fend off foul fungi on ornamental *and* edible plants.

1/2 cup of molasses
1/2 cup of powdered milk
1 tsp. of baking soda
1 gal. of warm water

Mix the molasses, powdered milk, and baking soda into a paste. Place the mixture into an old panty hose toe, and let it steep in the warm water for several hours. Strain, then pour the remaining liquid into a hand-held mist sprayer, and spritz your dahlias and other fungus-prone plants every week during the growing season. (For related text, see page 110.)

GARDEN CURE-ALL TONIC

When you need bad-guy bug relief in a hurry, mix up a batch of this rapid-acting remedy.

4 cloves of garlic
1 small onion
1 small jalapeño pepper
1 tsp. of Murphy's Oil Soap®
1 tsp. of vegetable oil
Warm water

Pulverize the garlic, onion, and pepper in a blender, and let them steep in a quart of warm water for two hours. Strain the mixture through cheesecloth or panty hose, and dilute with 3 parts of warm water. Add the Murphy's Oil Soap and vegetable oil, and pour into a hand-held mist sprayer. Then take aim, and polish off the bugs that are buggin' you! (For related text, see page 212.)

GRANDMA PUTT'S SIMPLE SOAP SPRAY

This old-fangled solution kills off just about any soft-bodied insect you can name.

1/2 bar of Fels Naptha® or Octagon®
soap,* shredded
2 gal. of water

Add the soap to the water and heat, stirring, until the soap dissolves completely. Let the solution cool, then pour it into a hand-held mist sprayer, and let 'er rip. Test it on one plant first, though—and be sure to rinse it off after the bugs have bitten the dust. (For related text, see page 94.)

*You'll find Fels Naptha and Octagon in either the bath soap or laundry section of your supermarket.

GREAT-GUNS GARLIC SPRAY

This'll halt an aphid invasion faster than you can say "Hold it right there!"

1 tbsp. of garlic oil*
3 drops of liquid dish soap
1 qt. of water

Mix these ingredients together in a blender, and pour the solution into a hand-held mist sprayer. Then, take aim and fire. Within seconds, those aphids'll be history! (For related text, see page 25.)

*To make garlic oil, mince 1 whole bulb of garlic and mix it in 1 cup of vegetable oil. Put the garlic oil in a glass jar with a tight lid and place it in the refrigerator to steep for a day or two. To test it for "doneness," open the lid, and take a sniff. If the aroma is so strong that you take a step back, you're ready to roll. If the scent isn't so strong, add half a bulb of garlic, and wait another day. Then, strain out the solids, and pour the oil into a fresh jar. Keep it in the fridge, and use it in any Miracle Mix that calls for garlic oil.

HAPPY HERB TONIC

No matter what temperatures your climate delivers, keep all of your herbs healthy and chipper with this nifty elixir.

1 cup of tea
1/2 tbsp. of bourbon
1/2 tbsp. of ammonia
1/2 tbsp. of hydrogen peroxide
1 gal. of warm water

Mix all of the ingredients together in a bucket. Then dish up hearty helpings every six weeks throughout the growing season. (For related text, see page 261.)

HERB BOOSTER TONIC

Even herbs enjoy a nice, cool drink when the going gets hot. Quench their thirst with this summertime pick-me-up.

1 can of beer
1 cup of ammonia
1/2 cup of Murphy's Oil Soap®
1/2 cup of corn syrup

Mix all of these ingredients in a 20-gallon hose-end sprayer. Then spray your herbs every six weeks during the growing season. (For related text, see page 278.)

HERB SOIL BOOSTER MIX

When you plant your herbs, add some of this marvelous mix to the soil. Those youngsters will be sure to get off to a rip-roarin' start.

5 lbs. of lime
5 lbs. of gypsum
1 lb. of 5-10-5 garden food
1/2 cup of Epsom salts

Mix all of these ingredients together, and work the formula into each 50-sq.-ft. area of herb garden to a depth of 12 to 18 inches. Then let it sit for 7 to 10 days before planting. (For related text, see page 255.)

HIT THE TRAIL MIX

This spicy concoction will make any critter hightail it away from your garden.

4 tbsp. of dry mustard
3 tbsp. of cayenne pepper
2 tbsp. of chili powder
2 tbsp. of cloves
1 tbsp. of Tabasco® sauce
2 qts. of warm water

Mix all of the ingredients together, and sprinkle the solution around the perimeter of your perennial beds. (For related text, see page 44.)

HOT BITE SPRAY

When furry munchers are after your flowering plants, whip up a batch of this timely tonic.

3 tbsp. of cayenne pepper
1 tbsp. of Tabasco® sauce
1 tbsp. of ammonia
1 tbsp. of baby shampoo
2 cups of hot water

Mix the cayenne pepper with the hot water in a bottle, and shake well. Let the mixture sit overnight, then pour off the liquid without disturbing the sediment. Mix the liquid with the remaining ingredients in a hand-held mist sprayer. Keep a batch on hand as long as new tulip buds are forming, and spritz the flower stems as often

as you can to keep 'em hot, hot, hot! It's strong medicine, so make sure you wear rubber gloves while you're handling this brew. (For related text, see 116.)

HOT BUG BREW

This potent beverage will deal a death blow to maggots, grown-up flies, and any other bug that's buggin' your plants.

3 hot green peppers (canned or fresh)
3 medium cloves of garlic
1 small onion
1 tbsp. of liquid dish soap
3 cups of water

Purée the peppers, garlic, and onion in a blender. Then pour the mixture into a jar, and add the dish soap and water. Let stand for 24 hours. Strain out the pulp with cheesecloth or panty hose, and use a hand-held mist sprayer to apply the remaining liquid to bug-infested plants, making sure to thoroughly coat the tops and undersides of all the leaves. (For related text, see page 133.)

HOT PEPPER SPRAY

This hot toddy will say a loud, strong "No!" to any Japanese beetle that starts to munch on your roses—and the recipes don't come much simpler than this one!

1/2 cup of dried cayenne peppers
1/2 cup of jalapeño peppers
1 gal. of water

Add the peppers to the water, bring it to a boil, and let it simmer for half an hour. (Make sure you keep the pan covered or the peppery steam will make you cry a river of tears!) Let the mixture cool, then strain out the solids, pour the liquid into a hand-held mist sprayer, and spritz your rosebushes from top to bottom. You'll have to repeat the process after every rain, but it's a small price to pay for beetle-free roses! (For related text, see page 88.)

JERRY'S LIME RICKEY

Back in my Uncle Art's day, lime soda pop rickeys were all the rage. Well, this rickey isn't made with soda pop, but it *will* make cabbage maggots rage!

1 cup of lime
1 qt. of water

Stir the lime into the water, and let it sit overnight. Then, pour the solution around the root ball of each maggot-plagued plant. Before you can say "Put a nickel in the jukebox," those maggots'll be history! (For related text, see page 182.)

KNOCK-'EM-DEAD INSECT SPRAY

This potent mixture will deal a death blow to squash bugs or any other foul felons that are after your veggies.

6 cloves of garlic, finely chopped
1 small onion, finely chopped
1 tbsp. of cayenne pepper
1 tbsp. of liquid dish soap
1 qt. of warm water

Mix all of these ingredients together, and let the mixture sit overnight. Strain out the solids, pour the liquid into a hand-held mist sprayer, and knock those buggy pests dead! (For related text, see page 161.)

LETHAL LEAFHOPPER SPRAY

Even hard-to-get bugs like leafhoppers kick the bucket when you hit 'em hard with this stuff.

1/2 cup of alcohol (any kind will do)
2 tbsp. of liquid dish soap
1 gal. of warm water

Mix all of these ingredients together, and pour the solution into a hand-held mist sprayer. Then, saturate your plants from top to bottom, especially the undersides of leaves, where leafhoppers love to hide. (For related text, see page 60.)

LETHAL WEAPON TONIC

If ants have turned your fruit tree into an aphid ranch, don't pull any punches. Grab your trusty hose-end sprayer out of its holster, and load it with this magic bullet.

3 tbsp. of garlic and onion juice*
3 tbsp. of skim milk
2 tbsp. of baby shampoo
1 tsp. of Tabasco® sauce
1 gal. of water

Mix all of these ingredients in a bucket, and pour the solution into a 20-gallon hose-end sprayer. Then spray your tree every 10 days until the aphids are lyin' 6 feet under Whiskey Boot Hill. (For related text, see page 205.)

*To make garlic and onion juice, put 2 cloves of garlic, 2 medium onions, and 3 cups of water in a blender and purée. Strain out the solids and pour the remaining liquid into a jar. Use whenever called for in a Miracle Mix. Bury the solids in your garden to repel aphids and other pesky pests.

LIQUID BANDAGE

This elixir works just like a bandage to keep germs and pests from moving into newly pruned trees or shrubs.

½ cup of interior latex paint
½ cup of antiseptic mouthwash
1 tsp. of cayenne pepper

Mix all of these ingredients in a small bucket, and paint the solution on pruning wounds to keep bugs and other thugs away from the tender tissue. (For related text, see page 197.)

MAGICAL MILDEW CONTROL TONIC

At the first sign of mildew—or whenever the weather is damp and humid—spray your mildew magnet plants with this timely tonic.

4 tbsp. of baking soda
2 tbsp. of Murphy's Oil Soap®
1 gal. of warm water

Mix all of these ingredients together. Then pour the solution into a hand-held mist sprayer and thoroughly douse your plants when you see tell-tale signs of mildew. (For related text, see page 247.)

MARVELOUS MELON SOIL

Melons are mighty particular about the ground they call home. This mixture suits 'em to a T.

2 parts coarse builder's sand (not beach or "sandbox" sand)
1 part compost
1 part professional planting mix
1 cup of my Mouthwatering Melon Mix*

Mix all of these ingredients together. Pour the soil mixture into each of your melon planting holes, and get ready to modestly accept your town's Most Mouthwatering Melon award! (For related text, see page 238.)

*To make Mouthwatering Melon Mix, combine 5 pounds of earthworm castings (available in catalogs), ½ pound of Epsom salts, and ¼ cup of instant tea granules.

MIGHTY MITE RHUBARB SPRAY

This potent potion will make mites mighty sorry they ganged up on your plants!

1 lb. of rhubarb leaves, chopped
2 tsp. of liquid dish soap
1 qt. of water

Boil the rhubarb leaves in the water for about half an hour. Then strain out the solids, and pour the liquid into a spray bottle. Mix in the dish soap, and spray away! When you're done, bury the soggy rhubarb leaves near your cabbage-family plants to fend off clubroot. **Just one word of caution:** Rhubarb leaves are highly poisonous, so never use this spray on edible plants. (For related text, see page 22.)

NETTLE TEA

Stinging nettles pack a load of nitrogen that's as potent as manure. They also give off pest-repelling chemicals. So what are you waiting for? Brew a pot of this powerful tea, and double your firepower!

1 lb. of stinging nettle leaves
1 gal. of water

Put the nettles in a bucket, pour in the water, and let the mixture steep for at least a week. Strain out the leaves, and water your plants with the brew. Then toss the leaves on the compost pile, or bury them in the garden. (For related text, see page 334.)

NO MO' NEMATODES TONIC

This simple elixir'll polish off nasty nematodes, lickety-split.

1 can of beer
1 cup of molasses

Mix these ingredients in a 20-gallon hose-end sprayer, and thoroughly soak any area where nasty nematodes are doin' their dirty work. (For related text, see page 155.)

OIL'S WELL THAT ENDS WELL MIX

This oily potion is just the ticket for wipin' out scale, aphids, and other little pests that suck the sap from your roses.

1 tbsp. of Basic Oil Mixture*
2 cups of water

Combine these ingredients in a hand-held mist sprayer, and spray your roses from top to bottom. (Shake the bottle now and then to make sure the oil and water stay mixed!) Repeat the process in seven days. Those scale babies'll never wake up! (For related text, see page 84.)

*To make Basic Oil Mixture, pour 1 cup of vegetable oil and 1 tablespoon of Murphy's Oil Soap® into a plastic squeeze bottle (an empty ketchup or mustard bottle is perfect). Then, measure out whatever you need for a Miracle Mix recipe, and store the rest for later.

ORANGE AID

You'll love the aroma of this citrusy spray—but caterpillars *hate* it!

1 cup of chopped orange peels*
¼ cup of boiling water

Put the orange peels in a blender or food processor, and pour the boiling water over them. Liquefy, then let the mixture sit overnight at room temperature. Strain the slurry through cheesecloth, and pour the liquid into a hand-held mist sprayer. Fill the balance of the bottle with water, and spray your plants from top to bottom. (For related text, see page 170.)

*Or substitute lemon, lime, or grapefruit peels.

OUT-TO-LUNCH MIX

Every spring, serve up this hearty lunch to your hardy bulbs—it'll give them all the nutrition they need to put on a *really* big show! (This recipe makes enough for 100 sq. ft. of soil.)

10 lbs. of compost
5 lbs. of bonemeal
1 lb. of Epsom salts

Mix all of these ingredients in a large container. Then spread the mixture on the soil where your bulbs are planted, and work it in just under the surface. For an extra treat, add up to 15 pounds of wood ashes to the mix. (For related text, see page 113.)

PEPPERMINT SOAP SPRAY

This brew is a nightmare-come-true for hard-bodied insects like weevils. The secret ingredient: peppermint. It cuts right through a bug's waxy shell, so the soap can get in and work its fatal magic.

2 tbsp. of liquid dish soap
2 tsp. of peppermint oil
1 gal. of warm water

Mix the dish soap and water together, then stir in the peppermint oil. Pour the solution into a hand-held mist sprayer, take aim, and fire! Those weevils'll never know what hit 'em! (For related text, see page 135.)

QUACK-UP SLUG COOKIES

Slugs will think it's time to party when they get a yeasty whiff of these tasty treats. But after a couple of bites, they're sure to have a killer of a hangover!

1 part dried quackgrass blades,
finely chopped
1 part wheat bran*
1 can of beer

Mix the quackgrass and bran in a bowl, then slowly add the beer, stirring until the mixture has the consistency of cookie dough. Run the dough through a meat grinder, or chop it into small bits (roughly ⅛ to ¼ inch thick). Let the "cookies" air-dry overnight, sprinkle them on the ground among your plants, and let the good times roll! (For related text, see page 260.)

*Available in supermarkets and health food stores.

QUASSIA SLUG SPRAY

Stop slugs in their slimy tracks with this potent potion. It helps fend off aphids, too!

4 oz. of quassia chips (available at health food stores)
1 gal. of water

Crush, grind, or chop the chips, add them to the water in a bucket, and let steep for 12 to 24 hours. Strain through cheesecloth, then spray the liquid on strawberries and other slug and aphid targets. (For related text, see page 232.)

REPOTTING BOOSTER TONIC

Once you've repotted your rooted cuttings, give them a drink of this elixir. It'll give 'em a good start in their new home.

1/2 tsp. of all-purpose, organic plant food
1/2 tsp. of Vitamin B₁ Plant Starter
1/2 cup of weak tea water*
1 gal. of warm water

Mix all of the ingredients together, and gently pour the mixture through the soil of your repotted cuttings. Let it drain through for 15 minutes or so, then pour off any excess liquid that's in the tray. (For related text, see page 42.)

*Soak a used tea bag in a mix of 1 gallon of warm water and 1 teaspoon of liquid dish soap until the mix is light brown.

RHUBARB BUG REPELLENT

Here's a potent spray that'll say "Scram!" to just about any bug.

3 medium-size rhubarb leaves
1/4 cup of liquid dish soap
1 gal. of water

Chop up the rhubarb leaves, put the pieces in the water, and bring to a boil. Let the mixture cool, then strain it through cheesecloth to filter out the leaf bits. Mix in the liquid dish soap. Apply with a hand-held mist sprayer. Just remember, rhubarb leaves are highly poisonous, so never use this spray on edible plants. (For related text, see page 104.)

ROBUST RHUBARB TONIC

Grandma Putt served this nutritious slop to her rhubarb plants twice a year. I still feed it to her grandplants.

1 cup of tea
1 tbsp. of Epsom salts
Vegetable table scraps (all that you have on hand—but no meat or fats)
1 qt. of water

Mash all of these ingredients together until you've got a sort of slurry. (Or do the job in a blender or food processor.) Then pour the mushy mix over the soil in your rhubarb bed. Serve up one meal in spring and another in fall. Then stand back, and watch those plants go! (For related text, see page 241.)

ROSE AMBROSIA

If your roses could talk, they'd ask for big helpings of this nifty elixir, which gives them just what they need to grow big and strong and fend off any trouble.

1 cup of beer
2 tsp. of instant tea granules
1 tsp. of rose/flower food
1 tsp. of fish emulsion
1 tsp. of hydrogen peroxide
1 tsp. of liquid dish soap
2 gal. of warm water

Mix all of these ingredients together, and give each of your rosebushes 1 pint every three weeks. Dribble it onto the soil just after you've watered, so it'll penetrate deep into the root zone. (For related text, see page 86.)

ROSE APHID ANTIDOTE

Give your plants a good blast of water, and wait about 10 minutes. Then deal the aphids a final death blow with this elixir. The secret ingredient is the citrus oil—it makes rose aphids knuckle right under!

1 lemon or orange peel, coarsely chopped
1 tbsp. of baby shampoo
2 cups of water

Put these ingredients into a blender, and blend on high for 10 to 15 seconds. Use a coffee filter to strain out the pulp, then pour the liquid into a hand-held mist sprayer. Thoroughly spray all the rosebuds and young stems. Repeat after four days, and your aphids will be history. (For related text, see page 93.)

ROSE REVIVAL TONICS

This dynamic duo will get your bare-root roses off and growing like champs. First, wash the bushes, roots and all, in a bucket of water with the following added:

1 tbsp. of liquid dish soap
1/4 tsp. of liquid bleach

Then, for about an hour before planting (or replanting), soak your bare-root rosebushes in a clean bucket filled with the following:

2 tbsp. of clear corn syrup
1 tsp. of liquid dish soap
1 tsp. of ammonia
1 gal. of warm water

(For related text, see page 81.)

ROSE START-UP TONIC

Here's the perfect meal to get your roses off to a rosy start.

1 tbsp. of liquid dish soap
1 tbsp. of hydrogen peroxide
1 tsp. of whiskey
1 tsp. of Vitamin B_1 Plant Starter
1/2 gal. of warm tea

Mix all of these ingredients together in a watering can. Then pour the solution all around the root zone of each newly planted (or replanted) rose. (For related text, see page 82.)

RUST RELIEF TONIC

Use this terrific tonic to keep your rust-prone plants in the green all summer long.

6 tbsp. of vegetable oil
2 tbsp. of baking soda
2 tbsp. of kelp extract (available at garden centers and health food stores)
1 gal. of water

Mix all of these ingredients together, and pour the solution into a hand-held mist sprayer. Then, give your formerly rusty plants a weekly shower throughout the growing season. Make sure you spray in the morning, though: You want that foliage to dry out before nightfall. (For related text, see page 23.)

SCAT CAT SOLUTION

Surround your prized plants with this pungent potion, and pussycats will go elsewhere for munchies.

5 tbsp. of flour
4 tbsp. of powdered mustard
3 tbsp. of cayenne pepper
2 tbsp. of chili powder
2 qts. of warm water

Mix all of these ingredients together. Then sprinkle the solution around target plants that are in the ground or in containers. (For related text, see page 244.)

SEEDLING TRANSPLANT RECOVERY TONIC

Give your transplants a break on moving day by serving them a sip of this soothing drink. It'll help them recover more quickly from the shock of transplanting.

1 tbsp. of fish emulsion
1 tbsp. of ammonia
1 tbsp. of Murphy's Oil Soap®
1 tsp. of instant tea granules
1 qt. of warm water

Mix all of these ingredients together, and pour the solution into a hand-held mist sprayer. Then mist your little plants several times a day until they're off and growing on the right root. (For related text, see page 145.)

SEED-STARTER TONIC

No matter what kind of seeds you're planting, get 'em off to a rip-roarin' start with this excellent elixir.

1 tsp. of baby shampoo
1 tsp. of Epsom salts
1 qt. of weak tea water*

Mix the shampoo and Epsom salts in the tea water. Then bundle up your seeds in cheesecloth or an old panty hose toe (one kind of seed per bundle, unless you're aimin' for a casual mix). Drop the bundles into the liquid, and put the container in the fridge to soak for 24 hours. Your seeds'll come out rarin' to grow! (For related text, see page 4.)

*Soak a used tea bag in a mix of 1 gallon of warm water and 1 teaspoon of liquid dish soap until the mix is light brown.

SLUGWEISER

Beer is the classic bait for slug and snail traps. But what attracts the slimy thugs isn't the alcohol in the beer, or even the hops and malt—it's the yeast. So fill up your traps with this potion. After all, why waste a good brewski on the enemy?

1 lb. of brown sugar
¹/₂ package (1¹/₂ tsp.) of dry yeast

Pour these ingredients into a 1-gallon jug, fill it with warm water, and let the mixture sit for two days, uncovered. Then pour it into your slug traps, and watch the culprits belly up to the bar! (For related text, see page 280.)

SO LONG, SUCKER SPRAY

This fabulous formula is just the ticket for tiny insects, like thrips and aphids, that are too small to handpick and whirl in a blender all by themselves.

2 cups of thrip-infested flowers
or leaves*
2 cups of warm water

Put the plant parts in an old blender, and whirl 'em with the water (tiny bugs and all). Strain the goop through cheesecloth, dilute with 1 gallon of water, and pour the juice into a hand-held mist sprayer. Then spray your plants from top to bottom, on both sides of leaves and stems, and along all runners. Repeat the treatment after rain. If you have any extra juice, freeze it right away before bacteria can get a toehold. Be sure to label it clearly—you don't want to have this stuff for dinner! (For related text, see page 71.)

*Substitute whatever pests are sucking the life out of your plants. Two notes of caution: Once you've used a blender to make this spray, don't use it again for either human or pet food—ever! And don't make this spray (or any other) from mosquitoes, fleas, or other blood-sucking insects that transmit human and animal diseases.

SQUIRREL BEATER TONIC

To keep pesky squirrels from stealing your crop, spray your fruit and nut trees with this spicy potion.

2 tbsp. of cayenne pepper
2 tbsp. of Tabasco® sauce
2 tbsp. of chili powder
1 tbsp. of Murphy's Oil Soap®
1 qt. of warm water

Mix all of these ingredients together. Then pour the mixture into a hand-held mist sprayer, and coat your trees from top to bottom. (For related text, see page 218.)

STRAWBERRY SUCCESS SOLUTION

Just before you plant your strawberries, give them a bath in this root-rousin' tonic.

1 can of beer
¼ cup of cold coffee
2 tbsp. of liquid dish soap
2 gal. of water

Mix all of these ingredients together in a bucket. Then soak your berries' bare roots in the solution for about 10 minutes before you tuck them into their holes. When you're finished planting, dribble the leftover solution on the soil around your plants. (For related text, see page 222.)

SUPER SOIL SANDWICH DRESSING

When you've got your ingredients all stacked up, top off your "super soil sandwich" with this zesty condiment. It'll kick-start the cooking process, and by the following spring, your super soil will be rarin' to grow!

1 can of beer
1 can of regular cola (not diet)
½ cup of ammonia
¼ cup of instant tea granules

Mix all of these ingredients in a bucket, and pour the solution into a 20-gallon hose-end sprayer. Then spray your "sandwich" until all the layers are saturated. (For related text, see page 306.)

SWEET SUCCESS SPRAY

This sugar-packed spray will lure bees to your veggie plants and ensure pollination. What's more, it'll kill nasty nematodes in the soil. So with this mixture, you get two benefits for the price of one!

½ cup of sugar
2 cups of water

Pour the sugar into the water and boil, stirring, until the sugar is completely dissolved. Let the mixture cool, dilute it with 1 gallon of water, and pour the solution into a hand-held mist sprayer. Then spritz your bloomin' plants. Before you know it, willing winged workers will fly to your rescue! (For related text, see page 165.)

TEA TIME FOR APHIDS

Aphids start showing up near the end of spring, and they love tasty new herb leaves. If the pesky pests are making a mess of your future medicine, give them a sip of this tantalizing tea.

½ cup of parsley flakes
2 tbsp. of minced garlic
3 cups of water

Mix all of these ingredients together, and boil down to 2 cups. Strain and cool. Put 2 cups of the tea in a 20-gallon hose-end sprayer, and drench your herbs until the aphids are history. (For related text, see page 283.)

TIMELY TOMATO TONIC

This powerful powder will help your tomato plants fend off dastardly diseases on the double.

3 cups of compost
1/2 cup of Epsom salts
1 tbsp. of baking soda
1/2 cup of nonfat dry milk

Combine the compost, Epsom salts, and baking soda in a bucket, then add a handful of the mix to the planting hole. After planting, sprinkle a little of the dry milk on top of the soil. Repeat every few weeks during the growing season. (For related text, see page 149.)

TOODLE-OO TERRORS TONIC

Our ancestors thought tomatoes were poisonous, so they avoided them like the plague. Flea beetles still do. Just spray your plants' leaves with this timely tonic, and kiss your flea-beetle battles good-bye!

2 cups of tomato leaves, chopped
1/2 tsp. of liquid dish soap
1 qt. of water

Put the leaves and water in a pan, and bring the water to a simmer. Then turn off the heat and let the mixture cool. Strain out the leaves, and add the dish soap to the water. Pour the solution into a hand-held mist sprayer, and spritz your plants from top to bottom. This potent potion also repels whiteflies, asparagus beetles, and cabbageworms. (Like all repellent sprays, though, you need to renew the supply after every rain.) (For related text, see page 246.)

TRANSPLANT TONIC

This terrific tonic is perfect for getting roses and all sorts of other transplants off to a super-fast start!

1/2 can of beer
1 tbsp. of ammonia
1 tbsp. of instant tea granules
1 tbsp. of baby shampoo
1 gal. of water

Mix all of the ingredients together. Then add 1 cup of the solution to each planting hole at transplant time. (For related text, see page 75.)

TREE PLANTING BOOSTER MIX

Start your trees off on the right root with this powerful powder. It'll help the soil drain well *and* hold moisture—and that's exactly what a fruit tree needs to grow strong and produce well.

4 lbs. of compost
2 lbs. of gypsum
1 lb. of Epsom salts
1 lb. of dry dog food
1 lb. of dry oatmeal

Mix all of these ingredients together in a bucket. Then work a handful or two into the bottom of the planting hole, and sprinkle another handful over the soil after planting. (For related text, see page 193.)

TREE TRANSPLANTING TONIC

For a fruit tree, being transplanted is a shocking experience. This soothing drink will ease the stress of going from a nursery pot, or the bare-root wrappings, to the wide-open spaces of your yard. (It works great for fruit-bearing bushes, too!)

$1/3$ **cup of hydrogen peroxide**
$1/4$ **cup of instant tea granules**
$1/4$ **cup of whiskey**
$1/4$ **cup of baby shampoo**
2 **tbsp. of fish emulsion**
1 **gal. of water**

Mix all of these ingredients in a bucket, and pour the solution into the hole when you transplant a fruit tree or bush. (For related text, see page 195.)

TREE WOUND STERILIZER TONIC

Anytime you cut diseased tissue from a tree or shrub, or even prune healthy branches, kill lingering germs with this powerful potion.

$1/4$ **cup of ammonia**
$1/4$ **cup of liquid dish soap**
$1/4$ **cup of antiseptic mouthwash**
1 **gal. of warm water**

Mix all of these ingredients, pour the solution into a hand-held mist sprayer, and drench the places where you've pruned trees or shrubs. (For related text, see page 198.)

VINEGAR FUNGUS FIGHTER

This simple-to-make elixir will help keep your plants fungus-free all summer long.

3 **tbsp. of apple cider vinegar**
1 **gal. of water**

Mix the vinegar and water, pour the solution into a spray bottle, and let 'er rip—it's as easy as that! Just be sure to spray your plants in the morning, so they have time to dry off before nightfall. Fungal spores *love* dark, damp flowerbeds! (For related text, see page 18.)

WEED WIPEOUT

When you've got weeds that won't take no for an answer, knock 'em flat on their backs with this mixer.

1 **tbsp. of gin**
1 **tbsp. of vinegar**
1 **tsp. of liquid dish soap**
1 **qt. of very warm water**

Mix all of these ingredients together, and pour the solution into a hand-held mist sprayer. Then, drench the weeds to the point of run-off, taking care not to spray any nearby plants. (For related text, see page 289.)

WILD MUSTARD TEA

Potato beetles, cabbage moths, and cabbage loopers will all give your garden a wide berth if you spray your plants with this tangy tea.

4 whole cloves
1 handful of wild mustard leaves
1 clove of garlic
1 cup of boiling water

Steep the cloves, mustard leaves, and garlic in the boiling water for 10 minutes. Let the elixir cool, then pour it into a hand-held mist sprayer, and let 'er go! (For related text, see page 129.)

WINTER WONDER DRUG

To keep your herbs and other perennial plants happy and healthy all winter long, douse them with this terrific tonic throughout the growing season.

1 tbsp. of liquid kelp, a.k.a. seaweed extract
1/8 tsp. of liquid dish soap
1 gal. of water

Mix all of these ingredients together, and mist-spray your herbs and other perennial plants from top to bottom every two to three weeks throughout the growing season. (For related text, see page 265.)

WINTERIZING TONIC

To head off trouble next spring, zap budding bud weevils and other bugs with this marvelous mixer.

1 cup of Murphy's Oil Soap®
1 cup of tobacco tea*
1 cup of antiseptic mouthwash

Mix all of these ingredients in a 20-gallon hose-end sprayer, filling the balance of the jar with warm water. Then saturate your berry beds, and the rest of your garden and lawn, too. They'll be pest-free and rarin' to grow come spring. (For related text, see page 233.)

*To make tobacco tea, wrap half a handful of chewing tobacco in a panty hose toe or a piece of cheesecloth. Soak it in 1 gallon of hot water until the water turns dark brown. Pour the liquid into a glass container with a tight lid for storage.

WOODY SEED STARTER TONIC

Seeds with woody coats, like beets and parsnips, get off to a faster start when you treat them to a dose of this powerful potion.

1 cup of vinegar
2 oz. of liquid dish soap
2 cups of warm water

Mix all of these ingredients together, and soak your seeds in the mixture for 24 hours. (For related text, see page 120)

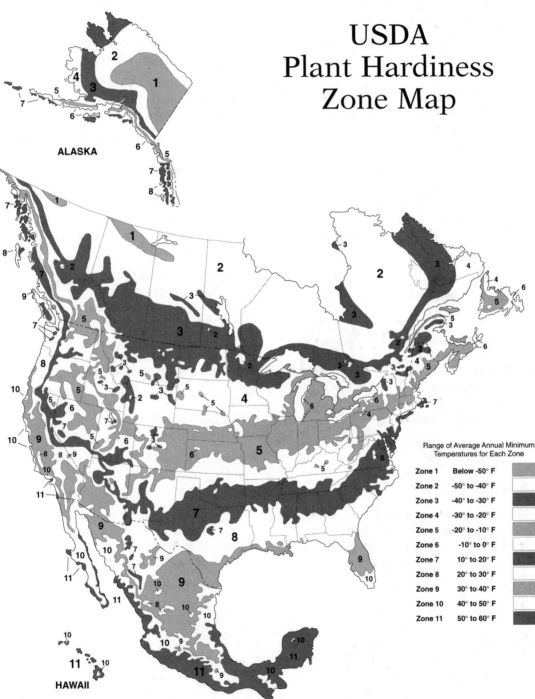

USDA Plant Hardiness Zone Map

ALASKA

HAWAII

Range of Average Annual Minimum
Temperatures for Each Zone

Zone 1	Below -50° F
Zone 2	-50° to -40° F
Zone 3	-40° to -30° F
Zone 4	-30° to -20° F
Zone 5	-20° to -10° F
Zone 6	-10° to 0° F
Zone 7	10° to 20° F
Zone 8	20° to 30° F
Zone 9	30° to 40° F
Zone 10	40° to 50° F
Zone 11	50° to 60° F

Index